MEDUSA'S HEAD

MEDUSA'S HEAD

The Rise and Survival of Joseph Fouché, Inventor of the Modern Police State

RAND MIRANTE

ARCHWAY PUBLISHING

Archway Publishing books may be ordered through booksellers or by contacting:

Archway Publishing
1663 Liberty Drive
Bloomington, IN 47403
www.archwaypublishing.com
1-(888)-242-5904

ISBN: 978-1-4808-1071-6 (sc)
ISBN: 978-1-4808-1069-3 (hc)
ISBN: 978-1-4808-1070-9 (e)

Library of Congress Control Number: 2014916589

Printed in the United States of America.

Archway Publishing rev. date: 1/27/2015

Anonymous, 19th century. Joseph Fouché (1759-1820), Duke of Otranto, Minister of Police. Oil on canvas. Photo: Gérard Blot. Châteaux de Versailles et de Trianon, Versailles, France. © RMN-Grand Palais/Art Resource, NY

And when death, opening its fatal ledger,
Asks me: — What throw you now into the sinister basket?
The head of the people, or the head of the king?
I say: — Neither one nor the other . . .

Victor Hugo, *Le Verso de la page*, 10:271-72

Let me have men about me that are fat;
Sleek-headed men and such as sleep o'nights:
Yon Cassius has a lean and hungry look;
He thinks too much: such men are dangerous.

William Shakespeare, *Julius Caesar*, Act I, scene 2

Preface and Acknowledgments

The roots of this work are traceable to a long-ago Christmas back in the 1950s, when my parents, always seeking new ways to kindle intellectual curiosity, presented me with a slipcase edition of Sir Arthur Conan Doyle's swashbuckling short stories, *The Exploits and Adventures of Brigadier Gerard*. This collection — undeservedly too little known today and overshadowed by the Sherlock Holmes saga — featured a supremely vain and thick-headed French cavalryman, Étienne Gérard of the Hussars of Conflans, who blundered his way to glory across Europe with *la Grande Armée*. I was enthralled by the lost world Conan Doyle had brought to life; the work displayed the same consummate attention to detail that marked his tales of the great detective.

The Conan Doyle book was accompanied by a gift of German *Zinnfigüren*, so-called "flat" toy soldiers, which I deployed in incongruous battle settings with Scottish and Russian troops arrayed together against their French nemeses. Thereafter, my nascent interest in this stirring period was fanned by a visit to the Toronto home of an extraordinary uncle, Roger Breen Sammon, a veteran of fifteen Pacific invasions and the decorated survivor of a *kamikaze* hit on his destroyer off Okinawa. Roger had amassed an incredible collection of several thousand books about the Napoleonic era, and in browsing through them, I first encountered the plethora of memoirs that were the outpouring of that era; my interests thereupon began to evolve beyond heroic adventure fiction and tabletop battles.

Many years later, after working as an attorney at McGraw-Hill, the New York-based media company, I found myself back at my alma mater,

Princeton University, pursuing a quite different second career, in development. One day in early 2002, an unexpected opportunity flashed across my computer screen: the University's brand-new freshman writing program issued an all-points bulletin asking for course proposals. They wanted ideas for offerings well suited to instruction in academic essay writing with an emphasis on effective, persuasive argumentation. Not being a Ph.D., but equipped with a Harvard Law J.D. and my previous experience in publishing, I decided to throw my hat into the ring and submitted an outline for a topic examining the nature and bounds of the crime of treason. This topic was not only timely but sufficiently disputatious, with one person's traitor being another's freedom fighter, and vice versa. To my everlasting gratitude, my proposal was accepted by the program's then-director, Dr. Kerry Walk, to whom I owe the great privilege of teaching for five fall semesters a course titled *Treason: from Henry V to John Walker Lindh.*

At some point in my serendipitous faculty turn, it occurred to me that for the sake of credibility I should write something myself, a work pertaining to the subject matter of my course. Mentally reviewing a rogues' gallery of real and purported traitors, and then homing in on those from the historical eras with which I had the greatest familiarity, the spectral and sinister figure of Joseph Fouché, the white-haired and gaunt grand inquisitor of the First Empire, suddenly came to mind. (Some credit for the occurrence of this idea should probably go to the fine English actor Albert Finney, who had a memorable cameo role as Fouché, despite looking nothing like him — Finney appears quite overweight and sports a beard — in Ridley Scott's riveting first movie, *The Duellists*, based upon a Joseph Conrad short story.) Fouché was certainly woven into most historical accounts of Napoleon's rule, but in English-language works he usually is a briefly noted and superficially treated background presence, an elusive éminence noire. But had anything been written in English in recent years that was actually focused on him? Not for over forty, as it turned out.

Questions soon proliferated. I knew that Fouché was a regicide, but then how had he successfully navigated the anti-Jacobin backlash of the Thermidorian Reaction? How had he not only survived the Bourbon

Restoration, but actually wound up serving in the cabinet of Louis XVIII, in spite of his responsibility for the death of the King's older brother? What accounted for a Jacobin radical and terrorist being graced with the aristocratic title of the Duke of Otranto? How was his Ministry of Police organized and how did it operate on a daily basis? Why did Napoleon keep giving him responsibility for state security and public order when he was clearly not to be trusted? What was it about Fouché's character and career, his accomplishments and abilities, that made him the first policeman, the first intelligence chief anywhere, of whom history seems to take any real note?

I commenced my research for *Medusa's Head* in early 2007. I pored over original issues of the newspaper *Le Moniteur Universel*, bound in their pungent and disintegrating leather covers, on the subterranean C floor of Princeton's Firestone Library. I immersed myself in a wide variety of memorialists' score-settling and slanted renditions of their experiences of the years of terror, turmoil, and tyranny spanning the Revolution, the Directory, the Consulate, the Empire, and the two Restorations. I held in my hands Fouché's 1793 pamphlet, *Réflexions sur le jugement de Louis Capet,* in which he stridently called for the immediate execution of Louis XVI, and I leafed through his correspondence displaying the strange and vaguely ominous logo of his Ministry of Police.

I knew from the start that I had selected an unusual individual to write about, but I soon became astounded by the trajectory and the contradictions of Fouché's career: from cleric-in-training to de-Christianizer, from scholarly physics instructor to the "Butcher of Lyon," from non-descript and frail son of a merchant mariner to a catalyst of the downfalls of Louis XVI and Maximilien Robespierre, from creator of Napoleon's sprawling state security service to an equivalent role as the Bourbon dynasty's watch-dog and mole. My subject was a man everyone feared and mistrusted but also one whom most everyone apparently thought they desperately needed on their side. I was stunned by the scope and multitude of his serial and perhaps pathological betrayals; by the pervasive, sophisticated, anticipatory nature of his policing establishment; and by the peculiar way in which his long career of rise and survival suddenly came to a crashing and ignominious end in that exotic haven for exiles,

Trieste on the Adriatic. And, while I did undertake on-site research in France (in particular, in Lyon, where there were some revolutionary rumblings during my visit in 2010), by the time I had completed the research phase of my project in 2012, issues of *Le Moniteur Universel* had become available via the Bibliothèque nationale de France's "Gallica" internet service, *sans* their distinctive musty C floor fragrance.

So, I submit to you the results of my investigation and assessment of the life, works, and misdeeds of the chameleonic chief investigator. First, however, I wish to recognize the much-appreciated assistance I have received along the way, in addition to the great influence of my parents, Albert and Irma, for fostering a lifetime of interest in reading and in history. My writing and argument have benefited from the perceptive, thorough, and challenging commentary of another brilliant uncle, William J. Burke, and I believe that no professional editor could have served me better than he did. I also wish to express my thanks to two other close readers for their helpful suggestions and commentary, a fellow-attorney and good friend, Allen Barringer, a true renaissance man, and my sister, Edith Mirante, a noted author and expert on indigenous peoples of South and Southeast Asia. When I started working on *Medusa's Head*, Edith forewarned me that, as a first-time author, I would need to triple my maximum estimation of the time and effort it would take to get it published. She was quite right; if anything, her prediction would have been a gross underestimate had not salvation appeared in the form of the new age of self-publishing and the guidance of a fellow Princetonian, Don Seitz, Class of 1979. Thanks are also due to my dear friend, classmate, and colleague, the redoubtable H. Kirk Unruh, Jr., Rear Admiral USN (Ret.) for his interest, encouragement, and perceptive insights throughout the course of this endeavor, and also for the backing and support of my classmates Paul Haaga, Bill Neidig, Mickey Pohl, and Rick Smith; I am a fortunate man indeed to be able to count these gentlemen as my friends. Finally, this work could not possibly have come to be without the support and suggestions of my patient and loving wife, Chris, and of my wonderful daughter, Alexandra.

Contents

Prologue: Terror in the Rue Nicaise

It was Christmas Eve, 1800, in the de-Christianized capital of France. To the rest of the Western world it was the cusp of a new century, but in Paris the revolutionary calendar had set the date as 3 Nivôse in the Year IX. As night enveloped the city, pedestrians stopped and stared at the elegant state carriage of First Consul Napoleon Bonaparte clattering down the cobbled streets along the right bank of the Seine. Behind his coach trailed an armed escort of plumed, green-jacketed cavalry from the elite guard unit which would later be known as the Chasseurs à Cheval. After them, at a widening interval, came a second state coach carrying Napoleon's consort, the former Josephine de Beauharnais, and her high-fashion entourage, including Napoleon's sister Caroline and his stepdaughter Hortense. This small procession had left the Tuileries Palace, the scene of revolutionary tumult just a few years before, and was making its way to the opera house. There, Napoleon and Josephine were to attend the Paris premiere of Joseph Haydn's great oratorio based on The Book of Genesis, *Die Schöpfung,* or *The Creation.*

Bonaparte was the de facto ruler of France in the Year IX, thanks to a military coup d'état known as the 18th Brumaire (again, a date on the new calendar), which he had somewhat clumsily conducted thirteen months before (in the Year VIII). He was the unifying force who on the one hand had come to embody the French Revolution with its sweeping changes and bloody excesses and, on the other, the strongman who had brought the turmoil and upheaval to an end. Contemplating his grand ambitions to remake the world, Napoleon was perhaps looking forward to mentally transposing Haydn's musical rendering of the Supreme Being bringing Order out of Chaos onto his own past and future career of creative, cathartic destruction.

The First Consul's carriage wheeled at considerable speed onto the narrow Rue Nicaise, hurtling past the startled early evening street traffic and vendors. Napoleon, whose sleep habits were always erratic, began to doze off. Then, Terror on a grand scale made its return to Paris.

A tremendous explosion directed from the side of the street blasted away part of the cavalry escort, devastated buildings the length of a block, and inflicted mayhem on pedestrians. As fires broke out, roofs collapsed, and people screamed in panic, Napoleon's driver whipped the frightened team of horses ahead and brought the coach out of harm's way and onto the broader Rue Honoré. The glass in its windows was shattered, flames leaped around it, and debris cascaded overhead, but its illustrious occupant and the two future Marshals of France who were accompanying him, Berthier and Lannes, were unharmed. The same close escape was true of the slower, trailing carriage containing Josephine and her attendants. The timing of the ignition of the massive bomb — later to be referred to as the "*Machine Infernale*" — had been ever so slightly off, and it had been detonated when the widening space *between* the two carriages had been aligned opposite it.

A distraught Josephine caught up with her husband on the steps of the opera house. Accompanied by the surviving members of the military escort in their charred pelisses, the couple purposefully strode into their box and looked out upon an audience already permeated by the Ministry of Police's special agents. The performance had of course been delayed, as both sound and word of the great explosion had preceded the Bonapartes' arrival. The crowd, reassured that the assassination attempt had not succeeded, rose and wildly cheered the First Consul and his aristocratic Creole wife. As the orchestra launched into Haydn's tremulous overture depicting Chaos and the creation of the primal light, the guests of honor — the survivors of a very modern act of chaos and terror — thereupon abruptly left their seats and under heavy guard swiftly returned to the Tuileries Palace.

There, a shaken and angry Napoleon summoned his political and military advisors and demanded immediate vengeance. The perpetrators of this abominable act — he was very certain of this — were the surviving ultra-radical, left-wing Jacobins who had heretofore not been consumed by their own Reign of Terror or by the vengeful "Thermidorian Reaction" which had followed it, and who had not yet accepted the fact that their Revolution and their Republic had been supplanted by effective one-man rule. A reflexive chorus of agreement echoed from the officers and politicians waiting upon the First Consul.

All save one. A sallow, thin, ascetic-looking figure with penetrating yet opaque eyes stepped forward. His name was Joseph Fouché and he was a policeman, although certainly not an ordinary one. If he looked somewhat like a priest, it was because he had at one time been slated to become a man of the cloth, leaving the Congregation of Oratorians at the altar, as it were. That was before he turned against his king and against the clerics who had taught him, and against Christianity and against the enemies of the Revolution with a brutality that shocked even the Jacobins who had set him loose on the rebellious city of Lyon in 1793. In that terrible year, Fouché had become one of the most feared men in France. He would be greatly feared again, the next time with a European stage.

Going against the tide, Fouché firmly stated that he believed that the Rue Nicaise assassins were not creatures of the left as Napoleon had charged.[1] Rather, he opined that they were monarchist reactionaries known as "*Chouans*" (after the owl call they used to signal each other when lying in ambush). These royalist émigrés and their Catholic peasant followers were concentrated in the departments of the Atlantic coast of France, north of the Loire River. They were funded by Prime Minister William Pitt's spy service to further Britain's own ends. Through insurrections and guerilla warfare, the leaders of the *Chouans* sought to recover the rights and privileges of their class from the Corsican usurper who had taken advantage of a decade of destructive radicalism to seize power, power which the royalists and their followers believed was rightfully theirs.

On hearing the conflicting opinion from his Minister of Police, Bonaparte was derisive and dismissive. He insultingly accused Fouché of seeing the world inflexibly, through his own Jacobin-tinted glasses. This to Joseph Fouché, the man who after being an avenging agent of the revolutionary

Terror, had helped to bring down the feared Robespierre himself. This to Fouché, who had personally locked up the Jacobin Club in Paris, scattered its membership, and shut down the radical presses in the service of the very Directory which he had subsequently permitted General Bonaparte to overthrow. This to Fouché! The upstart Napoleon, who was to become Emperor of the French and the ruler of all Europe, would learn to his lasting regret that his renegade policeman-advisor had no preconceived affiliations or loyalties, except perhaps to his own perversely and flexibly evolving world view, in which it was his consistent aim to be at the center of a web of intrigue, surveillance, and deception. To achieve his overarching objective of clandestine control of the French nation, Fouché would betray any cause, would abandon any individual without hesitation, and would do so before the person betrayed knew of it — if indeed he or she ever did.

Fouché quietly exited the Tuileries and assigned the chief prefect of the Paris police and a crack team of forensic investigators to the case. Working diligently amid the bloody detritus and debris scattered about the Rue Nicaise, his team found the shattered bones of a horse. This had been the horse that had dragged into position the cart carrying the massive roadside bomb consisting of gunpowder and scrap iron hidden underneath a tarpaulin. And on the remains of the shattered horse's extremities strewn about the street, the searchers found pieces of horseshoes and harness. The painstakingly collected and reassembled fragments, in turn, carried marks which enabled a grain merchant to identify them to the investigators. The merchant and an intermediary in the transaction remembered the man who had purchased the cart from them, and the police thereupon swiftly traced the customer to his Paris lodgings. [2]

So it was that a small group of assassins, monarchists all, were quickly and efficiently rounded up by Fouché's men. The cell of *Chouans* was rapidly tried, and all were thereupon executed. But for good measure, over one hundred Jacobin leftist radicals who had had nothing to do with the attempt and who had once thought that Fouché was one of them were also arrested by the Minister of Police's men and transported across the Atlantic in chains to French Guiana on the north coast of South America. This harsh penal colony was at that time referred to as "*la guillotine sèche*" — "the dry guillotine" — because its inmates were in effect sentenced to slow and excruciating deaths by disease and malnutrition in a torpid jungle setting.[3]

In the years to come, Napoleon as Emperor would greatly value the services of Fouché and at the same time both deeply mistrust and grotesquely underestimate the man, whom he periodically removed and then repeatedly returned to power, fatally overlooking his betrayals and remaining dependent upon his intelligence services. And the Corsican ruler of France would also well remember that it was the Bourbons (and their agents, backed by English gold) that had sought to extinguish his star of destiny on the Rue Nicaise.

Part I

Revolution

CHAPTER I

Oratorian

At first, Julien Fouché expected that his son Joseph would become a merchant mariner like himself. The Fouchés lived in the small village of Pellerin, on the outskirts of the great port city of Nantes, on the Loire River, which passes through the surrounding marshlands and opens into the nearby Atlantic. They were prosperous Bretons: the father was involved in a thriving business as a spice importer and owned several properties in Santo Domingo. At the time, Nantes was also a center of the triangulated slave trade; it is not certain whether Fouché *père*'s cargoes ever were human ones, but it can be assumed that his Caribbean plantation workers were not free men.

Joseph's birth on May 21, 1759 followed those of his three older sisters, two of whom died at young ages. Joseph himself was also sickly and weak, and in a few years it became evident that he was not destined for the rigors of a life of maritime commerce. Throughout his adult life, many would comment upon his wan and sallow complexion, his unsettling, almost wraith-like appearance, upon his hooded yet penetrating eyes. And he would himself use his delicate constitution as an excuse when he felt it expedient to avoid people and situations that menaced him; we shall see him exhibit this defense mechanism on future occasions and in his own words.

Thus it was soon determined by his parents that Joseph should be directed towards the considerably less strenuous calling of the priesthood. The once-dominant Society of Jesus had been driven out of France in 1764 by royal edict. A rival Catholic entity, founded in 1611 and known as the Oratorian Congregation, had quickly moved to fill the resulting gap. By the time of the Revolution, there were approximately one hundred Oratorian colleges and other institutions in France. It was to study and board at two of these establishments that the adolescent Fouché was sent, first to the college at Nantes and later on to the one in Paris.

Like the expelled Jesuits, the Oratorians were also known as able teachers. By the 1780s, the congregation had increasingly become caught up in modern influences. Their pedagogy branched out into the sciences and mathematics, so as "to instill in students all the religious and social virtues."[4] Some of the group's more liberal priests even became advocates of Constitutionalism in France.

The young Fouché displayed great aptitude as a scholar, and he was soon pointed towards a career in teaching in the Oratorian colleges. He had strong quantitative skills, particularly with respect to Euclid's solutions based on data and logical analysis, and he also displayed a real affinity for Tacitus's history of the corrupt Roman Empire.[5] He inexorably gravitated away from religious instruction. (In order to teach in an Oratorian college, it was not necessary actually to be a priest. Whether or not Fouché in fact took the vows would later become a matter of some controversy, not surprisingly when we contemplate the strange and contradictory course his life would take. But there is no solid evidence that he ever did so.)

After Fouché completed his training in Paris, the Oratorians sent him on a series of tutorial assignments. In 1788 he was appointed to their college in Arras, a city in northern France which was the center of what was known as the Artois region. There, the young instructor became a popular teacher of logic and physics. He also even proved to be a bit of a showman on one occasion, when he made a noteworthy balloon ascension witnessed by his highly impressed students.[6]

The real importance of Arras, however, was that it had become a vital hotbed of new social and political thinking. The city boasted many prominent scholars, scientists, and philosophers, and a group of them had formed a literary society for comradeship in wine-laced rationalist discussions. This group referred to themselves as the Rosati, which was a juxtaposition of the letters in "Artois." The intellectual Fouché was soon welcomed into this elite group, and it was at a Rosati meeting that he met a brilliant young attorney who was a native of Arras, Maximilien Robespierre. (Joseph also became acquainted with Robespierre's sister, Charlotte, and the pale, thin, and unhealthy teacher from Nantes seems to have at one point briefly pursued an unsuccessful courtship of her.)[7]

France at this time was engulfed in a ferment of new ideas, with the tides of change coming in the wake of economic collapse caused by royal and aristocratic interference with commerce, by oppressive and inefficient taxation, and by the crushing debts incurred by Louis XVI's decision to support America's independence. To address this growing crisis, the King in December 1788 called together representatives of the three Estates of France — the nobility, the clergy, and the merchant and professional classes — to meet at the royal palace at Versailles, where one thousand deputies of the Estates-General convened in May 1789. It was the first such assemblage of Frenchmen since 1614.

What had initially been envisioned as a forum for some meaningful but limited reforms — to be of course carefully guided and managed by the Crown and its adherents in the first two Estates — was soon to spin out of control, with power first devolving upon the Third Estate and with absolute rule becoming constitutional monarchy. All this was swiftly followed by revolutionary republican government, war, terror, despotism and near-anarchy. Present at the creation, as the delegate to the National Assembly of the Estates-General from Arras, was Robespierre. He was from relatively modest circumstances and, during his legal career, he had frequently represented downtrodden *pro bono* clients in their claims against entrenched interests. His Spartan outlook was matched by an equally Spartan existence, and he would come to be known as "the

Incorruptible." Robespierre received help in meeting his considerable expenses of attending the assembly at Versailles from his fellow Rosati society member Joseph Fouché; the Oratorian teacher had by then inherited substantial wealth from his father.[8] Fouché's own progress towards his eventual, if finite, affiliation with radical Jacobinism was significantly influenced by his exposure to Robespierre's revolutionary zeal. But the seeds of the later fierce enmity between the two men could also be traced back to Arras, with Charlotte Robespierre remaining unimpressed with the gaunt young Oratorian instructor and, worse, with the Incorruptible feeling uncomfortably financially dependent upon, and perhaps even resentful of, his sister's unwelcome suitor.

While the Estates-General met and popular passions rapidly increased throughout France, the Congregation of Oratorians became concerned that a disconcerting level of free thought and radicalism was developing in their college at Arras. In October 1790, they transferred instructor Fouché back to Nantes, where he was to teach at the order's prestigious institution there. But the port city was also becoming politicized, although much of its mercantilistic and devout citizenry would ultimately become opposed to revolutionary radicalism, and the place would soon come to be viewed by the Jacobins — and by native son Fouché — as a depraved refuge for priests, royalists, and backward Bretons. The consequences of this perception for the citizens of Nantes would later prove negative in the extreme.[9]

Catalytic events in Fouché's life happened in quick succession upon his return home to Nantes. He first joined and then soon became the head of the local Constitutional Club. (There, however, one of his first acts was highly reactionary, and likely traceable to an initial desire to ingratiate himself to his wealthy local constituents and perhaps also to his understanding as to the source of a sizable portion of the Fouché family fortune: he argued *against* abolition of the slave trade, which was then being suggested in the National Assembly at Versailles.[10])

Following his entry into politics, Joseph Fouché married one Bonne-Jeanne Coiquaud, the homely and pious daughter of a well-to-do Nantes administrator and prosecutor. He would be steadfastly loyal to her over the years until her death in 1812, throughout the course of his otherwise changeling existence; they would have five children to whom Fouché the family man was much devoted.[11] And yet another change in his life soon occurred: the Oratorian Congregation, previously the anchor to Joseph's career, suddenly found itself *in extremis*. The new French government broke relations with the Vatican, religious orders were suddenly suppressed by the authorities, and all Catholic priests had to give their vows to the Constitution of 1791 instead of to Rome in order to avoid being classed as enemies of the State.

Fouché's presidency of the Nantes Friends of the Constitution Club and, somewhat ironically given his evolving radical politics, his acquisition of additional wealth through marriage, proved to be the twin engines that propelled him onto the national stage. He was elected as a delegate to the new Republic's National Convention, from the Department of Loire-Inférieur. In October 1792 — now the beginning of Year I, the dawn of a new age marked by the official abolition of the French constitutional monarchy — he journeyed to Paris to represent his coastal constituents.

At the very first, the deputy from Nantes' observable politics seemed cautious and conciliatory. Fouché the political novice sought the company of men of letters who were exceptional thinkers and comparative moderates such as the Marquis de Condorcet, the esteemed mathematician and champion of universal public education; professor and fellow Oratorian Pierre Daunou; and the great rhetorician Pierre Vergniaud. (During the Terror, the first would be poisoned, the second imprisoned but survive, the third guillotined.) But there quickly came a defining moment that directed an intense and individual spotlight on each and every delegate to the Convention: the trial of King Louis XVI, and the concomitant rounds of balloting as to guilt and as to whether the death penalty should be immediately exacted. This pivotal event would force Joseph Fouché to make a momentous public decision which would permanently brand and inexorably follow him for the rest of his life, as it did to every other like-voting representative.

Chapter II

Regicide

King Louis of the proud House of Bourbon had been transformed from an all-powerful, divinely sanctioned monarch into a constitutional one in 1791. He might have even been a satisfactory ruler — or at least a survivor — had he been a man more inclined and able to influence if not control events. However, he was driven out of the Palace of Versailles by a savage mob; he was encouraged by his Queen to flee from his residence in the Tuileries in Paris disguised as a servant in an attempt to seek safety with royalist allies across the Rhine in Coblenz; he was subsequently captured at a coaching station in Varennes just short of his immediate objective; and in the end the royal fugitive and his family were unceremoniously escorted back to Paris, where Louis was cast in the diametrically opposed roles of head of state and virtual prisoner. The credibility and future of the constitutional monarchy had thus been irrevocably damaged.

This climate of crisis was heightened further when, in the summer of 1792, the Duke of Brunswick, the commander of hostile forces comprised of Prussians, Austrians, Hessians, and émigré monarchists which were massing along France's borders, issued a manifesto. In it, he warned the revolutionary Parisians what their fate would be if the members of the royal family came to any harm:

> [I]f the chateau of the Tuileries is taken by force or insulted, . . . if the least violence is done to it, the least outrage to their Majesties the king, the queen, and the royal family, if their safety, their preservation and their freedom are not immediately provided for, they [Brunswick's forces] will wreak an exemplary and ever-memorable vengeance by delivering up the city of Paris to military execution, and total destruction, and the rebels guilty of assassinations to the executions that they have earned.[12]

Thus threatened and provoked by a foreign aristocrat, a huge disorderly crowd stormed the Tuileries on August 10 1792, and the King's Swiss guard was hunted down and annihilated after initially inflicting heavy casualties on the invading *citoyens.* Louis sought the protection of the National Assembly, but he was instead confined in the prison of the Temple (the former headquarters of the medieval Knights Templar) with his family. He was forced to abdicate his functions under the Constitution of 1791, and elections were held for a replacement representative body, called the National Convention. The members of the Convention were tasked with writing a new constitution for a new republican form of government, although the one they actually drafted would be immediately suspended upon its completion with the onset of the monumental crises of 1793.

In spite of this violent uprising in Paris, it nevertheless appeared that the rescue of the King and his family was both probable and imminent, as the royalist-backed Prussian army under the Duke of Brunswick's personal command methodically advanced westward across the frontier on the road to the French capital. The great fortress strongholds at Longwy and Verdun quickly fell to this highly professional, intimidating force. Panic prevailed in Paris, as bloodthirsty mobs of Jacobins burst into various prisons and summarily executed aristocrats, priests, and other suspected enemies in order to prevent them from aiding their prospective Prussian liberators. Known as the "September Massacres," this extra-legal butchery led to a growing rift between, on the one hand, the radical Jacobins with their Parisian power-base, and on the other, relatively more moderate representatives from the provinces, the "Girondins," named after the department from whence some of that faction's leaders came. The Jacobins despised the Girondins as conciliatory compromisers who would betray the Revolution, and the Girondins loathed the Jacobins as anarchic rabble-rousers whose actions and rhetoric would lead to the destruction of authority and the ruination of France. Personal vendettas amongst the delegates raised the level of friction even higher.

The Oratorian physics instructor from Nantes, Joseph Fouché, would initially be viewed as naturally aligned by background and temperament with the more moderate Girondins. His actions, however, would reveal his political stripes to be quite otherwise, to the delight of the extremist faction.

What appeared to be the inevitable and ignominious end of France's revolutionary experiment was suddenly and shockingly averted on September 20. Near the village of Valmy, in the Argonne region, the Duke of Brunswick's seemingly invincible army of Prussian professionals was stopped dead in its tracks by the massed artillery of a highly motivated French army under the command of Generals Dumouriez and Kellerman. The defeat was more psychological than material, as casualties on both sides were surprisingly light. The Prussian force, goaded on by émigré members of the House of Bourbon, simply had not expected troops deemed little better than an armed rabble to mount any kind of determined resistance. When they in fact encountered it in spades from the inspired defenders, the invaders quickly melted away, fleeing back across the Rhine. The eminent writer Johann Wolfgang von Goethe, who was accompanying the Duke of Brunswick's suddenly demoralized troops as an observer, famously and correctly opined about the cannonade at Valmy: "From this place and this day forth commences a new epoch in the world's history, and you can all say that you were present at its birth."[13]

The news of the astonishing triumph over the Prussians completely transformed the situation back in Paris. On the equinox of September 21, the newly elected Convention unanimously voted for the abolition of the monarchy and the very next day was marked the beginning of the Year I, the dawn of Goethe's new epoch indeed. But the display of unanimity in removing royal rule was soon to be fractured and each and every delegate, including Fouché of Nantes, put to the test by the pressing question: what was to be done with the dethroned Louis?

The crimes with which Louis XVI would be charged were both existential and real. Louis' downfall marked the end of the divine right of kings and its theoretical replacement with rule by popular will as embodied in the Nation. Despite the stunning victory at Valmy, the new Republic and the Revolution were still threatened by a restoration of the monarchy by France's foes, internal and external, and the deposed Louis and his family were an obvious rallying point for counterrevolution and a return to pre-1789 feudal France. And Louis could not be trusted: in his role as a constitutional monarch he had vetoed acts against revanchist émigrés and renegade priests; he had unsuccessfully tried to flee the Tuileries Palace; his two younger brothers, the Comte de Provence and the Comte d'Artois (respectively, the future Louis XVIII and Charles X), with their aristocratic entourages and foreign allies still menaced France from their safe-haven in Coblenz across the Rhine; and he had allowed (albeit by an act of omission) the Swiss guards to fire upon the citizens of Paris (granted that his home had been invaded). To underscore his betrayals, a search conducted by a Girondin deputy to the Convention of Louis' former rooms at the Tuileries had revealed, in a secret compartment in an armoire, quasi-incriminating correspondence between the Bourbon ruler and various foreign and domestic enemies of the Republic. Treason was in the air. The prisoner-King, now disparagingly renamed against his will "Louis Capet" after the ancient dynastic forebears of the House of Bourbon, would be put on public trial.[14]

Into this maelstrom entered Joseph Fouché, ex-Oratorian, as one of eight elected representatives to the National Convention from the newly created coastal department of Loire-Inférieur. The Convention's meeting hall and the place where the riveting drama of the deposed King's trial would unfold was the Salle du Manège, located close by the Tuileries Palace, which had once been the royal riding school. It had a vaulted ceiling, bad acoustics, and its atmosphere alternated between severe drafts and oppressive heating. Its steeply tiered seating was arranged arena-like around the long oval of its former equestrian track. In his first days as a delegate Fouché sat with some of his moderate Girondin friends like Vergniaud and Daunou; soon, however, he was to move away from them and into the upper tiers of the Manège where the most radical and bloodthirsty Jacobins like Pierre-Gaspard Chaumette and Jacques Hébert sat, and from which lofty position they and their allies assumed the collective title of "*la Montagne*" ("the Mountain").

Louis's trial before the Convention in the Year I took place in several stages. First, investigators made a report to the deputies on October 4 on documentary evidence against the King which they had feverishly assembled and were holding in 95 cartons plus several wheat sacks.[15] The verbal attacks on the ex-monarch commenced in late November when the former wastrel turned Jacobin ideologue, Louis Antoine Saint-Just, denounced all royalty as enemies of mankind and questioned even the necessity of a trial ("Caesar was immolated in the Senate without any other formality than twenty-one dagger thrusts, without any other laws than the liberty of Rome").[16] Saint-Just was followed to the podium by Maximilien Robespierre, who intoned that the King "will be condemned, or the republic will not be acquitted," and added, threateningly, "If the king is not guilty, then those who deposed him are."[17] On December 10, a 35-count indictment listing the monarch's crimes was read out.

The next day, "Louis Capet" was escorted to the Convention by guards from the Temple prison and brought before the delegates sitting in the great hall of the Manège to defend himself. He heard the president speak the awful words: *"Louis, le peuple francais vous accusé d'avoir commis une multitude de crimes, pour établir votre tyrannie en détruisant la liberté."*[18] ("Louis, the French people accuse you of a multitude of crimes, committed in order to establish your tyranny and destroy liberty.") His legal defense during a subsequent session on December 26 was quite ably conducted, given the situation, by a hastily recruited trio of attorneys (one of whom would also be guillotined). They contested the jurisdiction of the Convention to try the constitutionally empowered King, while also attempting to argue that his actions were proper under the circumstances of threats to his safety, and that they were in any event privileged under the powers legally entrusted him. Louis, when put under examination during this session, his last appearance before the Convention, proved quite hard to trip up as he consistently pleaded ignorance of the crimes of which he was accused — although his evasive replies to questions about his knowledge of the secret compartment of papers in the armoire in the Tuileries, to which he had initially possessed the keys, undermined his credibility. But in any case, the likelihood of his conviction for treason against the Republic was never really in doubt. Rather, the more difficult question posed was: what would be done with him?

In response, there was a series of alternatives: execute him immediately, execute him later, hold him prisoner until peace came, exile him, or, most complicating, put his guilt and his resulting sentence to a vote by the people of France ("*appel au peuple*") instead of leaving the second and dicier of the twin issues to the members of the Convention. This last option, offering nervous deputies the ability to avoid personal responsibility altogether, was an absolute anathema to the radical Jacobins who prided themselves on being the embodiment of the popular will and civic virtue. They wanted the head of Louis Capet to roll and many of them agreed with Saint-Just that the trial itself was superfluous. These Jacobins of the Mountain were to find themselves an unexpected but most welcome ally in the person of Joseph Fouché, who had at first seemed to them to be another weak-kneed Girondin with a mercantile-clerical taint from the suspiciously moderate — and therefore counterrevolutionary — city of Nantes.

The Convention had decreed that any delegate who had anything to say about the trial and the fate of Louis could have his opinions printed at the public's expense. Fouché, whose feeble and reedy voice would have vanished into the lofty airspace of the Manège had he attempted to make a speech, took advantage of this perquisite. He quickly had a pamphlet produced titled "*Réflexions de J. Fouché, (de Nantes), sur le jugement de Louis Capet.*" (This was likely done during the week of January 7, 1793, as it was then that the Convention adjourned for several days to permit pamphlets of this nature to be printed and circulated.) In this short piece of several pages' length, Fouché argued strongly against the popular vote option, against giving the moderate delegates an easy way out:

> We waver before the shadow of a king, and the first fires of republican virtue are ready to be extinguished in our hands. Citizens, the course of justice, like that of the sun, cannot be turned back by interminable discussions. . . . If his head does not fall promptly under the blade of the law, brigands and assassins can walk with their heads held high; the most frightening disorder will menace society.

The former Oratorian scholar went on: ". . . [W]e are judges, and we should be impassive like divinity. The least act of weakness can begin a horrible succession of calamities." And he concluded by demanding the instant, definitive, and merciless resolution by the Convention of the two pending questions: "1. Has Louis betrayed the nation? 2. What punishment should he incur?"[19]

The delegates reconvened on January 15 to give their answers. The evasive appeal to the people was voted down. Then, the next day, to the first question posed, the answer of the majority was, as expected, affirmative: the traitor Louis Capet was guilty as charged.

However, the second question addressed by Fouché in his pamphlet proved to be a good deal thornier. Perhaps because of latent reservations about regicide and its implications both for the delegates personally and for their constituents, perhaps because of the supposition that Louis might conceivably be worth more to the survival of the Republic alive rather than dead, perhaps because of a last-minute reluctance to take the final step into the abyss, the voting as to the King's punishment ran very close between the death sentence and the variety of options mentioned earlier, ranging from mercy to death with a stay or delay of execution. (Thomas Paine, the American radical propagandist of revolution and author of *The Rights of Man*, was a voting delegate at the Convention; at very nearly the cost of his own life he actually argued in a speech before the January

7 adjournment that Louis Capet be shown clemency by being banished to the United States, noting favorably that the "monarchical organ" had "certainly performed a good, a great action" by intervening on behalf of the thirteen colonies' struggle for independence.)[20]

The fault lines within the Convention ran very deep between temporizing, concerned Girondins and ardent, vengeful Jacobins. There was no hiding place in the Manège for any of the delegates from voting on the fate of Louis Capet and the nature and direction of the revolutionary Republic. Each department of France was called in alphabetical sequence by the president. Each member had to come down from his seat, in the order of seniority within his department as determined by his date of election to the Convention, and each one had to approach the tribunal's podium. There, the delegate was required to announce his vote throughout the cavernous hall to the 720 other members as well as to the crowd of onlookers in attendance. As the time came for the eight-man delegation from the department of Loire-Inférieur to step forward to declare publicly their individual positions on the fate of Louis Capet, the vote for and against immediate execution was running close to even. The gaunt, sallow-complexioned teacher-deputy from Nantes, likely dressed in his trademark suit of jet black, approached the podium. As he had recommended in his pamphlet, he was impassive like divinity. In his thin and feeble voice he uttered just two words: "*La mort*."

Thus, Joseph Fouché, at the age of 33, had helped to eliminate the King of France. When the overall vote was completed, thirteen hours after it had commenced – 361 in favor of immediate death without recourse, 360 for the various other options – Fouché was a regicide, by the very narrowest of margins. His pamphlet had urged that no weakness be displayed in order to avoid calamities, but calamities would nonetheless most certainly ensue.

The final act in this drama was transformational in world history. Louis was taken from his family in the Temple prison on January 21, 1793 (in what had become 2 Pluviôse in the Year I) and was transported by carriage through the fogbound streets of the capital to the Place de la Révolution, formerly the Place Louis XV and today the Place de la Concorde. A forlorn-hope royalist rescue attempt was botched, and the once omnipotent Bourbon king mounted the scaffold before assembled throngs of Parisians and the massed troops of the Convention's National Guard. He tried to speak words of forgiveness, but those words were drowned out by the terrible drum-roll of the Guard. The fat-necked Louis was pushed beneath the blade of the guillotine, the blade fell, and then, amidst a profusion of spurting blood, the executioner raised the severed head of Capet for the crowd of liberated citizens to behold.

It has been claimed that at the time of the vote in the Convention, Fouché had confided to his ostensible friend, the moderate Girondin delegate from Pas-de-Calais and fellow former Oratorian professor Pierre Daunou (who himself had voted for Louis' exile), that he had originally intended to take a position for clemency but was worried about threats to his family back in Nantes if he did so.[21] Whether or not any such threats were actually intimated cannot be definitively established, but in any event the excuse itself does not ring true: the Bretons of Nantes were much more conservative than their Parisian counterparts, and five others in the eight-man delegation from Loire-Inférieur had found it in themselves to take a stand against the immediate execution of Louis Capet.[22] Rather, we have an early example of Fouché deviously attempting to keep a back channel open to the Girondins should the relentless Jacobins eventually fall from power and, moreover, perhaps even demonstrating an eye to attempting to twist the future historical record, however unconvincingly. In the short term, his fateful vote assured his survival. For many of those delegates inclined towards clemency or at least more measured punishment of the sovereign, moderation in a time of war and internal terror would constitute a vote for their own extinction.

The Emperor Napoleon once commented derisively to his Minister of Police about his lingering and unsavory status as a regicide. Fouché is said to have coolly retorted, "Sire, that is merely the first service which I have rendered your Majesty."[23] But, as will be seen, the regicidal mark was to hound Fouché, much as it would relentlessly hound so many other delegates to the 1792-93 session of the National Convention — at least those who survived the cataclysmic events that were to follow. Revenge would ultimately be exacted on them when the House of Bourbon was finally able to reclaim power twenty-two years later, although in Fouché's case the reckoning would be delayed and far more complicated than for most of the others.

Chapter III

Missionary

After the cannonade of Valmy and the execution of Louis, there was to be no turning back for the National Convention, no chance for peace or moderation, nor could there be any room for mercy or for compromise. The Jacobins of *la Montagne,* led by the ascendant Robespierre and his acolyte Saint-Just, gained supremacy, and they embarked upon a death struggle with France's enemies, internal and external, who were synonymous with their own. Their means to the end was the Terror, the ruthless elimination of all threats to the Republic, and their ideal was revolutionary Virtue, to be achieved by the creation of a new and selfless citizenry from a mold unlike any other in the world. One of their most potent weapons would turn out to be Joseph Fouché until, in the end, denounced and hunted, he would turn upon them.

In the spring of 1793, the Convention commenced spreading terror and propagating virtue throughout the country and even beyond its borders, as revolutionary armies were locked in combat with France's many foreign foes. The chosen instruments were the *représentants en mission,* trusted agents of the Jacobin overlords tasked with enforcing discipline, rewarding the virtuous (which of course meant the overlords themselves), and eliminating all vestiges of the *ancien régime.* According to the instructions of the Convention's fearsome Committee for Public Safety, operating under the command of Robespierre and Saint-Just, "You have in your spirit and in your heart the necessary resources to direct public opinion. Spread out into the popular societies, speak the language of philosophy and reason, unmask, engage in surveillance, denounce."[24] The *représentants* were expected to be in constant communication with the Convention but, as we shall see in the case of Fouché, they were also quite capable of acting unilaterally with broad discretionary powers, unless and until their actions resulted in disapproval and the dreaded recall to Paris. Their specific tasks were as follows: (i) to raise soldiers for the revolutionary armies fighting external enemies and insurrections against the Revolution, the authority of the Convention, or the Jacobin supremacy (although all these could be viewed by the Committee as one and the same counterrevolutionary offense); (ii) to requisition the materials and supplies required for those armies' operations and the funds to sustain the Republic; and (iii) to stamp out monarchists, aristocrats, "non-juring" or "refractory" priests (those men of the cloth who had refused to take the requisite oath of allegiance to the Constitution of 1791), and "brigands" (at that time, the catch-all term for anyone deemed rebellious or potentially rebellious by reason of background, word, or deed).

Like the proconsuls of the Roman Empire, the *représentants* fanned out from Paris during the spring and summer of the Year I; they were vested with the ability to act with unlimited authority (although not all of them in fact did so). Some of them were sent to accompany French armies fighting the forces of Prussia and the Habsburg Empire along the Rhine and in the Low Countries. These tribunes' objectives were to indoctrinate the Republic's troops and to uproot treasonous officers with links to the monarchy, the aristocracy, or the Girondist foes of *la Montagne*; they acted much like the Stalinist NKVD officers who motivated, monitored, and purged Red Army units during the Second World War. Others were sent into the western coastal countryside regions of France, where a full-scale, brutal civil war raged with the royalist-populist *Chouans* north of the Loire and the Vendeans to the south, and where Britain's Royal Navy lurked just offshore, looking for opportunities to lend support to the *ancien régime.* Still others were sent to the south of France, where great cities were in rebellion against the Jacobins' dictatorial authority, or into the central, heartland regions of the country. It was for one of these latter domestic missions that Joseph Fouché, deputy to the Convention from Loire-Inférieure, was selected by the Committee for Public Safety.

Actually, to a large extent Fouché selected his *mission* for himself, thereby demonstrating the significant powers that a duly appointed *représentant* could wield. The Committee for Public Safety at first believed that he would be exerting his efforts in Brittany against the *Chouans*, and Fouché initially went there as instructed. But, for reasons not entirely clear but perhaps attributable to the area's anarchic turmoil (it would be very difficult to raise sufficiently inspired troops from a region of counterrevolutionary rebels), as well as to his sense that better career opportunities existed elsewhere, he self-confidently and unilaterally elected to alter his assignment. So it was that in July 1793, Fouché on his own initiative arrived in Nevers, a town in central France on the Loire River.

The *représentant en mission* was not expected simply to operate on his own, without indigenous assistance. Among the local resources typically available to him (depending upon where he was stationed or stationed himself, of course) were a plethora of popular societies and clubs that had sprung up throughout France since the heady days of 1789 and the General Assembly at Versailles. Most useful to the *représentant*, were the Jacobin clubs, stocked with avid supporters of the policies of *la Montagne*, and in direct correspondence with the mother club on the Rue Saint-Honoré in Paris. However, other societies that were gathering places for "Friends of the Constitution" could also serve as fertile grounds for recruitment, once they had been brought under control and purged of reactionary or moderate elements. (A sample questionnaire utilized by Fouché to that end contained questions which the interrogated party would obviously need to answer correctly, such as: "In 1789 were you a patriot or were you not?"; "Have you frequented with nobles, the rich, or the sans-cullottes [the Parisian proletariat]?"; "Have you approved of all revolutionary laws?"; "Have you advocated the death of the tyrant [King Louis] and have you expressed any regret as to his death?"; and, "Have you carried on any trading in *assignats* [paper currency] in exchange for silver?")[25] Working swiftly under threatening circumstances, the *représentant* would select reliable revolutionaries from the available talent pool. He would use them to form committees of surveillance which would provide him with informants, and to staff revolutionary tribunals to administer justice to those accused of counterrevolutionary actions or sentiments. Enforcement muscle was supplied by detachments of National Guard troops, which the *représentant* could call upon as needed; he could supplement their numbers as his diligent efforts to recruit and equip troops from amongst the local populace gained momentum.

This template for exercising local authority was followed by Fouché in Nevers and elsewhere throughout his journeys in central France. Nevers also provided Fouché with a significant ally from the Convention, as it was the hometown of Pierre-Gaspard Chaumette, a fellow Jacobin deputy with whom Fouché had become increasingly aligned since the onset of the trial of Louis Capet. Chaumette had been a medical student in Paris, but with the outbreak of the Revolution he was elected President of the Paris Commune, the extremely radical municipal governing authority in the capital which also served as a power base for the Jacobins. He was a fellow regicide, in fact having been one of the most ardent proponents for executing the King, delivering bloodthirsty speeches in the Manège. He was also an equally ardent atheist.

The former Oratorian, now *en mission*, came under the increased influence of Chaumette in preaching a doctrine of apostasy. Fouché had in very short order made the transformation from a teacher in the service of a religious order, to a fervid denouncer of refractory priests (again, those priests not swearing loyalty to the Constitution), to anti-Catholicism, to aggressive and propagandizing atheism, all accomplished in breathtaking time. Some of this was doubtless very pragmatic on his part: the Church had long been an ally of the monarchy in France, although with the collapse of the Estates-General in 1789, fissures had quickly appeared between many in the church hierarchy, populated on the one hand by sons of the aristocracy, and on the other by parish priests who were frequently more in tune with the needs of their congregations. Now, weakened further by the schism between juring priests and refractory priests, and by the death of the divinely empowered Louis XVI, the Church was an extremely tempting source of revenue and plunder. With his de-Christianizing initiatives, Fouché would take the assault upon this vulnerable target to extremes.

On August 10, Joseph and Jeanne Fouché (Christian names, those) celebrated the birth of a baby daughter. That they named her Nièvre, after a river in central France was symbolic. Also symbolic was the girl's civil baptism in Nevers before the "altar of the country," replete with a detail of National Guardsmen as witnesses. (No church bells rang; they had already been melted down for bronze cannons.) This secular family ceremony was followed by an official, grander one on September 21 in the great cathedral of Nevers, during which Chaumette and Fouché placed upon the altar a bust of Brutus, the Roman tyrannicide who served as an exemplary hero to regicidal Jacobins.[26] And on September 23, *représentant* Fouché decreed that priests had for too long avoided the "obligations of true citizens" and that they had displayed egotistical attributes *"contraire aux principes d'un régime républicaine."* Henceforth, he ordered, any priest in his department must, within one month, marry, adopt, or take in an elderly indigent. Any who failed to comply would not be permitted to perform their religious functions, and their pensions would be terminated.[27]

This civic event and accompanying proclamation were but a foretaste of what was about to come.

The picturesque town of Moulins is located in the Department of l'Allier, which administrative region, like the Fouchés' newborn daughter, had also recently (in the Year I) taken its new name from that of a river. (Formerly the region had been called Bourbonnais, which had been erased from the map for obvious reasons.) Moulins, as a regional hub, had already been on Fouché's itinerary in central France; it is here in late September that we shall see him come into full flower as *représentant en mission* shortly after he revisited the town in the company of his new role model, Chaumette, and a cohort of National Guardsmen.

Fouché first ordered several arrests, including an inspector of army manufactures, the inspector's secretary, and a local aristocrat. Next, up went the obligatory statue of Brutus. This was followed by a wholesale renaming of the streets and squares in the town once traversed by Saint Joan of Arc: "Rousseau," "Marat," "Sans Cullottes," "Marseilleais," and "Voltaire" (this last literary designation still remains in situ), replaced the preexisting monarchical and ecclesiastical nomenclature. Fouché issued decrees in rapid succession, imposing taxes on the wealthy with dire consequences promised for evaders, and requisitioning precious metals from churchmen and aristocrats to be sent to Paris. Food and supplies were expropriated for the army, recruits for its ranks were demanded, and the needy of Moulins were also provided for from confiscated properties. *Représentant* Fouché directed that any citizen not bringing to market the quantity of grain required was to be put on public display before punishment was meted out, wearing a placard identifying him as "starver of the people, traitor to the country."[28] The committee of surveillance met daily. And Fouché next decreed that a revolutionary festival would be held in Moulins.

Fouché's fete (which anticipated a larger one which took place in Paris in November and was led by Chaumette, the so-called "Festival of Reason" which desanctified the Cathedral of Notre Dame) was set, not un-coincidentally, on what used to be a Sunday under the old calendar. The date was 8 Vendémiaire in the Year II (September 29, 1793). The ostensible purpose was to honor the memory of Louis-Michel le Peletier (ironically, an aristocrat by birth), who was a regicide deputy assassinated by a former member of King Louis' bodyguard after the fatal vote. The commemorative event was carefully choreographed. The day started with a cannon volley at 6 AM and drummers beating assembly two hours later. Part parade and part funeral cortege, a procession commenced with National Guardsmen under arms. Behind them was a delegation of the old and infirm, to whom Fouché intended tribute be paid as sympathetic victims of the old order. Workers carrying sledgehammers followed, and under the direction of revolutionary officials they intermittently smashed roadside symbols of religion and royalty. There was a choir chanting hymns to *"Liberté,"* there were wives and children of volunteers off fighting at the front, there were workers from the armaments industry. There was a bust of the martyr le Peletier, preceded by children tossing garlands. Chillingly, there were the members of the local *comité de surveillance*. Bakers carried trays of bread, fashioned from the requisitioned grain and advertised as *"Pain de l'Égalité"*; revolutionary troops demeaningly dragged emblems of the church and crown into the Place Brutus; martial music blared.

And then, surrounded by a phalanx of Guardsmen, along strode Joseph Fouché, resplendent in full *en mission* regalia, dressed in dark blue with a tricolor sash and scarf, with immense red, white, and blue ostrich plumes bedecking his bicorn hat, and with a saber hanging at his side. As he strutted through the renamed streets and headed toward an immense bonfire consuming the symbols of Bourbon rule and Catholicism, he approvingly listened to chants and saw placards which proclaimed not only *"Vive la Montagne!,"* but also *"Vive Fouché!"* The procession culminated with Fouché leading the marchers in a macabre and surreal dance circling around the bonfire. [29] Had the poet Goethe witnessed the fete of 8 Vendemiaire in Moulins as he had witnessed the cannonade at Valmy, he might have had not just a glimpse ahead into the nineteenth century, but into the twentieth as well.

After his fete, Fouché issued more orders and decrees at a furious pace. Seventy-six priests, many elderly, were deported to Guiana; very few survived. Houses were searched in nighttime raids for fugitives and for hidden gold, silver, and jewelry. A second prison was created to handle overflow from the holding area in the fifteenth century Chapelle Sainte-Claire. The committee of surveillance continued to hear informers and to extract information, while the revolutionary tribunal awaited delivery of a guillotine to la Place Brutus.[30] At this point, Fouché had finished his work in Moulins, leaving it to trusted and hardened subordinates with whom he would remain in close contact. The *représentant en mission*, having had the benefit of the experience of his laboratory experiment in Moulins and elsewhere in central France, would soon be headed to the south, to the city of Lyon, where the presence of a merciless Jacobin enforcer was urgently required by the Convention.

Before he left, there was one more decree to be promulgated, and it was a strange one indeed. Fouché issued it from Nevers on October 9, 1793, and after a preamble stating that only law, justice, liberty, and the cult of "universal Morality" were to be accorded privileged status, here is what he proclaimed:

> Article I: All cults of diverse religions may only be practiced in their houses of worship.
> Article II: The Republic does not recognize any cult as dominant or privileged; all religious signs found along the roads, in public squares, and generally in all public places will be destroyed.
> Article III: It is forbidden under penalty of imprisonment to all ministers and priests to appear in their costumes other than in their houses of worship.
> Article IV: In each municipality, all deceased citizens, from whatever sect, will be taken to a place designated as a communal cemetery, covered with a funeral cloth which will be marked "*le sommeil*" [sleep], accompanied by a public official . . .
> Article V: The common place where their ashes repose will be isolated from all habitation, planted with trees, under the shade of which will be raised a statue representing *le sommeil.* All other signage will be destroyed.
> Article VI: One will read on the gate of this field . . . this inscription: "*La mort est un sommeil éternel.*"[31]

Thus, in the region under his control, the former Oratorian student had substituted, for the Civil Constitution of the Clergy of 1790, atheism as the preeminent doctrine, enforced by the powers of the State. While the effects of his Nevers decree were somewhat circumscribed due to Robespierre's abhorrence of this kind of frontal assault upon his own deistic beliefs and his concerns over the perceived threat posed to public order and morality, *représentant* Joseph Fouché had anticipated the advent of another Joseph who would reject his religious training at the Tiflis Seminary and enshrine atheism and his own cult of personality: Josef Dzhugashvili, a.k.a. Stalin. The deputy from Loire-Inferieure, continuing his odyssey *en mission* and laying plans for his next committee of surveillance, would go on to create further such dark parallels during the next stage of his career.

Chapter IV

Butcher

Before the events that led to its very name being stripped away from it, Lyon was a magnificent place. At the outset of the Revolution, it was the second largest and arguably the most prosperous city in all of France. Two hundred and fifty miles to the southeast of Paris, it occupied the heights overlooking and surrounding a peninsula formed as well as bounded by the Saône River to the west and by the Rhône River to the east. Over the centuries it had naturally expanded from its ancient Roman site as its wealth, commerce, and fine arts flourished and grew. While the city had become an important banking center by the eighteenth century, the mainstay of Lyon's economy since the Renaissance was its silk industry, with its artisans producing exquisitely fine clothing, accoutrements, and furnishings for the aristocracy of Europe. While these artisans labored for the benefit of an oligarchy of mercantile houses, they owned their own looms and shared — to a significantly greater degree than did the laborers of Paris — in the wealth which flowed into their city and their region, known since the beginning of the Revolution as the Department of the Rhône-et-Loire.[32]

With the rise to power of the Jacobins and the execution of the King, the populace of the city of Lyon in the catastrophic year 1793 increasingly felt the burden of radical rule, which to a large extent was externally imposed upon them from Paris. The governing body, the Municipality of Lyon, came under the thumb of a homegrown and ferocious Jacobin, Joseph Chalier, who had previously been a traveling salesman for one of the silk houses. As head of the revolutionary tribunal in Lyon, Chalier zealously supported the demands of the Jacobin Convention in Paris for requisitions of troops and supplies and for the uprooting of political moderates as well as monarchists. In the case of Lyon in particular, the National Convention ordered that funding be expropriated from the local aristocrats and merchants to support its external and internal wars against the enemies of the Republic. Chalier enthusiastically complied. Under such pressures, the economy of the great city and its surrounding areas soon began to collapse.

Peaceful attempts by a broad-based coalition of the people of Lyon to remove Chalier electorally (the popular opposition candidate won election while in jail and unsurprisingly remained there), and to send representatives to the Convention to decry misrule and to request that a more moderate regime in the city be established, were successively thwarted. Consequently, the Lyonnais, led by elements of the local National Guard, staged an uprising on May 29. The insurgents seized Chalier, and they tried and executed him, using the very guillotine which he had requisitioned from Paris and threateningly erected in the grand public square. Back in the capital city, the Jacobin-controlled National Convention and the members of its intimidating enforcement unit, the Committee of Public Safety, were stunned and infuriated. The highly disturbing events in Lyon had occurred just as Paris and the Convention were about to be submerged in Robespierre's purgative Reign of Terror, and while foreign armies were threatening the French Republic from every quarter. The populace of vast sections of western coastal France, north and south of Loire, continued to be engaged in massive insurrections against Jacobin authority, and other great cities to the South, most notably Toulon and Marseilles, were unremittingly hostile to the radical government in Paris. Lyon was also a critical supply center for the French armies engaged in combat from the eastern Pyrenees to the Alps. While the people of Lyon insisted that theirs was not a revolt against the Republic, their actions were inevitably seen by the Jacobin Convention as part of a sweeping, collective, and unpardonable treason in time of war, a war for the Revolution's very existence.

Thus it followed that fierce retribution was visited upon Lyon in the summer of 1793: the Jacobin rulers of France sent an army of 16,000 men with orders to lay siege to the apostate second city. At first, the Lyonnais defenders enjoyed some degree of success. Their commander, the Comte Perrin de Précy, had royalist credentials, but their ranks were constituted by members of all social classes. The radical representatives of the Convention, shocked by the uprising's implications for the survival of the Revolution (at least as they had envisioned it), removed their own army commander, General Kellerman of Valmy fame, and accused him of lassitude. They poured in fresh reinforcements,[33] and put a stop to their besieging forces' sporadic offers to negotiate with the rebels. "Open your gates or the vengeance of the people is ready to burst over you," was the pointed threat that the Convention delivered to Lyon.[34] The city, however, continued to resist, with its leaders declaring fealty to the Constitution, while hoping for aid from elsewhere in France (which never materialized), and insisting that they were ignorant of whatever it was they had done to have armed repression so viciously visited upon them by the Republic.

From August into October of 1793, the promised vengeance did indeed burst upon Lyon. The Convention's artillery pounded away day and night with mortar rounds and incendiary shells, and great fires raged within the city's walls. Supplies ran low, famine set in, and panicked noncombatants fled through steadily narrowing gaps in the Convention army's lengthening siege lines until the constrictive circle of death was finally closed and escape routes were largely cut off.

Finally, after more than two months of relentless bombardment and mass starvation, the city of Lyon prepared to surrender. The Comte de Précy, correctly sensing what would be in store for a captured rebel garrison, led a near-suicidal breakout of about 700 defenders under an illuminated night sky just before the white flag was raised on October 10. The commander and a small contingent of survivors eventually succeeded in reaching safety over the border in Switzerland; they were the fortunate ones.

As the conquered city smoldered, the Convention in Paris took several never-to-be-forgotten steps to apply the coup de grace to the southern uprising. First, on October 12, it issued a proclamation: "*Lyon fit la guerre à la liberté, Lyon n'est plus.*" ("Lyon made war on liberty, Lyon exists no more.") [35] In a message of chilling import, the Jacobins thereupon summarily severed the city's name from it. The Convention decreed that no longer would the metropolis on the Rhône and Saône be referred to as Lyon, its name since the very Dark Ages which were now returning in the Year II, but rather as "Ville-Affranchie" ("Liberated City").

The next vengeful step against the rebellion would not be so symbolic. The National Convention's dreaded Committee of Public Safety swiftly dispatched to the scene not one but two new *représentants en mission* to take charge of the situation in the prostrate city. Its appointees arrived resplendent in their trademark revolutionary tricolor ostrich plumes and sashes. The first was a radicalized and dangerously bitter actor, dramatist, and underappreciated former director of the Grand Theater of Lyon named Jean-Marie Collot d'Herbois; he had recently overseen mass arrests in the Oise region. The other proconsul was Joseph Fouché of Nantes, most recently of Nevers and Moulins.

Fouché and Collot had been sent to Lyon as replacements for a Committee of Public Safety representative named Georges Couthon, who had balked at going beyond executing the Lyonnais ringleaders and re-indoctrinating their benighted followers. To the Convention, and to Robespierre and his colleagues on the Committee of Public Safety, smarting from the escape of the most-wanted Comte de Précy, the revolt of Lyon called for a solution that went well beyond the usual repressive measures. Fouché now was a proven fanatical commodity, and Collot, whose pre-revolutionary theatrical performances had not been well received in Lyons, had, literally, a vengeful axe to grind.[36]

The core problem was that the entire city had held out for nine weeks, repelling numerous Convention attacks and putting up a fierce resistance. This was not the work of a small coterie of aristocrats and recalcitrant priests at the forefront of a brief and minor uprising; rather, the rebellion of France's wealthy second city had all the hallmarks of a cross-class mass insurrection against the revolutionary authorities. It could not be tolerated or dealt with leniently. In the words of Joseph Fouché, it was "a slander against Nature and against the Revolution to believe that the mass of the people could be so corrupted."[37]

In his cover letter forwarding the October 12, 1793 (21 Vendémiaire in the Year II) decrees to his representatives in Lyon, the chief architect of the Reign of Terror, Maximilien Robespierre, admonished: "It is necessary to unmask the traitors and to strike them without pity . . . execute the decrees with relentless severity." [38] (This edict puts the lie to Robespierre's later attempts to distance himself from the havoc his own appointed agents wrought.) To carry out the spirit and intent of these instructions from the chief Terrorist, Fouché and Collot, along with some other Jacobin henchmen, expanded upon the standard operating procedures for *représentants en mission*. First they formed an entity called the *Commission Temporaire de Surveillance Républicaine*, which in turn set up revolutionary tribunals to mete out swift and brutal "justice" to the herd of prisoners. This Commission soon received 2000 heavily armed National Guard reinforcements from Paris and promptly set about its work. The houses of the city's rich were systematically demolished with pickaxes, sledgehammers, and explosives (rather than being given over to the poor). The property of the aristocrats and the *haute bourgeoisie* was seized and sold at state auction. Confiscatory revolutionary taxes were imposed upon a prostrate population and a ruined economy. Priests were arrested and de-Christianization programs were initiated by the by-now-expert Fouché. But most terrifying of all, mass executions began in earnest.

"The people must strike down all their enemies at once, and we will work to forge the lightning bolt," pronounced the Fouché-Collot Commission.[39] But the people's enemy *was* the people. Throughout November 1793, a steady stream of inhabitants of the Ville Affranchie were dragged before revolutionary tribunals and their death sentences were rapidly handed down. At first the victims — who came from all social classes, for such was the nature of the rebellion — were guillotined. The instrument of death was set up on a bridge over the Rhône, so that the heads and bodies could be readily slung into the river, whereupon they would float southwards as grim warnings to any restive Frenchmen downstream.

However, this one-at-a-time method, which had worked so well in Paris (the guillotine had actually been seen by the first wave of revolutionaries as a rather humane engine of death given its exceptional swiftness), was not well suited to the immediate mass executions which were demanded by the Committee of Public Safety to punish rebellious Lyon. So, Fouché and Collot thereupon commenced having the Lyonnais enemies of the state chained together and marched to a grassy area adjacent to the Rhône known as the plain de Brotteaux. There, artillerists of the Parisian Revolutionary Army fired repeated volleys of grapeshot into the mass of fettered human beings, causing the maximum amount of carnage. Grievously wounded survivors were thrown onto heaps of mutilated dead. As vultures circled overhead, the executioners were required to move in with bayonets and sabers to carry out the sentences of extermination. One prominent ninenteenth-century retrospective French illustrator, Dennis Raffet, who was not alive at the time of the Revolution, depicted Fouché resplendent in his plumed *en mission* garb, impassively watching over the Convention's cannoneers blasting away at the helpless prisoners.

The death toll from this post-siege mayhem neared 2000 citizens of the Ville Affranchie. (Of that number, thirty-three had been transported down from Moulins by Fouché's henchmen so that they could be dispatched at the site of this festival of mass murder.[40]) After several days of slaughter, repugnance for the horrific work was even beginning to erode the morale of battle-hardened National Guard troops. The Commission finally halted these executions by cannon fire, which became known as "*la mitrailleuse*," stating that a better way to extirpate Lyonnais traitors needed to be found.

The list of the condemned citizens of Lyon appeared on a monument erected many years later on the plain de Brotteaux, surrounded by weeping willows. The roll was a sobering one indeed. Here is a random sampling of some of the entries, complete with occupation and age: Jean-François Martin, captain of artillery (66 years); Jean Patural, priest (27 years); François Richard, grocer (40 years); Pierre LeClerc, postmaster (31 years); Jean-Marie Terrier, hatter (38 years); Antoine Courbon-Montviol, teacher (24 years); Jean-Claud Souchon, doctor (60 years); Hugues Durand, candle-maker (57 years); Jules Pommaray, clerk (18 years); Louis Reynard, silk-worker (32 years); Antoine Boivin, Justice of the peace (64 years); Jean Lebrecht, musician (26 years); Joseph Morin, wig-maker (32 years); Martin Foletier, student (17 years); Francois Lachaud, laborer (47 years); Jean Viamment, servant (21 years); Jean-Baptiste Vanderraghan, comedian (21 years).[41]

This was how the city on the Rhône and Saône lost its name, its stately homes, its silk and banking businesses, and much of its human population to war, repression, and reprisals.[42] However, as was the case with the excesses of the Terror in Paris and the massacres conducted elsewhere throughout France by the *représentants en mission*, the destruction of Lyon carried within it the seeds of the downfall of Robespierre and his fearsome Committee of Public Safety. But rather than being swept away as a most willing perpetrator, as the hideous "Butcher of Lyon," along with the whole lot of those responsible for ordering or sanctioning this fiendish retributive slaughter, Joseph Fouché would not only prove himself able to survive, but would soon demonstrate that he was clever enough to act as the agent for the demise of the higher-ups as well.

Chapter V

Nemesis

In the spring of 1794, that steely intellect of the French Revolution, Maximilien Robespierre, appeared to be in firm charge of the levers of power in France. He dominated the dreaded Committee of Public Safety, the National Convention, the municipal government of Paris ("the Commune"), and the revolutionary National Guard. His Jacobin party and its close allies had sequentially defeated and decimated each of their rivals.

First came the Girondins, whose delegates were driven from the National Convention and ruthlessly guillotined. Then it was the turn of the radical left-wing Hébertists, forerunners of the Bolsheviks, who were also crushed by Robespierre and his supporters on the Committee of Public Safety. (Fouché's atheist accomplice Chaumette would join the march to the scaffold by the members of this group.) Next in line were the Dantonists, who sought to moderate the excesses of the Terror and instead became the victims of it, along with their passionate and eloquent leader, Georges Danton, who is said to have presciently shouted from his tumbril as it passed the Incorruptible's lodgings: "You will follow us, Robespierre!"[43] While there were revolutionary tribunals which handed down sentences under a veneer of legal formality, the mechanisms of justice became increasingly swift and draconian until the accused, under the so-called Law of 22 Prairial, were essentially prevented from mounting any kind of defense of their alleged thoughts, words, and actions. The standard sentence decreed by the tribunals along with their waves of convictions was death, administered by the swift and relentless blade of the guillotine.

Robespierre possessed a consuming zeal for revolutionary virtue, coupled with the ability to inspire both acts of sacrifice in the name of the cause and to instill profound fear on the part of all those who crossed him or did not personify his lofty definition of a new morality. As "the Incorruptible" surveyed the scene in 1794, a different and less driven man might have decided that it was time ease up on the Reign of Terror: post-Valmy, the French Republic's armies had achieved additional great victories against the foreign invaders on the frontiers; Lyon and the other restive provincial cities had been effectively subdued; and opponents across the political spectrum were either eliminated or marginalized and cowering. But that kind of forbearance was not part of the make-up of Maximilien Robespierre. He would not shelve the Terror; he would redirect it against his former acolytes, most especially against a number of his wayward *représentants en mission,* including his erstwhile Rosati associate, Joseph Fouché.

As the savage repression visited upon Lyon and other French cities by the Convention's enforcers continued to exact enormous human and economic costs, local Jacobins began to find voice to complain. Robespierre, his brother Augustin, and other allies on the Committee of Public Safety, including his spartan comrade Louis Antoine Saint-Just and the same Georges Couthon who had initially advocated a somewhat more moderate approach to Lyon than had in fact occurred, listened to these entreaties and complaints with increasing and for the most part quite hypocritical sympathy. (Robespierre at one point declared, doubtless with Fouché and Collot specifically in mind: "Sometimes I have feared, I confess, that I will be sullied in the eyes of posterity by the unhealthy association with these perverse men.")[44] The result was that various *représentants en mission* began to be recalled to Paris at the behest of the Committee of Public Safety to account personally for themselves before the Convention, and to try to justify the extent of their Terrorist actions in the hinterlands.

Part of the reason for these recalls to the Manège was that the authorities in Paris were in fact becoming concerned that the Revolution's accomplishments could be disastrously undermined if unchecked excesses and economic ruination caused adherents in the provincial departments to have second thoughts about liberty, equality, and fraternity. But there was more to Robespierre's growing suspicion that something was out of joint than just that — after all, he had himself ordained and acclaimed the brutal punishment of the Ville Affranchie at the time. The basic problem was one of morality: Robespierre believed there was a God.

The ascetic architect of the Terror was not only convinced that the de-Christianization movement and its enforcers like Fouché and the recently eliminated Chaumette were creating unneeded enemies for the revolutionary Republic by pushing France's beleaguered Catholics well past the breaking point: he also believed that the prevalent atheistic rituals harking back to a distorted vision of Greece or Rome (exemplified by Fouché's adulation of Brutus) were insufficient to guarantee the requisite high standards of public morality. As Robespierre stated, "To invoke the name of Providence and to express an idea of the eternal being who essentially influences the destiny of nations, who seems to me to watch over the French Revolution, is not an ill-considered idea, but a sentiment of my heart." And, further: "If God did not exist, it would be necessary to invent Him."[45] This Robespierre was fully prepared to do.

The Incorruptible was fixated by the threats to revolutionary Virtue posed by bribery, graft, greed, and speculation. (The fall of Georges Danton had been linked in part to his supposed involvement in an investment bubble involving speculation in bonds of the French East India Company.) Rather than allowing the nihilistic desecration of churches and the blasphemous desecration of graveyards to continue, the sober Deist Maximilien Robespierre became determined to reintroduce the Creator and a stricter morality to atheistic, Jacobin Paris.

This determination to impose Virtue by making sacrificial examples is what put into motion the recall of *représentant en mission* Collot d'Herbois (who also served as one of the twelve exalted members of the Committee of Public Safety) and the return to Paris of the apostate Joseph Fouché from Lyon to explain their conduct to the Convention. At first, their justifications of their bloody repression seemed to be well received, and in June 1794 Fouché was even briefly elected president of the Jacobin Club in Paris. But Robespierre harbored great animosity towards Fouché, who was soon being termed the "Butcher of Lyon." His hatred stemmed in part, perhaps, from their initial acquaintance during simpler days in Arras, where Fouché had briefly courted Charlotte Robespierre and was the lender who had helped to finance Maximilien's delegacy to the National Assembly. Certainly, however, it was the former Oratorian's aggressive atheistic campaigns that now incurred the opprobrium of Robespierre, who immediately saw to it that Fouché was not just removed from the presidency of the Jacobin Club, but expelled from it as well. To the Incorruptible, Fouché's irreligious excesses throughout central France threatened the moral order by confusing the destiny of the good with the wicked, leaving "no other arbiter but the right of the strongest or cleverest."[46] At the Club, Robespierre denounced Fouché as the "conspirator-in-chief," and the Jacobins added accusations of "Caesarism,"[47] a stinging rebuke to such a fervent admirer of Brutus.

It appeared to most observers that the days of the representative from Nantes were numbered under any type of calendar. Fouché later wrote that Robespierre had said that "it will be my [Fouché's] head or his [Robespierre's] downfall."[48] Not many observers would have given Fouché any chance whatsoever of survival, notwithstanding his precautions of going into hiding and moving rapidly from place to place in that last summer of the Terror. But Joseph Fouché was not simply on the run: he was simultaneously and assiduously tying together the threads of a conspiracy to be carried out by a frightened group who had suddenly and unexpectedly found themselves to be on the wrong side of the Revolution. The plotters came to be known as the "Thermidorians," after the revolutionary month in which they hatched their deadly coup against Robespierre. The beleaguered proconsular instruments of Terror were to be organized and turned against the chief Terrorist.

After Fouché, first among this desperate group was his similarly bloodstained accomplice Collot d'Herbois, a native Parisian who wielded not inconsiderable power of his own because of his membership on the Committee of Public Safety. Stemming from the aftermath of the massacre of the Lyonnais insurgents, Collot had also become the enemy of Robespierre's ally, the wheelchair-bound fellow Committee of Public Safety member Georges Couthon. A second key compatriot in Fouché's plotting was Jean-Lambert Tallien, who had been *en mission* for the Convention in Bordeaux at the same time Fouché and Collot were in Lyon. There, Tallien had organized his own atheistic ritual, "the Festival of Reason," and sent many opponents of the Republic to their deaths. However, he had spared the life of one of them: Thérèse Cabarrus, the wealthy and beautiful former wife of an émigré aristocrat. He also made her his mistress. To the chaste moralist Robespierre, this was an abominable offense against the Revolution.

There were other recalled Convention enforcers who were now in danger of being proscribed and purged. Notable among them were Jean-Baptiste Carrier, who had eliminated by the thousands indigenous enemies of the State in Fouché's home town of Nantes by conducting horrific mass drownings in the Loire ("*les noyades*") using barges outfitted with trap doors, and Paul Barras, the libertine son of an aristocratic family who had helped subdue the counterrevolutionaries in the port city of Toulon. Carrier would ultimately follow Robespierre in his downfall, while Barras for a time would be ascendant and lift Joseph Fouché up with him, until Fouché would decide that it was time to stab his benefactor in the back.

The seemingly omnipotent Robespierre had another concern besides having earned the enmity of these Jacobin proconsuls whom he had decided to purge. Within the Convention, the Committee of General Security, an alternate and rival power center to the Committee of Public Safety, had also grown and flourished during the Terror. It was essentially a police organization responsible for administering revolutionary justice in Paris; it did not send out the *représentants en mission*, who were dispatched by the Committee of Public Safety. So Robespierre now had a dual problem: a second security force had established itself outside his direct control in the capital which was distrustful of the Committee which Robespierre dominated, and his own Committee, with a number of its agents suddenly transformed by panic into self-preserving conspirators, was no longer completely in the Incorruptible's back pocket.

Fouché was now at his clandestine best, hard at work tying together the survival instincts of the disparate conspirators and their potential allies on the two rival Committees and amongst the members of the Convention. In his memoirs, Barras recalls that "rising at early morn he [Fouché] would run round until night calling on deputies of all shades of opinion, saying to each and every one, 'You perish tomorrow if he [Robespierre] does not.'"[49] Fouché's paranoid listeners were extremely worried and highly attentive.

Although at the apparent apogee of his power, Robespierre made his first serious misstep when he decided to implement a "Festival of the Supreme Being" to reintroduce God to the city of Paris. Thus, May 7, 1794 (18 Floreal in Year II, the same day as Pentecost in the old ecclesiastical calendar) was proclaimed to be a day of ceremony and of celebration of the Deity, albeit not in a traditional Christian way. There were decorations by the renowned artist Jacques-Louis David (who later came close to losing his own head for having designed them), and a procession led by Robespierre in his powdered wig, tinted spectacles, and trademark light blue suit. The crowd, accompanied by 1000 musicians and 2400 choirboys snaked through the Gardens of the Tuileries and into the Champ de Mars, where a paper effigy of "Atheism" — along with the rather ironically designated images of "Ambition," "Egoism," and "Discord" — were ceremoniously ignited.[50] It was a fete, but one which in many respects was the antithesis of Fouché's fete in Moulins. While the weather on the day of the celebration was beautiful, and while portions of the sizable crowds seemed to display a degree of enthusiasm, albeit somewhat forced, and while The Incorruptible was transported by the vision that his new era of Virtue had arrived, there was also a subversive subcurrent, a noticeable atmosphere of unrest and derisive cynicism. A voice reportedly called out, "It's not enough for him to be king – he wants to be God!" Other such sarcasms subsequently were reported back to the singularly humorless Robespierre. These mockeries had occurred in overheard whispers and, less subtly, in clandestinely published broadsheets and journals, encouraged and planted by Fouché and his fellow conspirators. They were soon supplemented by other wild rumours that Fouché and his cohorts spread of the Incorruptible's purported moral transgressions, a foreshadowing of the kind of opinion-shaping that would in future years be perfected by Fouché's Ministry of Police.[51]

The head of the rival Committee of General Security, Marc-Guillaume Vadier, compounded the derisive undercurrent spawned by the Deistic extravanganza by using his agents to leak word that Robespierre was actually being influenced by a mad prophetess named Catherine Théot. The slanders spread by Vadier maintained that Robespierre himself was being worshipped as the Messiah by a secret cult. All this seemed to dovetail with Robespierre's ostentatious role in the Festival of the Supreme Being and consequently exposed him to further ridicule and innuendo.

In the wake of his Festival, Robespierre, perhaps exhausted and certainly feeling irritated and even somewhat humiliated, for the most part disappeared from public view for about a two month period, staying sequestered in his lodgings. (This curious withdrawal was to prove a fatal error, as it gave Fouché and his fellow plotters yet more time to organize and to sow distrust.) During that interval, Robespierre wrote a long, laborious defense of himself and his actions and expounded his vision for the future course of France and revolutionary Virtue.

Towards the end of his self-imposed retreat from the Convention, Robespierre became increasingly alarmed by word that was reaching him about the covert cabal being orchestrated by Fouché. He appeared at the Jacobin Club on July 9 to warn that "Someone is trying to persuade each member that he has been proscribed by the Committee of Public Safety. He wants to terrorize the Convention. I urge all members to be wary of the insidious remarks of certain people who, fearing for their lives, want others to share their fear." These remarks were a pointed threat and denunciation aimed at the elusive delegate from Nantes and to those who were listening to him.[52] On July 14, Robespierre had Fouché's name struck from the rolls of the Jacobin Club, after the fugitive had prudently declined to appear before it to answer charges against him and elected to remain in hiding. Fouché was soon on a proscription list drawn up by the Committee of Public Safety and he was certainly in the front rank of Robespierre's growing mental list of enemies of the state.[53]

Shortly before the culmination of the plot he was weaving together, Fouché wrote two letters, one to his surviving sister in Nantes and the other to his brother-in-law. He reassured his sister that "I have nothing to fear from the slanders of Robespierre. The Jacobin Club invited me to justify myself at their meeting; I am hardly going to present myself where Robespierre is the master . . . In a short time you will learn the outcome of this event which, I hope, will play out to the profit of the Republic." To his brother-in-law, he confidently stated: "Be calm, patriotism will triumph over tyranny . . . we will see the traitors unmasked."[54] The letter to his sister was intercepted by a proconsul in Loire-Inférieur who dutifully sent it back to the Committee of Public Safety. But by the time this final piece of damning evidence against Fouché had arrived in Paris, his conspiracy against his enemy had succeeded, and the Incorruptible and his Committee were to be feared no longer.[55]

On the 26th of July, 1794 (the 8th day of Thermidor in the Year II), Robespierre finally returned to the Convention hall. There, he stood and read his speech. In it he vehemently denounced the deputy Joseph Fouché to the other delegates: "No, Fouché, death is not an eternal sleep. Citizens, wipe from the tombs this impious phrase which throws a funeral shroud over nature and insults the dead! Write in its place this: death is the commencement of immortality!"[56]

The fearsome speaker also made other denunciations of enemies of the Revolution in the stifling hall of the Manège — he stated that there was "a criminal coalition which plots within the Convention itself"[57] — and he called for the awful justice of the Terror to be visited upon them, thereby striking at "the last heads of the hydra."[58] But here Robespierre made a grave mistake: he did not name any names of any other conspirators besides Fouché. The singling out of Fouché had an unintended and disastrous consequence for the speaker. A pervasive fear immediately spread through the listeners in the great hall of the Manège: *does the*

Incorruptible also mean me? The menaced deputies of the Convention sat in stunned and wary silence.

Because of the pervasive paranoia stemming from this sweeping condemnation of the Revolution's enemies — who were nameless and unidentifed except for Fouché — an unprecedented debate broke out as to whether Robespierre's speech should be publicly distributed or not, with a number of delegates arguing that it should be restricted to the eyes of members only. A courageous deputy demanded that Robespierre provide a list of names of the individuals to be proscribed and the Incorruptible compounded his earlier error by demurring, stating that he flattered no one, feared no one, and slandered no one. An unidentified voice thereupon shouted out "And what of Fouché?" Unused to this type of challenge, Robespierre evasively responded: "I do not want to talk about him at this moment."[59] Highly agitated, he thereupon left the hall of the Convention. He presented an address later that evening to the Jacobin Club of Paris. There he was greeted with great enthusiasm, Fouché and his unnamed band of co-conspirators against the Robespierrists were vilified, and Collot d'Herbois and an associate were forced to flee for their lives from the premises.

The next day at the Convention, however, Robespierre's attempt to reassert control of the deteriorating situation was completely thwarted, with a placatory and aphorism-filled speech delivered by his staunch ally on the Committee of Public Safety, Saint-Just, having no perceptible effect. Instrumental in this turn of events was the lurid performance of the recalled *représentant* and co-conspirator Tallien, who was furious over the arrest by the Robespierrists of his beloved mistress, the aristocrat Thérèse Cabarrus. Tallien brandished a dagger on the floor of the Convention, and delivered a histrionic speech while being abetted on points of order by the ex-playwright Collot (who happened to be the presiding official that day, and was ready to avenge his forceable ejection from the Jacobin Club the previous evening). With his feverish acting, Tallien was able to turn the emotional crowd against Robespierre. When his adversary tried to rise to respond, he was greeted with cries of "Tyrant!" from the Convention balconies, while most of Robespierre's own remaining allies from the Mountain — a number of them troubled atheists — sat silent. Collot rang the bell for order and Robespierre, angrily turning on his fellow Committee member, called him the "Speaker of murderers." The Incorruptible was then drowned out by a mob of delegates who had finally realized that there was safety in numbers. Someone shouted at him "the blood of Danton chokes you!"[60] The next thing Robespierre knew, he was seized and arrested by officers of the Convention. He was led off along with his brother, Augustin, and his staunch supporters Couthon and Saint-Just. The assiduous plotting of Joseph Fouché and his enlisted accomplices had seemingly succeeded.

But much drama remained. Robespierre and his fellow detainees were quickly released by their friends in the National Guard and the Paris Commune, and they all gathered at the Hôtel de Ville (the city hall) on the night of July 27-28 (9-10 Thermidor). Crowds of sympathetic Jacobins gathered at first. But as the hours passed and massive thunderstorms broke over the city, Convention forces led by co-conspirator Paul Barras marched on the municipal building. Robespierre's drenched supporters eventually began to melt away. The Incorruptible himself, showing vestiges of his stern moral compass and his legalistic proclivities, refused to sign a declaration of open rebellion against the Convention and the Republic. His last chance to install himself as a supreme dictator and to declare the Republic under an emergency state of siege consequently vanished. Convention forces thereupon burst into the Hôtel de Ville; havoc ensued. Robespierre was shot in the jaw (some say that he shot himself, but the better evidence points to an assailant), his brother Augustin was badly injured leaping from the building, and the invalid Couthon, in his wheelchair, crashed down the main stairway in a bizarre and forlorn attempt at flight. The lofty ideologue Saint-Just calmly surrendered. The National Convention had already summarily declared the Robespierrists to be outlaws, so there was no need for even the brief formality of a trial of the leading Terrorists before a revolutionary tribunal.

The next day, Maximilien Robespierre and his compatriots, including the gravely injured Augustin, the crippled Couthon, and the still-defiant Saint-Just were hauled through the streets of Paris to the same scaffold on the Place de la Révolution where the King of France, the Queen, and so many other enemies of the state had been executed during the Years I and II. The crowds jeered Robespierre mercilessly, and it is said that someone smeared blood on the door of his lodgings so that he could see it as the tumbril cart carried him past. The Incorruptible from Arras staggered up the ladder to the platform of death in the same light blue suit he had worn to the Festival of the Supreme Being some weeks before. The executioner ripped the bandages from Robespierre's fractured jaw and shoved his powdered head beneath the gleaming blade. The witnessing throng heard Maximilien Robespierre's last utterance: an unholy scream.

Eighty-six Jacobins joined the march to the scaffold, following Robespierre's small band of allies in a last paroxysm of vengeance. The Reign of Terror had come to an end. It was a conspiracy by its former chief enforcers — Carrier, Tallien, Vadier, Barras, Collot d'Herbois, and mastermind Joseph Fouché — who paradoxically were the unforeseen engines of its demise. And from that clique of desperate and impromptu plotters it would be Barras and Fouché who would have the cunning, foresight, and fortune not only to survive the storm they had unleashed, but to prosper.

Chapter VI

Survivor

Jean-Baptiste Carrier, one of Fouché's co-conspirators and a fellow *représentant en mission*, failed to anticipate the rapidity of Robespierre's shocking downfall on 9 Thermidor, and thus committed a fatal error. Carrier had been stationed in Fouché's home district, in the beleaguered city of Nantes, where he had conducted the aforementioned vicious and notorious mass drownings, wholesale prison massacres, and other indiscriminate depredations in the name of the Convention and the French Republic. There is speculation that Carrier had become completely deranged, perhaps because he had witnessed the aftermath of savage *Chouan* atrocities against the equally brutal republican forces.

Carrier's grave mistake was that for reasons unclear he had sent 132 of his Nantais detainees on a forced march to Paris to receive their revolutionary justice right in the capital city; it may be that he meant this offering as a form of Roman tribute and as proof of his earnest services on behalf of the Committee of Public Safety and the Convention. However, the 90-plus prisoners who survived the arduous journey turned out to be very fortunate indeed when the stunning overthrow of Robespierre brought the Jacobin Terror to an abrupt and unanticipated halt. Not only were all of them acquitted and released, but the lurid tales they had to tell of the brutality of Carrier's repression in Nantes, as well as the denunciations that came from other released prisoners who had similarly escaped torture and execution, led to a wave of public revulsion and outrage against the hideous crimes that had been committed in the name of the Republic.[61] (Among the eyewitnesses' accounts were those of *Vendéen* and *Chouan* prisoners of war being shot after they surrendered in reliance upon promises of amnesty, of one of Carrier's lieutenants pinning a severed ear to the cockade on his hat, and of the *noyades* having featured "republican marriages" with naked men and women being roped together, sabered, and drowned.)[62] The Jacobin Club in Paris was stormed by an angry mob. Rehabilitated survivors of the Terror, including Girondin deputies and other emboldened opponents of *la Montagne*, called for vengeance. (One accusatory pamphlet was entitled "Off with the Head of Carrier and All Those Who Resemble Him.")[63] The Thermidorian conspirators — not just Carrier, but Barras, Vadier, Tallien, Collot d'Herbois, and Fouché as well — suddenly found themselves in the midst of a battle for their own lives, in which they would desperately try to portray themselves as heroic topplers of the vile Robbespierreist dictatorship, while attempting with equal desperation and varying degrees of success to downplay their recent pasts as Committee of Public Safety enforcers.

Carrier posed an immediate problem for the survival of all of them. In response to charges which were brought by the Convention against his henchmen, the latter insisted that they had been acting under the orders of the *représentant en mission*, pointing their accusatory fingers at the man in charge: "If we are the agents of Carrier, it is necessary that Carrier appears . . . he who made the machine move is the sole one guilty!"[64] Calls for retribution against the "monster of Nantes" multiplied. One could readily envision a parallel scenario developing with respect to the perpetrators of the depredations in Lyon.

It was in this threatening environment of retaliation and revenge that Fouché exhibited his uncanny ability to change course and color instantaneously.

Fouché's first move was to be certain that all the anger and attention were focused on Carrier alone, and to ensure that he, Fouché, would be perceived as being amongst those demanding justice rather than someone who should quite obviously be the next in line to receive it. To achieve this end, Fouché reached out to a radical acquaintance of his, a man originally named François-Noel Babeuf (who had changed his given name while in prison to "Gracchus," after Tiberius Gracchus, a populist Roman martyr who had espoused agricultural reform). Babeuf was unusual amongst the Jacobin intelligentsia in that he was from a rough and impoverished background and was completely self-taught. As we shall soon see, his doctrinal outlook went far beyond anything any other faction, save perhaps for some of most radical of the previously guillotined communistic Hébertists, had been prepared to espouse. But, with the fall of the despotic Robespierre, Babeuf (who had recently been jailed for forging a document) was simply relieved to be alive. Fouché approached Babeuf and encouraged him to write a pamphlet attacking Carrier, which Fouché personally edited.[65] This pamphlet was entitled *La Guerre de la Vendée et le système de dépopulation*, and it reviled Carrier for having committed genocide (the word "*dépopulation*" was both an invention and an etymological precursor). Gracchus Babeuf alleged that Carrier had committed this heinous crime as part of a plot by Robespierre to deflate the number of Frenchmen who otherwise would have had to be fed in a time of extreme shortages.

On October 31, 1794, a commission of twenty-one deputies to the Convention was selected by lot to investigate the atrocities in Nantes and to draw up charges against Carrier, who was placed under arrest. Many witnesses were heard and the result was a sweeping and angry indictment:

> Citizen-representatives, faithful to our vows like you, we denounce to you the infamous Carrier; his crimes arise on every side against him; everything here bears witness to them; we denounce him to the national representation that he wished to degrade, we denounce him to the entire people whose faith he has betrayed.[66]

There followed a roll call vote by all deputies for committing the accused to trial. Fouché cast his own vote in favor of an accounting for his fellow regicide, who had obviously given a very bad name to all *représentants en mission*.[67]

Carrier was brought to trial before a special Convention Tribunal. In a proceeding that in some ways prefigured Nuremberg (although, unlike Nuremberg, the tribunal was largely constituted of the defendant's comparably complicit compatriots), he defended his conduct in Nantes as having been necessary at all times and as performed under orders from higher authority: "*Quelles ont pu être mes intentions? Certes, j'en ai pu eu d'autres que de sauver la république . . .Soumis aux décrets de la Convention nationale . . . En un mot, mes intentions étaient les votres. Si je pouvais m'être trompe, l'erreur serait entre nous, vous ne pourriez convertir entre un crime.*"[68] ("What have been my intentions? Certainly none other than to save the Republic. . . . Subject to the decrees of the National Convention . . . In a word, my intentions were yours. If I have been wrong, the error would be mutual, you cannot convert it into a crime.")

Carrier's argument that the blame must be shared up and across the chain of command was to no avail. The Convention's special tribunal sentenced him to death on December 16, 1794, and he angrily stared down jeering crowds as he was hustled to a guillotine in the Place de Grève that same day. But almost all of his agents and henchmen from the slaughter in Nantes were acquitted en masse; many of the deputies to the Convention sitting in judgment were no doubt already sufficiently discomfited by the precedent they had just set.

Inevitably, Fouché himself came under attack as a former tribune of the Terror, but he was able to sidestep adroitly the worst consequences — with the benefit of sheer good fortune to backstop his innate evasion skills. Not so Collot d'Herbois, who in the wake of 9 Thermidor had to witness the abolition of the Committee of Public Safety, which had served as his power base. Collot was impeached by the Convention along with a number of other Jacobin deputies on April Fool's Day 1795 (certainly not a date on the revolutionary calendar, but ironically à propos), and he was swiftly deported to the dry guillotine of the torpid, disease-ridden colony of Guiana. There, the theatrical terrorist and co-scourge of Lyon would die miserably within a year; it was rumored that the natives snatched his body from the military hospital in Cayenne and fed it to their pigs.[69]

Upon the news of Collot's arrest, Fouché hastily entered his lodgings and seized and destroyed a mass of potentially incriminating correspondence.[70] Perhaps because Fouché sensed that Collot could serve as a lightning rod for the bolt they had jointly brought down upon the Ville Affranchie, the deputy from Loire-Inférieure feverishly tried to reposition himself as a *moderating* influence in Lyon (there is precious little evidence to substantiate that he had been). In 1795 he published a pamphlet titled "*Réflexions de Fouché (de Nantes), sur les calomnies répandues contre lui*" ("Reflections of Fouché of Nantes upon the slanders spread against him"), in which he stated that he had all times fought against "the vile echoes of the kings, and against all of Robespierre's brigands." He continued to hammer away at the threat that had been posed by the Incorruptible: "Everyone knows with what devotion I have braved the axe of Robespierre, when the Terror prostrated all souls at his feet, to save, when I could, the city of Lyon, agonizing under the execrable power of brigandage." And then, after this breathtaking assertion that he had been a benevolent savior, rather than a brutal butcher, he alleged in a postscript that three deputations from Lyon to the National Convention since 9 Thermidor had asked for him, Joseph Fouché, to return to Lyon (the battered city's name prior to "*La Ville Affranchie*" by then having been restored to it), but that he had been unable to accept the assignment because of his all-purpose excuse, "the frail state of my health."[71] (The utter lack of attraction that these purported invitations to return to the doleful scene would have had to Fouché can only be imagined, given that a vengeful mob of 30,000 Lyonnais had recently stormed the prison where former Jacobin enforcers were in their turn being held; after first releasing the counterfeiters and petty criminals, the crowd had set fire to the jail and then slaughtered without pity their former oppressors, including those who had managed to flee onto the rooftop.)[72]

Despite Fouché's inimitable skills at changing his course and color, in this case it is somewhat unclear how effective Fouché's propaganda initiative to rehabilitate himself really was. Benevolent chance played a crucial role in sparing him from the consequences of his 1793 misdeeds. In 1795, like so many other Jacobins, he was made subject to an arrest decree, and he consequently forfeited his seat as a deputy.[73] He certainly would never be able to shake the gruesome reputation he had earned for his deeds in Lyon. But he was nevertheless most fortunate: even though deportation to join Collot in the deadly jungle prison of Guiana loomed as his likely fate, a sweeping amnesty was passed before the arrest decree could be carried out. He had bought himself just enough time to reap the advantages of good luck. Joseph Fouché thus remained a free man.

Almost destroyed by the Revolution as countless others had been, Fouché would henceforth find new ways to reinvent himself, to make himself useful to others of import, and to regain the surface of turbulent waters. Once afloat, he would prosper. But never again would he aim to serve as a selfless representative of the people. Henceforth, he would cynically utilize for his own ends and advancement the formidable skills of self-preservation he had already displayed in organizing the fall of Robespierre and in deflecting attention from — or at least attempting to avoid retribution for — his actions as a Jacobin *en mission.*

We now turn back to the man whom Fouché had ostensibly befriended, Gracchus Babeuf. After Babeuf's allegations of genocide had so helpfully charged the atmosphere against Carrier, the radical proselytizer next moved on to a new publishing venture and founded a newspaper called *Le Tribun du Peuple.* In it, he plucked from the tripartite motto of the Republic the word *"Égalité"* and espoused a novel theory, that of communism: all citizens of France would share equally in agricultural produce and manufactured wealth courtesy of a new government comprised of selfless tribunes who would effect the redistribution. (The irony — given Babeuf's hatred for Robespierre — is that only the Incorruptible may have possessed sufficient revolutionary virtue to carry out such a plan.) In late 1795 and early 1796 Babeuf and a number of surviving radical Jacobins began to organize an "Insurrectionary Committee" to help bring about the next revolution, a purer one that would create a new communist utopia and remake humanity, eradicating profit and privilege. It was called the "*Conjurations des Égaux*" ("the Conspiracy of Equals"). However, while the *Égaux* were infiltrating units of the French Army and assigning their agents to every section in Paris, their conspiracy itself also came under attack.

As we have seen, Babeuf considered Joseph Fouché, as an ardent Jacobin and expropriator of private property while *en mission,* to be his loyal friend and political ally. Babeuf had helped divert unwanted attention away from him with the collaborative pamphlet on *dépopulation*. Fouché even at one point was assailed in the Convention (by Tallien, with whom Fouché was now at odds) for his known connection with Babeuf, but he was able to deflect the criticism by asserting that he was in fact trying to serve as a moderating influence on the man and that he had actually succeeded in spiking one of his publications.[74]

Just how moderating an influence Fouché could be was evidenced when, at the request of his former co-conspirator Paul Barras, who was now one of the five Directors of France, he visited Babeuf to discuss the newspaper business and the editorial outlook of the *Tribun du Peuple*.[75] Fouché told a stunned Babeuf that he would guarantee him 6000 new subscriptions to his newspaper in exchange for official oversight of its content. Babeuf angrily rejected this insidious overture, in spite or perhaps because of Fouché's warning that several other publications had been similarly bought off by the new government.[76] In the very next issue of the *Tribun,* Babeuf denounced Fouché with piercing insight: "You have relations with those for and those against; you insinuate yourself with all parties; you do not pronounce your views in moments of peril . . . one does not know what to think of you." The communist editor thereupon defiantly proclaimed: "I do not wish any censor, any correcter, any prompter; I opt for persecution if necessary."[77]

Persecution was exactly what Babeuf got. Fouché had the police confiscate copies of the *Tribun*.[78] Then Babeuf and the members of his informant-ridden Insurrectionary Committee were rounded up. The radical publisher was brought in an iron cage to his trial before the High Court at the Vendôme, and he was convicted and executed in May of 1797.

Like his namesake (who had been beaten to death in the Roman senate), Gracchus Babeuf was the clear loser in his fight with established authority. The vanguard of the proletariat would have to wait for the "next and final revolution." In the interim, Babeuf would posthumously receive praise from the initiator of worldwide worker uprisings, Karl Marx.

Before he died, however, Babeuf wrote from prison that Joseph Fouché had visited his family and wept hypocritical tears.[79] The communist agitator bitterly accused his former friend of being "*un homme artificiaux qui pensait que la ruse était indispensable au triomphe de la démocratie.*" [80] ("He is an artificial man who believes that subterfuge is necessary to the triumph of democracy.") The doomed Babeuf's assessment was only half correct: Fouché no longer cared — if he ever really had at all — about the triumph of democracy. It was towards the realization of his own agenda, his own triumph in which he was now fully invested. He saw as his stepping stones the recent services he had undertaken for Paul Barras in pressuring Babeuf, and before that, in organizing the plot against Robespierre. Fouché sensed that in a fluid and corrupt setting like that of the post-Convention Directory, sooner or later his considerable skills at subversion and subterfuge would certainly be needed.

And Paul Barras would indeed prove to be an extremely helpful patron to his fellow regicide Fouché. The powerful Director was popularly known as the "Le Vicomte Rouge" — the Red Viscount — because of his aristocratic lineage and his radical Jacobin leanings; he espoused the latter until he was able to obtain executive powers for himself. Descended from feudal barons of Provence, Barras had a knighted ancestor who had led French forces during the Fifth Crusade, others who had been commanders of the Order of Saint Jean de Jerusalem, and another who had served as chamberlain to King Charles VIII.[81] As a young man, Barras had fought as an officer in the royal army of Louis XVI, seeing action against the British in the French enclave of Pondicherry, India, and again in the West Indies. In a rupture with his own past comparable to Fouché's break with his Oratorian upbringing, Barras had cast aside his lofty lineage and ostensibly converted to Jacobin radicalism;

also like Fouché, he had served the Convention and the Committee of Public Safety as a *représentant en mission.* He had been dispatched to the Mediterranean port city of Toulon, where he ferociously liquidated royalists and their fellow traveler enemies of the state who had sought assistance from Britain's Royal Navy during their city's revolt against the Convention in the bloody year of "'Ninety-three." While helping to direct the siege of the city, Barras had taken note of and encouraged the strategic and tactical vision of a young officer of artillery, Napoleon Bonaparte, helping to launch the Corsican onto his blazing trajectory of success and turning him, or so Barras foolishly thought, into a loyal and grateful apprentice. Like Fouché, Barras also had felt himself suddenly threatened by Robespierre and the Committee of Public Safety for his repressive actions while *en mission* and, as related, he had become a key member of the successful Thermidorian coup, leading the column of troops that surrounded and captured the Incorruptible and his supporters making their last stand in the Hôtel de Ville.

The sybaritic Director Barras was wily, unscrupulous, lucky, and quite determined — until the very end, when he would be betrayed, outwitted, and intimidated by his protégés, Bonaparte and Fouché, and would meekly leave the center stage of French politics. But until his abrupt exit in 1799, he was the only member of the five-man Directory to serve throughout all four years of the existence of that executive body. In part, his survival skills were simply attributable to an inveterate gambler's good fortune and ability to rig the betting: under the new Constitution, each year one of the Directors chosen by lot was required to stand down, also by lot, and once a Director had left office he was barred from resuming it for another five years. During Barras' tenure, other Directors came and went with dizzying rapidity, not only because they were not winning the annual drawing — unlike Barras, who had long courted Fortune at the gaming tables of Paris at establishments like the Palais Royal and Le Cercle des Étrangers — but also because they were the insufficiently agile victims of the succession of coups and purges that periodically crippled the new and unstable French government.

The Constitution under which Barras was supposed to operate came into effect in the Year III, shortly after the downfall of Robespierre. It was aimed at checking the excesses of authoritarianism that France had experienced at the hands of the Committee of Public Safety during the Terror. It provided for a bicameral legislature — the Council of Five Hundred and the Council of Elders — as well as the five-man executive Directory, but because of all of the myriad strictures in the 377 articles included in its 14 sections, the document in fact turned out to be a blueprint for deadlock and instability. Every year, one-third of the deputies in the legislature had to stand for re-election. Pendulum swings in the country between the fortunes of radical Jacobins and conservative elements, including royalists who had re-emerged after Thermidor, accentuated the revolving door aspect of this arrangement. The Directory — which itself was highly factionalized — had no legal veto power under the Constitution, but it did control much activity at the local levels and the Directors had taken upon themselves the illegal prerogative of influencing and annulling elections, and substituting their own candidates.[82] In a series of coups and counter-coups, the Directory mowed down rioting conservatives (with Barras appointing the seemingly reliable Brigadier Bonaparte to deploy artillery in the streets of Paris to give insurgents "a whiff of grapeshot") on 13 Vendémiaire in Year IV (October 5, 1795); it mobilized troops to remove legislative delegates, one of its own Directors, and a treasonous commanding general, Pichegru, on 18 Fructidor in Year V (September 3, 1797); it unseated Jacobins who threatened from the left on 22 Floreal in Year VI (May 11,1798); and, in turn, it was the subject of a retaliatory counter-coup by the legislature on 30 Prairial in Year VII (June 18, 1799) when two Directors — but not the resilient Barras — were expelled from office. Instability reigned.

All this factional, complex, and cumulatively paralyzing infighting at the top levels of government, between the executive and the legislative branches and within both bodies as well, was the inevitable fallout of six years of cataclysmic revolutionary upheavals. The Jacobins remained a very strong presence, but now they were faced with committed opponents with real staying power. The French countryside remained in turmoil, with escalating cycles of bloody reprisals between Jacobins and the groups they had suppressed during the Terror. Many of the senior leaders of the *Chouans* and Vendeans had been eliminated on battlefields and in ambushes in the *bocage* country of western France, but the Atlantic maritime and other regions along the Alps and the Mediterranean were still filled with armed insurgents who defied the Directory's tax and draft authorities, and who yearned for the official return of their Catholic religion. The Bourbons and their royalist émigré faithful watchfully remained on the borders, attempting to bribe and intrigue their way back into power. They prayed fervently to be carried back to the throne by the bayonets of Austrian and Russian troops and by the guns of the Royal Navy.

The overarching paradox amidst all this violence and turmoil was that after the austere years of Robespierre and the revolutionary fetes in honor of Reason and the Supreme Being, life in the French capital under the Directory had become one of luxury and vice for those who were fortunate enough to survive the Terror and the Thermidorian reaction and grasp the levers of power. These clever, fortunate survivors could amass staggering fortunes in a time of war, when diplomacy was conducted by bribery, and when complex conspiracies took root. Barras and his fellow Directors resided in the Luxembourg Palace; the Red Viscount also had a magnificent country manor outside Paris called "Grosbois," which he had acquired by virtue of his access to the national treasury.[83] In both these venues, Barras the erstwhile Jacobin immersed himself in wine and women, in games of chance and courtiers, in supplicants and sycophants. In his inner circle were Germaine de Staël, the brilliant daughter of King Louis' finance minister; the former bishop of Autun and devious aristocrat Talleyrand; Talma, the greatest actor of the day; Madame Récamier, of diaphanous dress and seductive couch fame; the revolutionary artist Jacques-Louis David, the impresario of Robespierre's Festival, who rivaled Fouché and Barras as a survivor and who had ingratiated himself post-Robespierre by designing the resplendent costumes of the Directors, with wide-brimmed Renaissance hats sprouting giant plumes, and red capes embellished with gold brocade; Thérèse Tallien who by this time was enjoying a ménage-a-trois with Barras and her husband, Jean-Lambert Tallien, the fellow Thermidorian; and another of Barras' mistresses, one Josephine de Beauharnais, the Creole widow of an aristocratic guillotine victim who herself had barely escaped the blade.[84] A fellow Director, La Révellière-Lépeaux — who would be forced from office in June, 1799 — painted in his *Mémoires* this savage image of the corrupt Barras and his entourage:

> Gallantry, debauchery, gaming, the dining table, and intrigue had perverted and dishonored his youth. His falsity and deep dissimulation, joined with his other vices, had only strengthened in him with age. At the Luxembourg, he was ever surrounded by the most toad-like anarchists, the most corrupt aristocrats, fallen women, ruined men, pimps, agitators, mistresses, and lackeys. He practiced the most infamous debauchery, by his own admission, in his home.[85]

It was into this mix that the temporarily adrift Fouché, without office or power, inserted himself as a supplicant and a useful tool to Barras.

In Barras' own set of *Mémoires*, just as vicious as La Révellière's and of even wider scope because Barras had many more scores to settle, the ex-Director explained the various appointments and emoluments he had directed to Fouché both as a tribute to the latter's persistence and to the sympathy he felt towards a man who had found no asylum outside the Revolution: "Joseph Fouché waited in my antechamber with a pitiable air, he spoke like a mendicant."[86] There may well be some truth to this description; this despite the fact that when Barras wrote his chronicle he burned with such fury regarding Fouché (as well as for Napoleon, Josephine, the rest of the Bonapartes, and Talleyrand, among a legion of others) that he engaged in corrosive personal invective, referring at one point to Madame Fouché's "horrible ugliness" and to Fouché's daughter as the "albino product of this hideous couple." He concluded about the subject at hand that "I have never known, during the Revolution, anything more ignoble than the conversation of this man."[87]

Beneath all of this well-after-the-fact diatribe, however, was the undeniable reality that Barras in times of crisis had greatly valued and promoted Fouché, and that he was under the profound misapprehension that he could facilely use and control him. He had seen what Fouché could do when Fouché had been personally threatened by Robespierre (which perhaps should have served as a warning to Barras). He had witnessed Fouché's skills when surgically applied to Carrier and Babeuf (and perhaps that should have similarly carried a warning message to him as well). Barras first deployed Fouché as his private investigator and informant ("to earn money he acted as my policeman"),[88] and soon came to appreciate the fellow ex-Jacobin's skills at building networks and distilling information and discovering leads. Barras conceded in his *Mémoires*, "Because he penetrated everywhere, Joseph Fouché stood in the first rank. . . . He procured the best information on all parties about whom the Directory had an interest in learning and in placing them under surveillance."[89]

Next the ascendant "mendicant" was appointed as a military commissioner to a French army; this was a rapid road to riches. Fouché eagerly availed himself of his new position after his years of Spartan service to the Revolution: "*de réparer le temps perdu*" — to make up for lost time — as he purportedly told subject-matter expert Barras.[90] Soon thereafter came diplomatic postings replete with opportunities for more pocket-lining. Barras recalled with regard to one undertaking to which he assigned his eager personal agent, "I believed the way to repulse our enemies . . . was *to present the Revolution itself to them and oppose it to them like Medusa's head*. I proposed Fouché for Italy." [Emphasis added.][91] There followed a mission to the French satellite then known as the Batavian Republic (Holland), where Fouché continued diligently to compile his list of useful future contacts, informants, and potential accomplices, derived from the ranks of the senior officer corps and military suppliers and from those of various other emissaries of the Directory.

Finally the time arrived for the ex-Oratorian's plum appointment, the real opportunity to pursue his true calling and his path to power. The Ministry of Police for the Republic had been established in early 1796, with its headquarters in the former Hôtel de Juigne, located at No. 17 on the Quai Malaquais, overlooking the left bank of the Seine. But the nine men who had previously headed it in less than a four-year period had possessed varying degrees of competence, and none of them had enjoyed a significant run: most fell victim to the vicious internecine struggles between Jacobins and anti-Jacobins in the government. In the summer of 1799, with economic, political, and military circumstances worsening daily for the Republic, Barras, and a forceful new fellow Director, the Abbé Emmanuel-Joseph Sieyès, both agreed that there was but one man for this important job: Joseph Fouché.

Sieyès, an anti-Jacobin and an Oratorian cleric who had barely escaped the Terror,[92] had at first been suspicious of such a candidacy, but Talleyrand — who in his diplomatic capacity for the Directory had been receiving valuable intelligence from Fouché, and who could readily recognize a talented kindred intriguer — reassured him: "At a time when the Jacobins are arrayed so boldly and violently against us, there is only one Jacobin who can battle them vigorously, attack them in hand-to-hand combat, and strike them down. You can do no better than Fouché."[93]

Another one of the Directors, Louis-Jérôme Gohier, protested that in the incumbent, police minister Claude-Sébastien Bourguignon, "you will never have a more honest man." The terse and chilly response came from Fouché's two powerful supporters: "That is not sufficient."[94] Thus it was that on July 20, 1799 — 2 Thermidor in the Year VII — Joseph Fouché became the French Republican Directory's Minister of Police. The Directory itself had less than six months to live. Fouché would help to dig its grave and in the bargain he would help to banish his benefactor, Paul Barras.

Chapter VII

Enabler

The new police minister would waste little time in exceeding the expectations of Barras and Sieyès. His two patrons' immediate target was the Left, which was enjoying a resurgence as France remained beleaguered, externally and internally, and the situation seemed to call for the extreme measures of 1792-93 to defend *la patrie en danger.* About half the deputies in the legislative Council of Five Hundred were Jacobins of varying degrees of ardor,[95] as were two of the five executive branch Directors, Jean-François Moulin and the honesty-prone Gohier. The Jacobin Club of Paris had reopened its headquarters in the drafty and haunted hall of the Manège, and thousands flocked to attend incendiary meetings there. The radical press was extremely vocal, launching daily attacks on the despised Director Sieyès in its flagship publication, *Le Journal des Hommes Libres.*

At first, Fouché intentionally lulled his leftist former compatriots into the complacent hope that one of their own was now in charge of internal security. But then, in person and accompanied by a phalanx of armed special agents and requisitioned troops, he suddenly descended on the Jacobin Club, scattering its occupants and padlocking the doors. He dramatically returned to the Luxembourg Palace, home of the Directors, and presented them with the keys to the Manège, exclaiming: "*Citoyens Directeurs, vos ordres sont exécutés!*"[96] This police raid took place on August

13, after Fouché was just two weeks on the job. He followed up with a crack-down on the opposition press, armed with decrees from the Directory. By early September, scores of editors, writers, and newspaper owners had been arrested and many were deported to the bleak prison island of Oléron off the French Atlantic coast, which at least enjoyed a considerably more temperate climate than Guiana. And while all this was happening, Fouché rapidly increased the number of his policemen and agents and exponentially expanded his ministry's network of paid informants. Streams of intelligence on political actors of every stripe flowed towards him and were assimilated and assessed. Astute political observers could readily sense that he was transforming himself into a power broker who could only be ignored at extreme peril.

While Fouché continued to take the pulse of his network of contacts and gather strength and influence, the power of the Directory as a political entity continued to ebb. The ambitious Abbé Sieyès was actively considering ways to supplant what he had concluded was a fatally flawed, dysfunctional system of government and to transform it under a new constitution, which he would devise himself, and which would possibly include an element of monarchy. To effect this end, this wily Director-cleric (and regicide, as well) cast his eyes upon the army's senior officers to find a man who could supply and lead the requisite armed force to carry out a coup d'état.

Sieyès first had the war minister, General Jean-Baptiste Bernadotte, removed as an untrustworthy Jacobin; Fouché had duplicitously forewarned Bernadotte not to be found at the Jacobin Club on the day of the police raid, or it would mean his head.[97] (We shall witness time and again Fouché's clever practice of keeping potentially useful people indebted to him, even to the point of manufacturing bogus threats against them if necessary, so that he could play the apparent role of surreptitious savior.) Bernadotte acidly wrote to the Directors that they had "accepted" his resignation even though he had not tendered it.[98] (We shall later encounter Bernadotte again, at an important juncture in Fouché's imperial career.)

Sieyès' initial overture was to General Jean Victor Moreau, who however appeared reluctant to break his oath of allegiance and engage in overthrowing the Republic. The Abbé next cast his eye upon General Barthélemy Joubert, then commander of the Army of Italy, as the man of the hour, but in August Joubert was killed fighting the Russians and Austrians at Novi, in the Italian Piedmont. As Sieyès continued to review his options, searching for the necessary spear-point, the answer — although it would be one he would ultimately regret — fortuitously stepped ashore on October 9, 1799, at the very place of the Abbé's birth, the ancient port city of Fréjus on the Côte d'Azur. General of the Republic Napoleon Bonaparte had unexpectedly returned from the Land of the Pharaohs.

That the heralded commander had left behind 12,000 of his exhausted and plague-stricken men of the Army of the Orient to suffer in the heat and pestilence of Alexandria, that a French fleet lay at the bottom of Aboukir Bay thanks to Admiral Horatio Nelson, that the General had taken it upon himself to return from his Egyptian expedition without express orders and, to top it off, that he had done so in violation of a mandatory quarantine, meant nothing to the cheering, adulatory crowds that lined his route from the coast all the way to Paris, much as they would in 1815 when the exiled Emperor escaped from the island of Elba.[99] They only knew that General Bonaparte had led the Army of Italy to a string of stunning victories over the foes of the Republic, and they had heard about his triumph on scorching sands against the Mamelukes at the Battle of the Pyramids. They fervently believed that he was the savior of France. Sieyès, initially distrustful, soon became converted to the idea that the Corsican officer could in fact be the pliable savior requisite to his own plotting and plans. An earlier warning about Bonaparte from a disgraced traitor to the Republic, the renegade General Pichegru, went unheeded: "The Directors think they are keeping a pet; he will eat them one fine morning without them expecting it."[100]

At first, Napoleon Bonaparte's attention was focused upon (i) convincing the Directory that his popularity outweighed his transgressions, and (ii) attending to the indiscretions — both amorous and financial — of his wife of less than three years, Josephine, widow of the executed aristocrat Alexandre de Beauharnais. The Directors accepted the reality of the first situation, and Josephine's former keeper and protector, Barras, eventually calmed Napoleon down with worldly advice regarding the latter. What Napoleon did not know, however, was that the Directory's Minister of Police had already turned his wife into an informant while her warrior was overseas. The looted treasures provided to her by Bonaparte's Italian victories had proved insufficient to maintain the Creole beauty in the luxury to which she had become very much accustomed, and the perceptive Fouché had swiftly exploited the situation. He put her on his police payroll for all the information she could provide him on her numerous contacts in the world of the Directory and throughout Paris society and, most importantly, regarding her ascendant husband.[101]

Thus it was with a certain amount of unsuspected familiarity that Fouché approached his first meeting with General Bonaparte, at the latter's home on the Rue Victoire, in early November. After keeping the policeman waiting for an hour, Napoleon proceeded to pick the brains (or so he thought) of the former Terrorist on the mood of the populace and the security situation confronting France.[102] The sweeping and detailed intelligence Fouché provided must have seemed most impressive to a military man just beginning to find his way politically; Napoleon, like Barras, would soon come to value greatly the abilities and insights of the Minister of Police. For his part, the attentive and perceptive Fouché concluded that it was worth placing a wager upon the rise of Bonaparte, a wager which, as always, Fouché would very carefully hedge against, in the event that the ambitious general met with failure.

The clever and devious Talleyrand had relinquished (actually, he was asked to relinquish) his position as Minister of Foreign Affairs at about the same time — in the mid-summer of 1799 — that Fouché had received his own police portfolio. Talleyrand was another confidante of Josephine's. As an aristocratic former bishop, he was trusted by Sieyès. He brought the Director Sieyès and General Bonaparte together in the common cause of overthrowing the government of France. The newly aligned duo needed allies, and an inner circle soon formed around them. It was comprised by Sieyès' compliant fellow Director, Roger Ducos; two of Napoleon's brothers, Lucien, an influential deputy in the Council of Five Hundred, and the good-natured, ineffectual Joseph; Jean-Jacques Régis de Cambacérès, a prominent lawyer who had become the Minister of Justice (and of whom we will see considerably more later as Archchancellor of the Empire). Around the perimeter there was a second, shadowy circle of merchants, financiers, and military contractors, eager to dispel forever the curse of Jacobinism and its Babeuvist-communist tendencies; this second conspiratorial circle was joined by the chief of the Paris police force, a Barras appointee, Pierre-Francois Réal.

Réal was already overshadowed by his boss, the new Minister of Police, but instead of being jealous Réal acted as an advocate for Fouché to the other plotters, citing his exceptional resourcefulness and enormous potential utility. While Fouché appears not to have been fully integrated into all the details of the Bonapartist conspiracy (although he had of course his own ways of keeping well informed about it, starting with Napoleon's bedmate), he was very much a player even before the coup was unleashed. He contributed important intelligence. He donated 900,000 francs of police funding[103] (the second-largest single contribution to the coup d'état, it seems). He provided other forms of encouragement: according to Napoleon's long-time personal friend and his private secretary at the time, Louis-Antoine de Bourrienne, Fouché advised him on 14 Brumaire (November 4): "Tell your General to be speedy; if he delays, he is lost."[104] And Fouché was part of a baleful and unnerving delegation — also comprising Réal, Talleyrand, and Joseph Bonaparte — that called upon Director Paul Barras at the Luxembourg Palace on November 6. This meeting did not result in Barras coming over to the conspiracy with fellow Directors Sieyès and Ducos, but it did begin the process of steering the Red Viscount into neutrality and marginalization. The final push into irrelevance and exile would soon be administered by Barras' two erstwhile and ungrateful protégés, Napoleon Bonaparte and Joseph Fouché.

Who then constituted the likely and possible obstacles to the success of this proposed attempt to extinguish the French Republic? First, the Jacobins, who despite having been thrown onto the defensive by Fouché still had a very considerable presence in the legislature, especially in the Council of Five Hundred. Second, the two Jacobin-leaning Directors, Gohier and Moulin. Third, several high-ranking officers, most notably the Jacobin hero Bernadotte (whose War Ministry portfolio, as noted, had recently been pulled by Sieyès and who was also now beholden to Fouché for his timely pre-raid warning), and Generals Pierre Augereau and Jean-Baptiste Jourdan (the latter had observed: "It is obvious that a regime that systematically nullifies elections . . . is no longer a republic, it is a dictatorship"[105]). Fourth, the traditional source of the radicals' strength, the working-class mobs from the Paris *faubourgs*, who had so many times in the recent past rallied to the calls of the leaders of the Commune in the ferocious defense of liberty, equality, and fraternity. Finally, there were some ambiguous but threatening fence-sitters: most notably, Barras himself, who had successfully faced down a dizzying series of upheavals and attempted coups starting with Thermidor and the Robespierreist threat; another hero-general, Jean-Victor Moreau, the popular commander-in-chief of the Army of the Rhine, he with the scruples about overthrowing the Republic; and finally, General François Lefebvre, commander of the Paris garrison, a Jacobin who had earnestly pledged to defend the Constitution but who could perhaps be influenced to do the polar opposite.

The plot itself was beautifully simple. The concept was to use the very provisions of the Constitution of the Year III to paralyze the government, and then to move in for the kill with the perpetrators operating under a cloak of purported compliance with legal procedures. The first step was to get the legislature out of Paris and well away from any possible direct assistance from the Jacobins and their disorderly mob of proletarian allies. The mechanism to accomplish it was a provision in the Constitution (Article 102) which permitted the Council of Elders to move its own sessions and those of the other chamber, the Council of Five Hundred, outside the city if there was an imminent threat of violent disruption. The plotters counted on using this gambit to cajole their friends and intimidate their enemies in both Councils into authorizing an emergency government; they would, of course, constitute and control this new entity if the executive branch, the Directory, could be liquidated. And the swiftest "legal" way effectively to eliminate the despised pentarchy was for three of its five members to resign.

But the actual execution of the plot, on the 18th and 19th Brumaire (November 9-10, 1799), was neither beautiful nor simple. The removal of the three Directors did in fact unfold as planned: Sieyès and Ducos, as conspirators, of course resigned. They were followed by a reluctant but suddenly spineless Barras, whom Talleyrand visited in the Luxembourg Palace on the 18th. It is unclear whether all or part of the large bribe Talleyrand carried with him went to Barras, and it is equally unclear how much of it the incorrigibly corrupt Talleyrand kept.[106] In any event, the result was the resignation of the Directorial majority, so the executive entity became moribund. (Barras, stating at the time that "I cheerfully return to the rank of a private citizen: happy, after so many storms, to resign,"[107] removed himself to his manor house of Grosbois, under the vigilant eyes of a cavalry detail sent after him by Napoleon.) For good measure, the other two Directors, Gohier and Moulin, were surrounded "for their own safety" in the Luxembourg Palace by 10,000 troops dispatched by Napoleon and under the immediate command of General Lefebvre; this malleable officer, no longer a potential obstacle, had tearfully accepted from Bonaparte a resplendent presentation sword from the Egyptian campaign, and he would eventually rise to become a Marshal of the Empire and receive the title of the Duke of Danzig.

The artificially induced decampment of the two legislative chambers from Paris also worked quite smoothly, at least at the outset. The Council of Elders fell prey to the alarming rumors of an imminent Jacobin uprising which the conspirators had strategically planted, and on 18 Brumaire (November 9) it collectively invoked Article 102 to remove itself and the other house of the legislature seven miles outside of Paris to the Palace of Saint-Cloud for an extraordinary session on the following day. As soon as the alarmed deputies hastily departed westward through the suburbs, Fouché's gendarmes erected barricades and roadblocks around the capital city. After the legislative exodus, no one was permitted to enter or leave Paris without a pass issued by the Minister of Police or by General Bonaparte, who had been able to have himself named commander-in-chief of the Paris garrison by the Elders before they left their meeting hall in the Tuileries.

On the next day, the 19th Brumaire (November 10), at Saint-Cloud, the conspiracy almost came undone. If it had collapsed, the fault would have been Napoleon's. His first mistake was to address the Council of the Elders in threatening tones and in his thick Corsican accent, without paying deference to the Constitution:

> Citizen Representatives, the situation in which you find yourselves is not normal, you are sitting on top of a volcano . . . Today slanders are already heaped upon me. There is talk of Caesar, there is talk of Cromwell, there is talk of military government. If I had wanted military government, would I have rushed to lend my support to the nation's representative body?

In response to a shouted query about compliance with the Constitution, the General angrily retorted:

> The Constitution! You have destroyed it yourselves. You violated it on 18 Fructidor; you violated it on 22 Floreal; you violated it on 30 Prairial. No one respects it any longer. . . Those who speak to you of the Constitution know very well that, assaulted at every moment, mutilated at every page, the Constitution exists no longer.

And he ended ominously:

> If I am a traitor, may you all be Brutus. And you, my comrades who accompany me, you, brave grenadiers whom I see surrounding this place, may these bayonets with which we have triumphed together be turned immediately against my heart. But also, should any orator in foreign pay dare pronounce against your general the word "Outside the law," let the lightning of war crush him instantly. Remember that I march accompanied

> by the god of war and the god of fortune. I am leaving. You go ahead and deliberate. Order and I will execute.[108]

Napoleon's next stop was an appearance before an even more hostile Council of the Five Hundred, with a good number of the Jacobin deputies having made their way to the Palace of Saint-Cloud despite efforts to keep them in the dark about the sudden relocation to the outskirts of Paris. Here, the god of fortune almost deserted Bonaparte, and his reference to the legislature as a collective Brutus came close to being fulfilled. He was shouted down by angry delegates who suspected that the rumors of a Jacobin uprising were the fraudulent pretense which they in fact were, and he was rushed and jostled by a number of them. His brother Lucien, who had maneuvered himself into serving as presiding officer of the Five Hundred that day, was unable to stem the fury by oratory. Napoleon had to be escorted out of the chamber by his bodyguard of grenadiers.

Outside the Palace, troops in massed formations shifted uneasily. Many were partial to Bonaparte or at least to his growing legend, but they were also hesitant to storm the Republic's constitutionally assembled, governing legislative body in what was obviously becoming a blatant coup d'état rather than an ostensibly legal transfer of emergency powers. Two men saved Napoleon's life and his star. Lucien delivered a histrionic harangue to the troops: he claimed that the deputies in the Five Hundred had tried to assassinate his brother and he pledged to run his sibling through with his own sword if he betrayed the Republic. Lucien's words had a perceptible effect. The actions of Napoleon's cavalry commander in Italy and Egypt, the highly volatile former Jacobin Joachim Murat (later to become Napoleon's supremely untrustworthy brother-in-law and Marshal, as well as the King of Naples), were also pivotal. Murat stormed off in the direction of the Council of the Five Hundred's meeting hall, and where he led, his troops enthusiastically followed. Waving his saber, he loudly announced, "Citizens, you are dissolved!" and shouted the energizing order to his men: "Throw these bastards out of here!"[109] The deputies fled in panic before the bayonets, scrambling out of windows as the ship of state swiftly sank beneath the waters.

Just twenty-four days had passed between Napoleon's triumphal return to Paris from Egypt and his overthrow of the Directory and the two Councils of the Legislature. Notwithstanding the end result, the coup d'état of 18-19 Brumaire had certainly turned out to be a near-run thing. On the way to Saint-Cloud, one of Napoleon's aides had noted sardonically, while passing through the Place de la Révolution, that the plotters could, by the end of the following day, easily wind up being escorted to the guillotine still positioned there.[110]

Of course, Joseph Fouché, from his Paris headquarters, had been attentively monitoring the progress of the coup to ascertain who would emerge victorious. The Minister of Police was very well aware of the risks associated with the gamble taken by the Bonapartist clique, and he directed his efforts towards appearing indispensably instrumental if it succeeded and vigilantly protective of the Republic if it failed. When the plot first began to get underway, in addition to ordering the placement of barricades around the entrances to Paris, he put out an ambiguous proclamation with vague references to countering threats from royalists. This clever proclamation could well have been interpreted benignly by the Jacobin opponents to the coup had it turned out that they gained the upper hand.

But Fouché quickly concluded that the Jacobins and their allies were supine, that the Corsican general had in fact succeeded in grasping the levers of power, and that the population of Paris, weary of the Revolution in general and the Directory in particular, was apathetic to the events happening just outside the capital. His 900,000 franc wager was about to pay off handsomely. Up went a new proclamation, one that would cement the career of Fouché under the new regime:

> *Le ministre de la Police générale prévient ses concitoyens que les Conseils étaient réunis à Saint-Cloud pour délibrer sur les intérêts de la République et de la liberté, lorsque général Bonaparte, étant entre au Conseil des Cinqs Cents pour dénouncer des manouevres contre-révolutionaires a faille périr victime d'un assassinat. Le génie de la République a sauvé ce général; il revient à Paris avec son escorte; le corps legislative a pris toutes les mesures qui peuvent assurer le triomphe et la gloire de*

> *la République.* [111]("The Minister of Police advises his fellow citizens that the Councils were meeting at Saint-Cloud to consider the interests of the Republic and of Liberty, when General Bonaparte, having entered into the Council of Five Hundred to denounce counter-revolutionary maneuvers, narrowly missed perishing as the victim of an assassination attempt. The Genius of the Republic saved this general; he returns to Paris with his escort; the legislative body has undertaken all measures necessary to assure the triumph and glory of the Republic.")

Thus did Fouché firmly and in a most timely and calculated fashion align himself with the winners, and in so doing he helped lend credence to the Bonapartes' hastily concocted story of dagger-wielding assailants in the Council of Five Hundred,[112] instead of the contrary and de-mythologizing image of an ambitious and cunning usurper being pushed back by determined defenders of the Constitution.

Minister Fouché did not solely rest his case for supporting the winning side upon his second proclamation. He swiftly rounded up the usual Jacobin suspects and herded them off for the time being to the ancient prison where Louis and his family had been held, the dreaded Temple. He carefully took the pulse of Paris and sent detailed reports along to the conspirators. His men cracked down hard on dissidents and malcontents. Seditious newspapers were harassed or shut down; new plays were now required to be submitted to the police for pre-performance reviews of their content. And, of considerable importance to Napoleon, Fouché would obligingly help their mutual former sponsor and protector, the once resourceful and resilient Paul Barras, step off into political oblivion.

Fouché's forceful actions, very precisely timed to coincide with the assurance of Napoleon's victory but not so obvious as such, won him the backing of the newly empowered Provisional Consul (before year-end to become First Consul) Bonaparte. Sieyès, now a Provisional Consul as well (along with the fellow conspirator-Director Roger Ducos, to make up a triumvirate), began to suspect Fouché was an untrustworthy Jacobin mole (perhaps as the result of the warning given to Bernadotte), and strongly suggested a candidate to replace him, one Charles Alquier, another regicide who had evolved into a middle-of-the-road deputy in the Council of Five Hundred. Alquier had no police experience, he had no network of contacts, nor did he possess any apparent ruthlessness, and Napoleon would have none of him. Sieyès backed off. Before long, he too would be gone. Fouché remained France's Minister of Police.

Perhaps feeling uneasy about the damage Barras might be able to do if opposition to the Saint-Cloud *putsch* ever began to crystallize, Napoleon dispatched Minister Fouché to visit the former Director at his "Grosbois" estate on 20 Brumaire (November 11), the day after the coup. Fouché came armed with a variety of enticing emoluments to play to the Director's well-known love of luxury and to lure him away from France, where he might yet do damage to Napoleon's future plans: ambassadorships to Madrid, to Dresden, and even to America's new capital of Washington were on offer. But Barras did not bite; the humiliation of 18-19 Brumaire was the end of the road for him. In the course of rejecting any such appeasing appointment, he bitterly cited to Fouché the example of George Washington as a successful general who did not seek to aggrandize himself by seizing dictatorial powers. Fouché, understandably concerned that Provisional Consul Bonaparte might well suspect that his Minister of Police had been engaged in some form of intrigue with his former sponsor instead of actually carrying out his assigned mission, extracted a letter signed by Barras and addressed to Napoleon confirming that the offers of diplomatic postings had in fact been extended and declined. On hearing about this rejection, Napoleon purportedly said to Fouché: "What does Washington have to do with this matter? And why does Barras speak to me of him? There is no other way to establish a government than to seize hold and not to let go. Barras is always immersed in Republican ideas: he rambles on like an old woman."[113]

Barras was grossly mistaken if he imagined that he would simply be left to cultivate his magnificent gardens at Grosbois. Fouché rapidly permeated the ex-Director's staff of servants with informers and agents[114] and Barras — who at one point before his fall from power had been accused of being in treasonous correspondence with the Bourbons, including Louis the Pretender, across the Rhine in Coblenz — quickly felt the chill of omnipresent surveillance; one of his closest aides was arrested.[115] Within a year, he was compelled to relinquish his beloved estate and take himself far away from Paris, as he came under the direct threat of being forcibly removed by the Ministry of Police to the Atlantic prison island of Ré. Thus, the once dominant *Vicomte Rouge* abruptly and ignominiously departed the world stage — at least until the posthumous publication of his vitriolic *Mémoires*. As Barras departed Grosbois, Fouché's agents scoured the former Director's hastily abandoned home, busily confiscating much of his correspondence with Napoleon.[116]

The impounded letters went into the exponentially expanding personal files of the Minister of Police. One can be certain that their contents were very carefully perused.

A new double-game had begun.

CHAPTER VIII

Entangler

Joseph Fouché served as Napoleon's Minister of Police for three separate terms; twice he was summarily dismissed. His first term at the ministry — when he continued as a holdover from the Directory in appreciation of his purported services rendered to the coup d'état — lasted from Bonaparte's seizure of power on 18-19 Brumaire in Year VIII (November 9-10, 1799) until September 1802. The official explanation for Fouché's first departure was that he was no longer needed as police minister since Consular France was enjoying a reduced threat level: it was temporarily at peace with all of Europe at that time — even with its arch-enemy Britain. But the chief underlying motives for the first removal of Fouché from office were that Napoleon, spurred by his brothers Lucien and Joseph, resented the fact that his Minister had made known his preference that the First Consul's term merely be extended for ten years rather than designating the incumbent "Consul for Life," as well as the more general principle that he seemed to be too dangerous and conniving a man to countenance having in one's inner circle during relatively tranquil times. The Ministry of Police was thereupon subsumed within the Ministry of Justice under Chief Judge Claude-Ambroise Regnier, and in this subservient role it quickly degenerated into at best, mediocrity, and at worst, embarrassing incompetence. Jean-Jacques-Régis de Cambacérès, the Brumaire plotter who had been transformed from Minister of Justice to Second Consul (and later to Archchancellor of the Empire) by Napoleon, and who was certainly no admirer of Fouché, commented in his *Mémoires* that "This project [the takeover of the police ministry] appeared to present difficulties. There is necessarily in the action of the Police a kind of arbitrariness which would be dangerous to encounter in the Minister of Justice." And he observed of Fouché's successor: "The good qualities of Regnier were offset by the uncertainty of his ideas and the weakness of his character."[117]

Fouché, as a reward for his assistance with the coup of 18-19 Brumaire as well as for his successful conduct of the investigation into the Rue Nicaise bombing, was named senator for the wealthy district of Aix, a personally lucrative office. However, in parting temporarily with his Minister, Napoleon accurately anticipated the future, saying of Fouché:

> *Le citoyen Fouché, ministre de la Police, dans les circonstances difficiles, a répondu par ses talents, par son activité, par son attachement au gouvernement, a tout ce que les conjonctures exigeant de lui. Placé dans le sein du Senat, si d'autres circonstances redemandaient encore un Ministre de Police, le Gouvernement n'en trouvaient point un qui fut plus digne de sa confiance.*[118] ("Citizen Fouché, Minister of Police, in difficult circumstances, has responded with his talents, with his activity, with his attachment to the government, to everything that situations required of him. Placed in the bosom of the Senate, if other circumstances should favor again a Minister of Police, the Government could not find one more worthy of its confidence.")

Within two years, circumstances once again favored increased vigilance. France and Britain had renewed hostilities. Britain was frantically attempting to line up allies and preparing to fend off invasion, while its Corsican nemesis was ordering the construction of landing barges and assembling a massive invasion force in the coastal camps of Boulogne. The counterrevolutionary Vendean and *Chouan* insurgents and the exiled diehard royalists scattered around the borders of France once again became assets of immediate interest to His Majesty's intelligence services, which envisaged them as sharp instruments capable of beheading the growing threat just across the English Channel.[119]

So it was that in early 1804, four years after the Rue Nicaise Christmas Eve assassination attempt, Napoleon once again came under direct personal threat from a new, and this time, a more widespread and complex conspiracy. The plot was set in motion by the convergence upon Paris of two disaffected French generals. The first, travelling from London incognito, was Jean-Charles Pichegru, who had offered his services to Britain and the Bourbons after he had made an against-all-odds, harrowing escape from the dry guillotine of the Guiana penal colony. The other discontented general was Jean-Victor Moreau, he who had declined Sieyès' invitation to overthrow the Directory in 1799, but who now ruefully and ambitiously saw himself as a rival to Napoleon, and who commanded substantial respect amongst elements of the French Army for his conduct in the field. These two veteran army officers were joined by the heavyset and fearless *Chouan* guerilla leader Georges Cadoudal, who was suspected of masterminding the Rue Nicaise bombing but who always steadfastly denied it, insisting that he preferred to kill the First Consul in direct personal combat. As many as fifty or sixty other royalist operatives and their fellow travelers secretly congregated in various safe houses throughout the capital.

Fouché may have had to relinquish the ministry and his gloomy offices on the Quai Malaquais, but he had not lost the core of his network of agents and informants which, exploiting his highly lucrative senatorial post, he continued to finance and deploy. He also kept up a steady stream of notes to his once and future boss on the failings of the official police under Chief Judge Regnier, as threats to the regime and to the First Consul's safety rapidly mounted.[120] From a variety of sources — including a particularly well-placed double agent who was able to implicate British spies and diplomatic representatives as well as the primary French conspirators — Fouché got wind of the general outlines of the budding assassination and coup attempt, and this time he squarely placed his bet on Napoleon, warning him that "the air is filled with daggers."[121] Orders quickly began to emanate from Bonaparte. On February 14, Moreau was arrested and charged with high treason. Two weeks later, Pichegru was seized in one of his Paris hiding places and hauled off to the Temple prison to await trial after putting up a furious struggle with the police. The crafty, elusive, and ever-dangerous Cadoudal was next. Following a tip, agents chased his carriage through the streets of Paris and after the *Chouan* leader shot two of them, he surrendered to his remaining pursuers without further resistance. Under intense interrogation, Cadoudal revealed that according to the plan a Bourbon prince was to join the Paris plotters and to lead the coup which would remove Bonaparte and restore the House of Bourbon to power. But he could not tell his questioners which Bourbon prince it was. It also was separately reported to Napoleon's investigators — perhaps accurately, perhaps not — that a mysterious individual whose name was not revealed but to whom utmost deference was paid had attended one of the secret meetings in Paris.

Suspicions were quickly focused on Louis-Antoine-Henri de Bourbon-Condé, bearing the title of the Duc d'Enghien. The Duke had been a youthful commander in the royalist counterrevolutionary army unsuccessfully led by his grandfather, the illustrious Prince of Condé, a relative of the martyred Louis XVI, in fighting along the Rhine in the 1790s. Since that time, the Duc d'Enghien had been striving to help restore the Bourbons to power, and he was certainly in league with the British. And he was known to inhabit the vicinity of Ettenheim, in the Grand Duchy of Baden, very close to the borders of France. However, this is where French external intelligence (at this time under the control of the foreign ministry) irretrievably broke down. First, spies noted the absence of d'Enghien from the Ettenheim area during the time frame in which the aforementioned mysterious attendee was alleged to have been in Paris. But it later — too much later — transpired that the young duke was actually visiting a woman whom he loved and who was living somewhere else in Baden. It further appears that it had been erroneously reported back by a surveillance agent that d'Enghien had held a secret meeting with General Dumouriez of Valmy fame, who, like Pichegru, was a revolutionary turned royalist. Being spotted together with Dumouriez could indeed have been compelling evidence that d'Enghien had been enlisted in a far-reaching subversive plot. But later — again, too much later — it developed that d'Enghien had actually been in the company of a low-level and innocuous émigré named Thumery, and that when pronounced by an informant with a thick German accent Thumery's name sounded to French ears just like "Dumouriez."[122]

On March 10, after the arrest of General Moreau and the captures of General Pichegru and Georges Cadoudal, Napoleon held a meeting of his top advisors at the Tuileries. Present were Second Consul Cambacérès; Third Consul Lebrun; Chief Judge Regnier, to whom, as noted, the police now reported; Foreign Minister Talleyrand; and Napoleon's unofficial special consultant on the matter, Joseph Fouché. The First Consul opened the session by stating his conclusion that the Duc d'Enghien was the Bourbon prince involved in the plot against his life, and asked his advisors to opine on whether his agents should reach out beyond France's borders to capture him and mete out swift and dramatic justice.

Minutes of this meeting were not kept and Napoleon's dutiful secretary, Méneval, was away from the palace at the time. Méneval nevertheless states that he learned that Lebrun and Cambacérès were "little disposed" towards the draconian action being proposed, and he also notes that Fouché (whom Méneval despised) "did not hide his opinion that it was necessary to make a prompt example, so as to finish with the conspirators." [123](Cambacérès actually wound up bravely pursuing Napoleon into his private chambers after the meeting to continue without avail his argument that making the abduction in neutral territory would be a grave mistake.)[124] However, even accepting Méneval's account as truthful, it is not at all clear that Fouché necessarily favored the summary and hasty execution of d'Enghien as opposed to a thorough police investigation (with himself back in the lead role, of course) of his ties to the conspiracy and to other potential plotters, or even whether Fouché might have secretly intended at some point to "save" d'Enghien, consistent with his habitual practice of keeping every one of his avenues open — a strategy which would be in evidence in many forthcoming situations.

It *is* quite clear from a number of sources that Foreign Minister Talleyrand strongly advocated, at the extraordinary session at the Tuileries and in at least one separate prior communication to the First Consul, that "the safety of the state requires that all conspirators be seized without exception," and that he pointed his finger in the direction of Baden.[125] And here the selfish interests of Fouché and Talleyrand do indeed seem to converge: by encouraging Napoleon to smear his own hands with a captive Bourbon's blood, he would be forever compromised. There would be no turning back for the First Consul, no accommodation with his enemies, no role for him in brokering a rapprochement with the royalists as General Monck had effected on behalf of Charles II of England 144 years before (an analogy in fact posited by Talleyrand and others). The option of restoring a Bourbon monarch to the throne of France was one which the regicide Fouché and the ex-bishop Talleyrand would jealously reserve for themselves.

In the end, an angry and fearful Napoleon was not to be deterred by any geopolitical or diplomatic considerations from eradicating the 32-year-old Duc d'Enghien. On March 15, he sent several squadrons of his elite gendarme cavalry racing a few miles over the French border to Ettenheim, violating the sovereign and neutral territory of the Grand Duchy of Baden. There they seized d'Enghien (who, preoccupied with his calls upon his lady friend, had rashly ignored warnings of the raid, despite his having ventured so close to the French border), and they brought the young royal back across the Rhine as a prisoner.

Napoleon immediately conducted a personal review of the papers which had been confiscated from d'Enghien, and realized to his chagrin that there was no evidence that he had actually been involved with either Cadoudal, the *Chouans*, or any of the suspect French generals, and that there were significant indications to the contrary.[126] Nevertheless, given the fact that he had ordered a high-profile Bourbon to be kidnapped by a sizable paramilitary force on foreign soil, he believed that too much had been set in motion to be abruptly reversed. The First Consul of France could not bring himself to admit that the entire operation had been an embarrassing mistake. Moreover, with assassination plots against him seemingly cropping up everywhere, Napoleon felt an acute need to send out a pervasive and unmistakable warning message. So, he resolved upon a course of secrecy, obfuscation, and the swift elimination of his hapless captive.

On March 20, in the great hall of the forbidding and fortress-like Château de Vincennes, just outside of Paris, a special, hand-picked military tribunal charged the Duke with plotting against the First Consul. Its member-officers thereupon summarily sentenced him to death. No time was granted to d'Enghien to prepare a defense, nor was he permitted to retain an advocate, or even to be visited by a priest. His request for an audience with Bonaparte was denied out of hand by Napoleon's trusted aide, the blindly obedient General Jean-Marie Savary (who would later be rewarded with the Ministry of Police portfolio in 1810, after Fouché abruptly plummeted from power for a second time).[127] Upon his sentence being pronounced in the middle of the night, the Duc d'Enghien was immediately hauled out and shot by a hastily assembled firing squad in the torch-lit moat of the Chateau, with his whimpering pet dog beside him (at least that is how it was portrayed in royalist depictions of the deed).

Strangely, when Savary was returning to Paris hours after the execution had taken place, he happened to encounter on the roadway then *conseiller d'État* (state counselor for security) Réal (still a close ally of Fouché despite — or perhaps because of — the folding up of the police ministry). Réal revealed to Savary that he was under new instructions from the First Consul to proceed to Vincennes to interrogate d'Enghien more intensively; Savary replied that the time for that was irretrievably past. It is possible that Napoleon had had second thoughts, even though he refused — right up to his own death on St. Helena when he included a last-minute, self-justifying special addition to his final will and testament — ever to express any kind of remorse over d'Enghien's fate. Or quite possibly the First Consul was simply trying to cover himself. Or perhaps it had occurred to Fouché himself that an enhanced, expanded, and intelligently conducted questioning of the Duke might reveal to Fouché's own personal advantage the authors of other conspiratorial probes that were being made in the Bourbons' direction, probes that might even be traced back to the French Foreign Ministry, and perhaps all the way up to its cunning and shameless bribe-taking head, Talleyrand.[128]

The summary execution of a *prince du sang* did put an abrupt end to any possibility — however remote — of any rapprochement by Napoleon with elements of the House of Bourbon. Bonaparte would never play the part of Monck; that would be left to Talleyrand and Fouché. It also set the stage for Napoleon's subsequent assumption, on December 2, 1804, of all the trappings of a Roman Caesar with his self-coronation as the Emperor of France in the Cathedral of Notre Dame (converted back to its ecclesiastical purposes after having served as the Revolution's atheistic "Temple of Reason"), with the Pope merely looking on. It should be kept in mind that prior to this watershed point, in many quarters of Europe, First Consul Bonaparte had been idolized as an iconoclastic liberator and a force of nature, the heroic destroyer of old regimes and the challenger of hereditary privileges across the Continent. Now, he instead appeared to have irretrievably unmasked himself as a new and formidable entry in history's endless line of despotic rulers.

The *Chouan* chief Cadoudal, who was soon publicly executed, caustically observed before the blade descended on him: "We came to give France a King [i.e., Louis XVIII, then living in exile], and now we have an Emperor."[129]

In performing his role as Napoleon's unswervingly loyal enforcer, General Savary had dutifully, tactlessly, and brutally followed his orders in executing d'Enghien. (Savary had grabbed the quill away from the officer nominally in charge of the military tribunal who was about to write Napoleon a post-conviction recommendation for clemency, brusquely advising him that his work was ended.)[130] Napoleon's paladin deservedly received a goodly share of the opprobrium — albeit not the ultimate blame — for *l'affaire d'Enghien* to the very end of his days.

With his usual adroitness and favorable fortune, Talleyrand emerged relatively unscathed for the time being from the whole unpleasant business, thanks in part to his having burned almost all of the self-incriminating evidence.[131] Not so with Napoleon: his reputation deservedly suffered greatly from the cruel and lawless nature of the damaging episode he had launched. According to Méneval, the d'Enghien fiasco "had a fatal influence on Napoleon's destiny."[132] Even Josephine — whose first husband was a guillotined aristocrat — was rumored to have pleaded for mercy for d'Enghien, and at the very least, she clearly was greatly distressed by it after the fact.[133]

Napoleon, who discussed the matter with his military aide-de-camp Armand de Caulaincourt (who had helped to oversee the raid into Baden) during their long trek across the Russian steppes in 1812, reportedly said "I would do again just what I did," but also then went on to aver bitterly that Talleyrand "made me arrest the Duc d'Enghien, who was not even in my thoughts . . . I attached not the slightest importance to his presence on the banks of the Rhine and had no designs whatever on him."[134] Much later, during the Second Bourbon Restoration in 1823, Savary would dramatically accuse Talleyrand of having withheld evidence which would have stayed the executioner's (i.e., his own) hand.[135] (Talleyrand, with equal dramatic flair, called for a formal investigation of Savary's charges by the Chamber of Peers, which he doubtless knew that Louis XVIII would quash, as the King immediately did.)[136] And Méneval — by then, he was Baron Méneval — would point to an incriminating letter which Talleyrand had written on March 8, 1804 and had meant to destroy along with the rest of his pertinent correspondence, but which had slipped behind a desk drawer and was discovered many years later.[137]

Joseph Fouché, who would shortly thereafter reassume control of the Ministry of Police, does not appear to have been directly operationally involved in the abduction and killing of the Duc d'Enghien. And despite Méneval's secondhand and unattributed account of the fateful meeting on March 10, it is unclear what Fouché's precise advice to the First Consul actually was regarding what needed to be done immediately *after* the kidnapping stratagem had been effected. Certainly, Fouché seems never to have been widely blamed for engineering this particular misdeed, unlike Bonaparte, Savary, and Talleyrand. But even if Fouché's own fingerprints are only faintly and ambiguously visible in the matter, he is nevertheless famously credited with an acid postmortem comment on this prefiguring episode of extraordinary rendition, lightning-strike conviction by military tribunal, and swift and unjustified execution, an episode which one could argue was traceable back to the after-effects of the abominable act of terror in the Rue Nicaise four years before, an episode which would reverberate for many years to come. The dour, sardonic policeman *redux* is said to have observed the following about

Bonaparte's revenge against the Bourbon royal: "*c'est plus qu'une crime, c'est une faute*" ("it is worse than a crime, it is a mistake").[138] This cynical comment rings true, and if the attribution is correct, Fouché neatly summarized the public relations constraints which unexpectedly create uncomfortable boundaries for official conduct, even for those at the very pinnacle of power. Also — and again, if the insidious remark is in fact correctly attributed, and if Méneval's account is accurate and Fouché in fact had counseled strongly in favor of the d'Enghien abduction in the first place — the *ex post facto* observation not only exemplifies Fouché's superb ability to cover his own tracks, but it also typifies Fouché's willingness, even his eagerness, to lure Napoleon to the edge of a precipice from which the Emperor of the French could subsequently be pushed.

Part II

Empire

Chapter IX

Minister

What then was the nature of Napoleonic France's police and state security service, as created and directed by Fouché? One primary attribute was that the Ministry of Police adopted as its core mission the surveillance of individuals and the prevention of threats to the Consulate and subsequently to the Empire, rather than reactively trying to suppress unrest and revolution after they had already coalesced and matured. In Fouché's conceptualization: "The police, such as I envision it, should be established to foresee and prevent crimes, to contain and stop those whom the laws have not foreseen."[139] The other chief attribute was a focus not only upon plots and conspiracies, but also upon the gauging and shaping of public opinion. To accomplish these interrelated ends, the necessary ingredients were strict centralized control, a wealth of informers and intelligence, and an all-seeing eye at the top of the structure to distill and discriminate amongst myriad symptoms and purported leads. The ministry's lifeblood was this flow and analysis of information, which pulsed through its network every hour of every day from within France, and from the territories of her possessions, her allies, and her adversaries.

The organization of Fouché's ministry should be comprehended from two angles: first, how it centrally controlled the regions, and second, how it allocated its work internally. As to the regions, the ministry worked partly through prefects who were personally appointed by Napoleon and who oversaw all the local mayors — who were also centrally appointed. The prefects conducted surveillance of the mayors and local administrators but they were flanked by police commissioners who themselves reported directly to the ministry on the Quai Malaquais. The greater the population of a town or city, the greater number of such commissioners it merited. Overseeing these police commissioners were commissioners general, who could call in muscular enforcement resources as needed locally; these resources included the paramilitary Gendarmerie Nationale, first under General Étienne Radet, with whom Fouché worked well, and subsequently under Marshal Bon-Adrien Moncey, with whom he did not, and the military reserve forces of the Garde Nationale.[140] The commissioners general expanded in number along with the burgeoning Empire, reaching twenty-six by 1808. They were located in major population centers, in ports, border strongholds, and crossing points, and in the capitals and major cities of France's allies (or vassal states, depending upon one's point of view, of course). Nice, Toulon, Marseille, Lyon, Rochefort, Cherbourg, Bordeaux, Strasbourg, Cologne, Geneva, Turin, Ostend, and Antwerp, among others, all qualified for direct internal oversight in this manner. The next level of control was exercised by Fouché's own lieutenants, with a Prefect of Police for Paris (staffed by the rather disloyal — to Fouché, of all people — but largely controllable Louis-Nicolas DuBois) and for the regions of France and Italy, headed by the more trustworthy henchmen Pierre-François Réal (the introducer of Fouché to Bonaparte, as will be recalled), Pelet de la Lozère, and Pierre-Marie Desmarest of the *haute police* (a description of which follows shortly).

The centrally controlled commissioners who constituted the base of this organizational pyramid acted as conduits for Fouché's orders, and they enabled the ministry both to circumvent and report on all local administrators. In Fouché's disparaging words to Napoleon regarding mayors, magistrates, and the like: "Experience has shown that one who administers is a poor inspector, as the details of his administration absorb all his attention . . . so that one comes to believe that in criticizing others, he will call attention upon himself."[141] The police commissioners also took on the task of putting down insurrections — which continued to break out in those western regions of France conducive to royalist plots (despite Napoleon's Concordat of 1801 — the Consulate's accommodation with the Vatican and the Catholic Church), or wherever there was resistance to conscription. Fouché's commissioners also fought endemic "brigandage" (the very serious problem of highway robbery and other forms of quasi-organized violent lawlessness), took charge of prisoners (of war and otherwise) and of prisons, and they oversaw the issuance of passports and identity papers. And the better ones were able continually to expand the huge network of informants that stimulated the ganglia of the organization with snippets of intelligence.

There is no reliable figure as to the number of informants who were tapped constantly or periodically by the ministry and who were paid for their insights and intelligence regarding enemies foreign and domestic, although it is estimated that there were 10,000 in Paris alone. Fouché burned entire archival lists of them when he was abruptly dismissed by Napoleon for the second time, in 1810[142] (see Chapter XII). But it is certain that their numbers were legion: the Ministry of Police paid very well. Informants were recruited from the aristocratic émigrés who returned to France in droves after proscription lists were drastically whittled down on Napoleon's orders, a decision based on Fouché's advice. They were recruited from the workers of the *faubourgs* of Paris. They were recruited from toll-takers, customs agents, and passport police, who would receive a 100-franc bounty for anything unusual they noticed.[143] They permeated the staffs of servants of the well-to-do and, yes, even those of Fouché's fellow ministers. (We have already seen Fouché's ready reliance on this method of surveillance with his infiltration of Barras' household.) They came from the netherworld of gaming houses and bordellos and they came from organized crime. They populated the prisons: wardens, guards, and inmates alike. And Fouché continued to include among his horde of informants the Emperor's wife.

The nexus for the vast information flow, which was gathered by this enormous army of stalkers, shadowers, and stool pigeons and filtered through the commissioners and commissioners general (unless they were being expressly bypassed on Fouché's orders) was of course the ministry's headquarters at No. 17 Quai Malaquais. Here the plethora of puzzle pieces were assembled and stored, with the work product distributed to those who had need to know. This puzzle-assembly process was a critical feature: in 1815, when Fouché surfaced for his brief third tour of duty for the Emperor Napoleon, the Minister of Police redux commented to his regional prefects: "*Tel événement, en apparence peu remarquable dans la sphère d'un départment, peut avoir un grand intérêt dans l'ordre général par ses liaisons avec des analogues que vous n'avez peu connaître.*"[144] ("Such an event, appearing unremarkable within the sphere of a [regional] department, can be of great interest in the general order of things by its connections with related matters of which you are scarcely aware.") Connecting the dots, in modern parlance.

To effect this sifting process and exploit the resulting intelligence, the ministry itself was organized into six divisions. The First Division was comprised by Fouché's office and his secretariat, and constituted the ganglion and the main communications node. The Second Division contained Fouché's experts on state security and was known as the "*haute police*" ("high police") under Desmarest (a former Benedictine priest who was highly adept at obtaining confessions); it received ample resources and Fouché's constant personal attention. Not only did the Second Division anticipate and track domestic plots, it also constantly assessed and sought to penetrate the ruling circles of the Empire's foreign enemies. Every French person living abroad was a potential member of the Second Division's information network; it deployed hundreds of agents in the capitals of St. Petersburg, London, Berlin, Vienna, Madrid, and Naples. In turn, the agents of the *haute police* sought to keep all foreign emissaries from ambassadors down to consular officials and their staffs under constant close surveillance. The *haute police* were experts at shadowing, tracking, and compromising their quarry. Here too, the many eyes of the ministry were watchful: in the shops and markets; in the inns and taverns; at the coaching stations and border checkpoints; in the domestic servant corps and the gaming establishments. It is said that in one instance Fouché accurately predicted that a war with Prussia would break out within months based in part upon an agent's observation that the Prussian ambassador had laid in only enough firewood at his residence for part of the winter.[145] It was also observed that "three men could not meet and talk indiscretely about public affairs without the Minister of Police being informed about it the following day."[146]

The Second Division (and often other police agents not permanently assigned to the *haute police* but acting in conjunction with it) was also armed with extraordinary powers of indefinite detention: under Article 46 of the Constitution of the Year VIII (adopted in December 1799 after the coup d'état and establishing the Consulate), and subsequently under the Napoleonic Code of Criminal Procedure, there was no writ of *habeas corpus*.[147] Detainees could languish indefinitely in the dank Temple prison (run by the Second Division), or elsewhere in Fouché's gulag, with ample time and incentives to encourage them to consider the advantages of cooperating with the authorities.

The next two divisions of the ministry reflected additional further modern aspects of Fouché's organization. The Third Division watched over and subverted the press and other means of expression, including booksellers, printers, theatrical productions, and even songs. We have previously seen how Fouché could personally put the squeeze on journalists, both in 1796 during the Babeuf conspiracy episode and in 1799 in the wake of the coup of 18-19 Brumaire. Napoleon himself possessed a profound contempt for the concept of a free press, and this was an area where his minister and his minions carried out their ruler's will with particular élan. Bonaparte was constantly dashing off letters to Fouché complaining about the journals' unfavorable or simply neutral coverage ("they write without an objective and the principal ones do not show any enthusiasm for the Government").[148] The Emperor demanded that censors be appointed, that editors be strongly reminded of their patriotic duties, that articles be planted, and he even went so far as to urge pointedly the use of specific caricatures (e.g.,"make them include an Englishman with a purse in his hand, supplicating the different powers to take his money, etc.").[149] During the first year of the Consulate, the number of newspapers in Paris shrank from 74 to 13, with a further contraction to 4 by the advent of the Empire in 1804.[150] Those few that survived were for the most part docile state organs like *Le Moniteur Universel*, for which Fouché and his Third Division staff would regularly ghostwrite articles.

The ministry's Fourth Division conducted ongoing surveillance of émigrés, those who had returned to France under amnesty as well as those who had not. These fugitives from the Revolution could be productive citizens or they could be security risks, and they could of course serve willingly or unwillingly as valuable informants. An English visitor named John Carr described "[t]he promptitude and activity of the French police, under the penetrating eye of Monsieur Fouché," observing that

> No one can escape the vigilance of this man and his emissaries. An emigrant of respectability assured me, that when he and a friend waited upon him for their passports to enable them to quit Paris for the South of France, he [the Minister] surprised them by relating to them the names of the towns, the streets, and of the people with whom they had lodged, at various times, during their emigration in England.[151]

The workings of the Fourth Division inexorably involved it more and more in foreign espionage.

The last two divisions evidenced the first glimmerings of the information age: accounting and archives. The nineteenth-century Russian socialist Alexander Herzen once prophesied that his native land would see the advent of "Genghis Khan with a telegraph"[152] (later to be embodied by Lenin's Cheka and Stalin's NKVD); by similar analogy, Fouché was the Grand Inquisitor with a data storage and retrieval system.

Accounting — the Fifth Division — wasn't simply a matter of adhering (or not) to budgetary constraints. The ministry supplemented what on the surface appeared to be a relatively modest published budget for an undertaking of such magnitude with a brisk business in passport and other documentation fees, firearms licenses, and a highly lucrative take from the licensing and profits of the gaming establishments of France, as well as from its universe of brothels.[153]

In 1806, Napoleon became concerned about the moral implications of widespread betting, and he issued a decree stating that "Houses in which games of chance are played are prohibited over the whole extent of our territory . . .". However, recognizing the lucrative off-the-books role that gambling revenues played in funding a first-rate state security service, his decree intentionally left an enormous loophole: "Our Minister of Police will draw up special regulations in this respect for places where mineral waters are found . . . and for the City of Paris." Thus, the casinos of the Palais-Royale, the Club des Princes, and the Club des Étrangers in the capital, and those in the fashionable resorts such as Spa, Aix-la-Chapelle, Plombières, Luxeuil, and Aix-les-Bains, continued to thrive, as did the Ministry of Police.[154]

Archives, the Sixth Division, stored and sorted the reams of information that flooded in daily from all quarters, with thousands of individuals' dossiers retrieved and supplemented on an ongoing basis. One example of the beaverish work of Fouché's archivists was their topographical atlas of Western France, hotbed of the only fitfully suppressed rebellions north and south of the Loire. The atlas contained extensive and detailed maps of towns, of assembly areas, of the locations of past attacks, of safe-houses, and of embarkation points and supply paths and escape routes through the dense *bocage.* It was supplemented by an exhaustive listing of thousands of names and biographies of anyone who had ever been involved in the Vendean or *Chouannerie* risings during the Revolution and the Directory, and of their parents and acquaintances.[155]

In addition to the six divisions, there was another shadowy operation referred to as "*le Cabinet noir*" ("the black office"), which worked closely with the *Directeur des Postes* and which opened and read the mails. Unlike many other features of Fouché's ministry, this was not an innovation, as the sanctity of private correspondence had on occasion been violated by agents of the *Ancien Régime.* But the practice became widespread and routine under Fouché. Even members of the fractious Bonaparte family began to resort to using private messengers (although these too could be bought off by the police), in order to attempt to communicate discretely.

Fouché also wielded a double-edged sword with respect to sensitive correspondence. He was able as the police minister to retrieve and destroy many of his own self-incriminating reports which he had sent to the Committee of Public Safety back in 1793 in order to keep them informed about his activities as a zealous *représentat en mission* in prostrate Lyon.[156] We shall witness again his uncanny ability to cover his own tracks.

It is, however, the tangible manifestation of the work of the six divisions and the *Cabinet noir* that is simply astounding: the daily (or, technically, six-days-per-week) reports generated by the Ministry of Police. The daily Bulletin concerned itself with not just the events of the day from the Empire and abroad — diplomatic, political, subversive, and criminal — although the sheer volume of reporting on those was staggering enough. The Bulletin also was concerned with trends and opinions that could and should act either as reassurances or as warning signals as to the impact of imperial policies. The daily Bulletin was edited by Fouché's staff of carefully recruited, well-educated and astute advisors (a number of them clerics, some even former Oratorians[157]), and it was often shaped and annotated in the margins by the pen of the minister himself.

This reportage was accomplished under the aegis of the ministry's unusual logo, which heralded official correspondance: a toga-clad woman seated on a chair with riddle-solving sphinxes for arms. In one hand, she holds aloft a torch dispelling the dark clouds of intrigue and deception, while with her other, she confronts a coiled viper with its reflection: holding the mirror up to crime and subversion.

Princeton University Library

From the Quai Malaquais, couriers brought the on-average twenty-page Bulletin across the Seine to the Emperor's then-current residence — the Tuileries, Fontainebleau, Saint-Cloud, or Malmaison — or, as was more often the case, to some distant site where the Emperor was lodged while on campaign — to Munich or Madrid, perhaps, or to the Schönbrunn Palace in Vienna, or to a bivouac on the banks of the Danube or of the Vistula. The daily Bulletin's primary reader was absolutely addicted to and in constant dialogue with it.[158] On one occasion when delivery was missed, Napoleon complained: "I have not received the police Bulletin – this is inconceivable negligence."[159]

A sampling of topics from the "*Table Analytique*" attached to just over one year's worth (April 1804 to July 1805) of the published collection of the Bulletins conveys the incredible scope of this quotidian briefing (this list is by no means exhaustive, and follows the French alphabetical order of the index): Accidents and fires, foreign affairs, English agents, Bourbon agents, foreign agents, agriculture, amnesties, anarchists, army conscriptions and desertions, arms and munitions manufacture, arrests, murders and assassinations, attacks on couriers, fraudulent bankruptcies, trading exchanges (Paris, Marseille, Bordeaux, and London), brigandage, riots, songs against the Emperor, the *Chouannerie*, commerce, contraband, plots and conspiracies, religious "cults" (still something of a post-revolutionary preoccupation of Fouché's), denunciations, disappearances, customs duties, duels, forest fires, émigrés, epidemics, public spiritedness, escapes, fetes and ceremonies, convicts, conduct of the *Garde Nationale* and the *Gendarmerie*, insurrections, gambling (broken down by reports on major winners and losers at *trente-et-un*, *roulette*, and *loto*, among other games of chance), newspapers (foreign and domestic) and repressive measures taken against them, insults to the Legion of Honor award, libelous pamphlets and placards, booksellers and literature, conduct of mayors and other local officials, naval actions and affairs (including burnings, combats, corsairs, desertions, enlistments, sanitary measures, captures from the English, captures by the English, shipwrecks, and prizes), counterfeiting, naturalizations, wage demands by workers, passports (irregular, lacking, false, and altered), poisonings, priests, prisons, royalists, surveillance, theaters (political allusions and public responses thereto, and also ticket sales figures), tribunals, and thievery.[160]

But to truly appreciate the reporting accomplishment of Fouché and his ministry, one should envision oneself as the imperial recipient, standing in his study or seated on a campstool and avidly opening the courier's green leather folder containing the latest edition. Following are excerpts from two quite typical examples of what Napoleon read daily. The first is taken from a Bulletin compiled near the beginning of Fouché's second ministry, at the Empire's inception:

BULLETIN OF 1 BRUMAIRE YEAR XIII
[23 October 1804]

453. Paris. Meteor. Public Spirit. Some observers have today collected the various comments by the curious, who gathered to watch the meteor, which appeared at 9 o'clock in the evening. Several of them said: "It represents blood, a sign of the continuation of war." Others, in greater number, said: "It represents fire, a sign of joy, which presages happiness for the coronation."
454. Turin. Situation. By a letter of 14 vendémiaire the Minister has asked General Menou to undertake a frequent correspondence with him about what is going on in Turin. The general, in his response of the 23rd, assures that the city actually enjoys great tranquility. The divisiveness caused by the two actresses is entirely ended. . . .
455. Nantes. Performance. The commissioner general of police for Nantes has given the information asked of him regarding the presentation, in the theater of Nantes, of "*La partie de chasse d'Henri IV*" ["The Hunting Party of Henry IV"] . . . He permitted it as a good means of recognizing individuals who might harbor a secret attachment to the Bourbon family. At the premiere, the actor who played the role of Henry IV was booed. Two other performances followed; there were hardly any spectators and there was great indifference. The director spontaneously retired the play. He was nevertheless made to understand the order of the Minister . . . .
457. Introduction of English Merchandise. As the result of correspondence seized from an English packet-boat on its arrival in Rotterdam [it appears that] the English are increasing their maneuvers to introduce

their merchandise. A number of the letters seized have been sent to the director-general of customs as proof-positive of this fraudulent commerce, as well as the situation with certain French merchant houses which received English merchandise, and as to several Dutch traders who favored its introduction, and he has been requested to take steps . . . .
459. Diverse Events.
Tours. . . . Johnston, an Irishman, seen at Tours, is instructed to remain there under surveillance without going to Verdun.
Vagabond. Mallard, 45 years of age, arrested at Fontainbleau, has been: a trappist [monk] (12 years), an émigré, a soldier of Condé [the Bourbon prince], arrested, detained at the Temple, under surveillance . . . returned to see his parents.
Sambre-et-Meuse. Conscription. Contingent complete. No concern regarding the next levy.
Spain. Epidemic in Cadiz confirmed. Maritime quarantine at Bayonne.
Suspicious Traveller. Going to Berlin, Vienna, Trieste, under the false name of Mauriet. To be sought and investigated by the *commissaire des Relations extérieures* in Trieste.
Intelligence. Under surveillance . . . le chevalier de Guer (returned émigré, fanatic, found out by numerous secret agents among the workers in his mines) . . . .[161]

The second example is a Bulletin produced towards the end of Fouché's second term as Minister, at the Empire's apogee:

BULLETIN OF FRIDAY 9 FEBRUARY 1810

550. Paris. [After discussing the likely opinion in French political circles as to an alliance with the defeated Austrian Empire, the item turns to the Polish reaction:] The instinct of the Poles is to see in this great event which is unfolding, the future reestablishment of the kingdom of Poland. This reestablishment appears to be too useful to the interests of France for it to appear doubtful to them . . . .
551. Paris. Russian Legation. At Monday evening's ball, at the residence of Prince Kourakin [the Russian ambassador], Cardinal Litta [a Papal emissary] arrived first. The prince, who dined at the home of the Duke of Cadore [Jean-Baptiste Champagny, the French Minister of Foreign

Affairs at the time, having succeeded Talleyrand], had asked the Princess Galitzin to receive the ladies. This princess proceeded to mock the cardinal in a most mystifying manner: she indirectly referred to his expulsion from St. Petersburg, she contrived to speak of madness, because the cardinal has an insane brother (he believes himself to be invisible); finally, the princess left the cardinal standing alone while she had the cardinal Maury seated next to her. The young Casimir, protégé or rather the son of Mme. De Genlis [a noted literary figure], had been invited to the party; Mme. De Genlis desires that he go to Petersburg, and there be patronized by the prince, whom she approached in a flirtatious manner . . . .

552. Sarthe. Brigandage. Competence. The prefect of Sarthe announces that he has arrested three individuals from the village of d'Arthezé, who have supported brigands last month. He observes that there are some uncertainties regarding the competence of the criminal court and of the military commission, that they are slow in coming to judgments. . . . Two deserters from Mayenne, accused of assassinating Launay and arraigned by this commission, have waited for a long time in prison while the general of the division decides whether the commission is competent to judge them . . . .

553. Diverse Events.

Holland. Report. Anxiety with which the decision of the Emperor is awaited on the incorporation of Holland into France.

Dyle. Details regarding the priest Stevens, head of a religious sect, sought for a long time. Someone is sheltering him. Names cited: his sister; another Stevens, François, curé and mayor of Wavre; Bouthon, lieutenant of the gendarmerie . . . .

Lorient. Enemy undertakings. [Fouché writes in the margin: "The agent who gave this information to the police wrote that the English have planted on the Ile d'Hoedic a Frenchman named Saint-Ange. This individual is without doubt Saint-Hubert, an old *chouan* chief in the Vendée, who has often taken the name Saint-Ange. I have given orders regarding this in all places habituated by this individual."]. . .[162]

These are just excerpts from two reports selected from thousands, but they demonstrate the breadth and depth of information being collected and weighed, with their content ranging from political analysis, to assessments of public opinion and of political and cultural media, to the performance of judges and administrators, to the status of foreign plots, to threats from commercial warfare and brigandage, and from a variety of other potentially subversive sources. The ministry's vast surveillance network yielded myriad threads and Fouché and his acolytes on the Quai Malaquais diligently and deftly tied them together into a web of intelligence, pursuant to the motto: "*veille pour le bonheur du peuple*" (safeguard the happiness of the people).[163]

But at what point might Fouché transgress the boundary between serving the Emperor as his minister and deciding for himself what should constitute and define the happiness of the French nation? As the number of Bulletins mounted and their dates progressed, to 1808, 1809, 1810 . . . the Minister of Police would himself determinedly draw closer and closer to that fateful line.

Chapter X

Schemer

On the evening of January 2, 1809, Napoleon began his review of the daily reports and dispatches delivered to him in his chilly headquarters in the Casa de Tepa in the town of Astorga in the remote northwestern corner of Spain. He had taken direct personal command of an army which was forging its way along the winding and treacherous Camino de Santiago, an ancient route of French pilgrims. The Emperor and his soldiers were in laborious but relentless pursuit of retreating British troops under the command of Sir John Moore. Napoleon's objective was to eliminate Moore's men before they could escape the Iberian Peninsula. He would thus deprive the Spanish *guerrilleros* of the conventional, professional force which had been supporting their national uprising against the French invaders and against the king whom Napoleon had forcefully foisted upon Spain the year before, his brother Joseph.

Napoleon's presence in Spain had been urgently required, because of the unforeseen breadth of the violence directed against his brother's regime, because his marshals were neither working in concert with one another nor with King Joseph, and because the commander of another French army had panicked and shockingly surrendered to supposedly inferior Spanish troops at Baylen in July of 1808. Napoleon was now on the verge of restoring some degree of order by personally seeing to the destruction of the British expeditionary force, which was desperately trying to reach an embarkation point in order to escape from the Peninsula and live to fight another day. But that evening, as the Emperor read his dispatches, he suddenly saw his immediate strategic plans being undermined by two items of very disturbing news.

The first item was not entirely unexpected or unpredictable. Emperor Francis I of Austria had perceived that the French military machine had become bogged down in Spain, and that Napoleon's attention and energies were largely directed toward salvaging the situation. Francis was chafing under the loss of numerous Habsburg territories and his title of Holy Roman Emperor due to repeated defeats inflicted on him by Napoleon, and he was now ready to engage in yet another round of warfare. The Austrian army was ordered into mobilization mode, and it would soon be able to threaten the Emperor's buffer zone of German allies and satellite states as well as France's recently established frontier along the Rhine.

The Austrians had learned from their stinging defeat by Napoleon at Austerlitz over three years earlier, in 1805. The Emperor Francis's determined younger brother, the highly competent Archduke Charles, had instituted wide-ranging organizational and tactical reforms in an army that, inspired by France's "nation under arms" ethos, was growing to truly formidable size. The Austrians were further emboldened by assurances from Britain that it would not only supply financial backing, but that it would also deploy the unrivalled power of the Royal Navy to create a second front (or, actually, a third front counting Spain) by landing an expeditionary force somewhere in Northern Europe. Prussia, which had been humiliated by Napoleon and his "Iron Marshal" Louis-Nicolas Davout, at the twin battles of Jena and Auerstadt in 1807, was sending signals that it too could well be enticed into joining a new grand alliance against the hated Corsican upstart. Moreover, the Habsburg rulers of Austria had it on excellent authority that Napoleon's new-found but perceptibly unenthusiastic ally, Alexander I of Russia, could be counted on not to intervene militarily on the side of the French. That excellent authority was in fact a mole operating at the very highest level of France's foreign ministry. Through argument and flattery, this mole had already been bolstering the Czar's inclination to resist Napoleon's bid for European dominance. Soon, he would also be secretively feeding precise information to Austrian diplomats about French troop strengths and deployments, and receiving vast payments in return.

The other disconcerting intelligence item that Napoleon found in his dispatch case on the evening of January 2 concerned a contingency which he had *not* anticipated. This unsettling development was made manifest by reports from Paris and messages intercepted in Italy by the Emperor's devoted stepson, Prince Eugène de Beauharnais (Josephine's son by her previous marriage to a guillotined aristocrat). As the Emperor worked by the fire in the Casa de Tepa, he absorbed the disturbing news contained therein and considered its implications. His Minister of Foreign Affairs, Charles Maurice de Talleyrand-Périgord, named by Napoleon just a year earlier as the Prince of Benevento, was in league with another minister, a minister with whom Talleyrand had engaged in an acrimonious running feud for a decade, a rivalry which spanned the Consulate and the first five years of the Empire: the Minister of Police. The intercepted communication forwarded by Prince Eugène demonstrated that the two ministers had not only patched up their seemingly irreconcilable differences, but that they had also had the temerity to engage in contingency planning for the childless Emperor's line of succession should any harm befall him. It was as though two mutually antagonistic senior corporate executives had suddenly decided between themselves the successor to their chief executive officer.

Fouché's and Talleyrand's widely known and profound distaste for each other had both personal and professional roots. Talleyrand came from aristocratic stock and Fouché's background was decidedly bourgeois-mercantile. Talleyrand had once been the Bishop d'Autun; Fouché was never more than a mere instructor in the Oratorian school system. While Talleyrand had played a very important role in the early years of the French Revolution, he had prudently fled the Terror to seek refuge, first in England, and not being very warmly received there, subsequently in America; Fouché had enthusiastically helped conduct the Terror.

Talleyrand was an affected libertine: when he was named vice-chancellor in 1804, Fouché sardonically commented that it was the only vice he had not previously possessed; Fouché was austere in his personal habits and in his family life. As to the professional contribution to the gulf between the two, the inexorable spread of Fouché's intelligence network, its infiltration of both the French and foreign diplomatic corps, and the flow of information regarding matters of diplomacy and international intrigues which the daily Bulletins directed to the Emperor, were all bound to create jealousy and even anxiety on the part of the Minister of Foreign Affairs, who concluded that the rival ministry's *haute police* had grossly overstepped their place in the hierarchy of government. The two adversaries did share common traits, however: unsurpassed deviousness, avidity for self-enrichment, and the ingrained habit of constantly calculating and re-calculating the likelihoods of all possible eventualities.

What then had brought these two men into at least a temporary, ostensible alliance? The answer was that last common trait, the fact that they shared both a concern for the consequences of Napoleon's inevitable death, and a strong sense of the enormous opportunities that the premature demise of the Emperor would provide to those who proved to be the smartest and most agile. Napoleon was fearless on the battlefield and he had often exposed himself to risk. While his days of personally leading troops across a bridge under enemy fire, as he had done during his first Italian campaign in 1796, were for the most part at an end, he made no effort to isolate himself from the stray shot or the skipping cannonball and, as we shall see later in this chapter, he remained a risk-taker with regard to his own safety. In addition to the ever-present chance of his being killed on the field of arms, threats from assassins abounded — from royalists, from *Chouans* and Vendeans, from Jacobin holdouts and, now, from swarms of fierce Spanish guerrillas who were dangerously indistinguishable from non-combatants. The possible, even probable, sudden death of France's warrior-emperor became a constant factor in the calculations of the two cunning ministers, who always carefully and unscrupulously prepared for any and all outcomes.

Fouché had already directly attempted to act upon his concerns over the Emperor's succession. In a very odd incident which had occurred in

November 1807, he had seemingly taken it upon himself to call on the Empress Josephine at the Palace of Fontainebleau, to the south of Paris. As we have noted, Fouché had been reading her incoming and outgoing correspondence for years with her connivance. In a private session, the Minister of Police suggested to her that in her non-fertile state she should request a divorce for the good of France and of her beloved, the Emperor. When the stunned Josephine inquired whether Fouché was speaking on behalf of His Majesty or on his own account, he responded to her that the latter was the case. She thereupon denounced him to her husband, who postured as being highly indignant over Fouché's actions. However, Napoleon also left Fouché in charge of his ministry. It was an inaction that spoke volumes to observers, and to Josephine herself: the Emperor was likely testing the waters, preparing and shaping the marital battlefield. In the telling words of his Archchancellor, Cambacérès, in whom Josephine had immediately confided about the incident: "One notes that he [Fouché] stayed in his position, that he continued to operate, at least apparently, with the confidence of his master, and that the affair of the divorce seemed entirely forgotten."[164]

The issue of succession went beyond issue. The Emperor's four brothers, Louis, Joseph, Jérôme, and Lucien did not even remotely share Napoleon's leadership talents; they were grasping, untrustworthy, and mostly ineffectual (Louis was something of an exception in this regard, as was sister Élisa). At the time of the coronation in 1804, Fouché — who had already feuded with Lucien in particular and prevailed — reportedly described the quartet of the Emperor's brothers as "revoltingly incapable."[165] So, replicating the thought processes of the Abbé Sieyès in his earlier search for a military man to act as the savior of France from the sclerotic Directory, Fouché and Talleyrand also cast about for a military man, especially one whom they could closely control. They soon focused upon Joachim Murat, the flamboyant cavalry officer who had routed the Five Hundred from the Palace of Saint-Cloud on 19 Brumaire. Murat, the son of an innkeeper, had his very rough edges, a colossal ego reflected in his peacock uniforms, and, as will be seen, most of the Bonaparte brothers' aforementioned negative characteristics. Nevertheless, both ministers were convinced (perhaps wrongly) that the cavalry officer and his wife, Napoleon's hyper-avaricious youngest sister Caroline, could be easily manipulated.

Joachim and Caroline Murat were apoplectic over Napoleon's recent placement of the eldest Bonaparte sibling, the docile Joseph, upon the throne of Spain. In addition, they were ungraciously resentful of their also-ran reward, the throne of the Kingdom of Naples. In the view of Étienne-Denis Pasquier, an insider and protégé of Cambacérès who would become counselor of state and a prefect of police, "M. Fouché had always been on the most intimate terms with him [Murat], and prided himself on being able to manage him. M. de Talleyrand considered that it would be even easier to overthrow him than to set him up . . . . As to Mme. Murat, the Emperor's sister, her ambition was so boundless that one could make her accept any and all terms."[166]

As noted, a message sent on behalf of the two ministers to the Murats initiating a line of communication for succession maneuvers in the event of Napoleon's death had been intercepted by Prince Eugène. The dutiful son-in-law forwarded it to the Emperor in Astorgas. This dispatch constituted extremely damaging evidence of a high-level conspiracy to engage in an unauthorized usurpation of the Emperor's prerogative to select his own next-in-line. But a separate, additional message Napoleon received from Paris in his Spanish headquarters on that frigid January evening was equally disturbing: Talleyrand and Fouché had publicly paraded their newly formed alliance before the astonished eyes of the Empire's elite and its foreign observers. The venue they had selected was an elegant dinner party given by Talleyrand on December 20, 1808 at his lavish mansion on the Rue de Varennes in Paris. After the multitude of dignitaries from the Empire and beyond had assembled, suddenly, as if on cue, the Prince of Benevento's *major domo* dramatically announced the arrival of Talleyrand's unexpected guest of honor. Pasquier recorded:

> I can still recall the effect produced at a brilliant evening party given by M. de Talleyrand, by the appearance of M. Fouché, on the day when he entered his former foe's dining room for the first time. No one could believe his eyes, and the wonder was far greater when the affectation of harmony was carried to the point of the two men linking arms and together walking from room to room during the whole course of the evening.[167]

This unwelcome report of unexpected amity between the two formerly bitter rivals prompted Napoleon to decide to scrap his plans to see personally to the destruction of Sir John Moore's retreating army. He handed the task over to Marshal Jean Soult, who in turn allowed the pace of the French army's pursuit to slow, permitting the British force to avoid annihilation by scrambling aboard Royal Navy rescue ships at Corunna and escaping from Spain, only to refit and return to fight again under a new commander, Arthur Wellesley, destined to become the Duke of Wellington.[168] In the meantime, Napoleon travelled to Valladolid, in north-central Spain, and from there he made a grueling journey over the snow-bound Pyrenees all the way back to Paris, stopping only to change teams of horses for his custom-built headquarters carriage. He arrived at the Tuileries Palace on January 22, just three weeks after having received the set of disconcerting dispatches at the Casa de Tepa.

First, and probably quite unfairly, an incensed Napoleon rebuked the doggedly loyal Cambacérès for not letting him know about the new concordance between the rival schemers. The Archchancellor recounts that he was thusly admonished: "How could you let me ignore the fact that after such a long enmity, Talleyrand and Fouché are reconciled? Don't you recognize the ambitious outlooks of these two, and can you not doubt that their reconciliation is highly prejudicial to me?"[169]

Next, on January 27, Napoleon gave a thorough dressing-down to Fouché, whom he had nevertheless already decided to retain in his post. With Spain in turmoil, Austria on the march and backed by Britain, and with Prussia wavering, now was not the time to remove his ruthlessly efficient Minister of Police. Also, Fouché's agents and the gendarmes had recently, during the summer of 1808, seemingly eradicated most of the last vestiges of the endemic rebellion in the Vendée by quashing multiple conspiracies and capturing their ringleaders.[170] This had very much pleased the Emperor. And, upon being confronted about his machinations, Fouché apparently coolly and rather persuasively argued that he had acted not against Napoleon himself, but only to preserve Napoleon's empire and accomplishments in the regrettable event that its ruler met an untimely and unfortunate end. As the Emperor contemplated his next move to confront the growing Austrian menace in Bavaria, he must have thought it prudent to leave at least one effective minister in place in Paris, albeit one who would from now on be very closely observed. Also, as Pasquier, at one point a prefect of police himself, astutely noted in his *Mémoires*, "It is always difficult to remove the occupant of the Ministry of Police, as the post naturally leaves many wires at the disposal of the man who has held it for any length of time."[171]

The Emperor's primary retaliation against the threat to his authority took place on January 28, in his chambers at the Tuileries Palace. In addition to Talleyrand, in attendance were the Archchancellor Cambacérès; the Archtreasurer and Duc de Plaisance, Charles Francois Lebrun; the Minister of the Navy, Denis Decrès; the Comte de Montesquiou-Fezensac (who unsuspectingly was about to be awarded Talleyrand's title of Grand Chamberlain); and a subdued Joseph Fouché, who was now in full survival mode.[172] Napoleon set the stage with general but threatening observations about the absolute power he wielded, the magnificent favors he had bestowed, and the binding loyalty he deserved from his subordinates: "*Vos honneurs, vos biens, a qui les devez vous? A moi seul; comment pouvez-vous les conserver? Par moi seul . . . Apprenez que, s'il survenait une révolution nouvelle, quelque part vous y eussiez prise, elle vous écraiserait les premiers.*"[173] ("Your honors, your property, to whom do you owe them? To me alone; how are you able to hold on to them? Thanks to me alone. . . . Understand that, if a new revolution comes about, whatever part you take in it, you will be the first ones eliminated.")

Napoleon thereupon turned vehemently on Prince of Benevento and Minister of Foreign Affairs Talleyrand, who had been insouciantly and impassively lounging about during these preceding remarks, in accordance with his ingrained aristocratic habits. With the hateful invective of an enraged Corsican cornering his adversary in a vendetta, Napoleon unleashed a diatribe in which he called his target a thief (Talleyrand had indeed pocketed vast amounts in bribes in the course of his negotiations on behalf of the Directory, the Consulate, and the Empire over the years), an atheist, an ingrate, a man without loyalty, ethics, or honor. (Napoleon may not have known for certain — but perhaps he instinctively sensed or had been pointed by someone knowledgeable towards the conclusion — that Talleyrand was the aforementioned mole, that his own Foreign

Minister and Grand Chamberlain of the Empire had devastatingly undermined his relationship and alliance with Czar Alexander at the conference at Erfurt in 1808.)[174] Bad advice given in the past by the Foreign Minister was dredged up and thrown back in his stolid face — namely, the kidnapping of the Duc d'Enghien and the removal of the Spanish royal family that had launched the Empire's costly Iberian adventure. Pasquier, who spoke to at least one eyewitness shortly thereafter as well as to a lady of the imperial court in whom Talleyrand had confided soon after the scene, wrote that the Emperor snarled: "You deserve that I should smash you like a wine glass. I can do it, but I despise you too much to take the trouble."[175] Then came the capper, the final, memorable insult directed at a man who was everything he was being accused of, and who was therefore already quite dangerous: the distinguished Prince de Benevento, upon whom so much prestige and rank had been bestowed by the victor of 19 Brumaire, was nothing more than "*un bas de soie étouffé avec la merde!*" — Talleyrand was "a silk stocking stuffed with shit." With that final insult, the blistering session was over and the Minister of Foreign Affairs, who would be immediately stripped of his portfolio and of his honorary and lucrative rank of Grand Chamberlain, was left behind to mutter that it was a pity that such a great man should be so ill-bred.[176]

Talleyrand's serene impassivity was legendary — according to Louis Bonaparte, "If he got a kick in the backside while he was talking to you, his face would never give you a sign of it."[177] But behind that stoic mask doubtless simmered deep mortification and outrage over a searing and humiliating event. Pasquier refers to the experience as the "mortal half hour" and comments that it "must have been . . . frightful . . .for him, if one is to judge of it by the suffering felt at it by those present, none of whom ever subsequently referred to it without shuddering at its recollection."[178] (One does find it hard to envision Fouché actually shuddering, however, unless he did it to disguise some degree of internal glee.) And, behind his mask, ex-Foreign Minister Talleyrand began to plot a devastating revenge, to be taken at his pleasure and leisure, without constraint of time.

While Talleyrand's calculations centered upon the toppling of the Corsican usurper-emperor, might he also have begun to consider a way to settle scores with the Minister of Police as well? For Fouché had survived and Talleyrand had not, and now the former was the only first-rate minister in the imperial galaxy. And might it have occurred to Talleyrand that there could have been a set-up in all this? Was it purely happenstance that Fouché had weathered his meeting with Napoleon on the 27th of January 1809, but Talleyrand had not survived the scorching counterpart on the 28th? Did Fouché know of the dangerous game that Talleyrand had been playing with the Czar, and did he use that information to escape Napoleon's wrath? The keen observer Cambacérès wrote, *"J'en tirai la conséquence que le prince de Bénévent avait été la dupe du minister de la Police, et que les manouevres de ce dernier l'avaient emporté sur la finesse de l'autre."*[179] ("I concluded that the Prince of Benevento had been the dupe of the Minister of the Police, and that the maneuvers of the latter had overcome the finesse of the former.")

In April 1809, the Archduke Charles and his revitalized Austrian army of over 200,000 men, without a formal declaration of war, invaded the territory of Napoleon's ally, the Kingdom of Bavaria. Confronting them there, to the northeast of Munich, was France's *Armée d'Allemagne.* This too seemed a formidable force with a troop strength of 170,000. But in the absence of so many experienced *Grande Armée* professionals who were deployed in the bloody attempt to subdue the mass uprising in Spain, it had in fact been cobbled together from inexperienced French conscripts and a hodge-podge of formations from Napoleon's buffer-states creation, the Confederation of the Rhine. In addition to Bavarians, other German-speaking units serving under the tricolor came from Württemberg, Westphalia, Weimar, Coburg, Baden, Berg, Nassau, Hesse-Darmstadt, and Saxony, filling out the ranks of the aptly named Army of Germany. For the time being, these Teutonic contingents were satisfied to be allied with what had up to that point clearly been the winning side.

Prior to leaving Paris to join his troops at the front, the heir-less Emperor met with his Minister of Police, who was also about to be awarded the portfolio of the Ministry of the Interior after the incumbent had suffered a breakdown. It is reported by Pierre-Marie Desmarest of the Ministry of Police that this exchange occurred between the two men:

Napoleon: "What would you do, Fouché, if I were to die from a bullet, or from some other accident?"
Fouché: "Sire, I would seize all the power that I could, so as to dominate events, and not be swept away by them."
Napoleon (apparently after a moment's reflection): "Get the jump, that is how the game is played."[180]

Despite considerable confusion at the outset of the renewed war with Austria over the receipt, interpretation, and execution of the absent Emperor's orders, France's Army of Germany successfully repelled Archduke Charles' invasion. With Napoleon personally on the scene by mid-April, the French-led forces went on the offensive and began to move through Bavaria and down the valley of the Danube River, with the Habsburgs' distant capital of Vienna on the south bank as their ultimate goal. The Archduke cautiously sought to break off combat and he pulled his army back, crossing to the north bank of the Danube at the fortress city of Ratisbon and leaving behind six of his battalions to cover his retreat. The Franco-German army pounded the medieval walls with artillery fire and sent infantry columns storming forward with scaling ladders to dislodge the defenders. Napoleon, on horseback, moved closer to observe the assault. Suddenly, a bullet fired from one of the parapets struck him, and he was quickly down on the ground. A cry swept throughout the French ranks: "The Emperor has been shot!"

But the projectile was a spent round, and it had wounded Napoleon only slightly, in the foot. He was rapidly bandaged up, he remounted his white Arabian, and with his staff and cavalry escort he rode through the Army of Germany's siege lines to demonstrate to his wildly cheering men that neither his life nor his leadership was in doubt.

By May 12, Napoleon's army had completed its long march through the Danube valley to Vienna, and the Emperor installed himself in the Habsburgs' hastily abandoned Schönbrunn Palace. However, the

Austrian army under the Archduke remained largely intact on the north bank, directly across from the capital. Napoleon was determined to bring his longstanding enemy to battle and finish it off for good. He ordered his engineers to build a series of pontoon bridges interconnecting the two riverbanks via a large island called Lobau in the middle of the Danube. Upon their completion, his troops began to march over them and to establish a bridgehead on the north bank where two rural villages, Aspern and Essling, were situated.

A sizable advance contingent had made it across the river when the vulnerable pontoon bridges behind them were suddenly broken up by fireships and debris (including an entire floating windmill) that had been launched at them from up-river by the Austrians. At the same time a far more massive attack than had been anticipated by the French command was hurled at the twin villages by the Archduke. Vicious house-to-house fighting took place throughout the entire day, and the Austrians brought to bear their huge local advantage in artillery (the Army of Germany's advance columns had transported few cannons with them). A Marshal of France and a longtime favorite of Napoleon's, who had accompanied him the night of the Rue Nicaise bombing, the Duc de Montebello, Jean Lannes, was killed and over 20,000 casualties were suffered by the Franco-German army; the remnants of the advance assault force limped away from the north bank across the increasingly precarious makeshift bridges, which were undergoing constant repair and replacement. At Apsern-Essling, Napoleon had suffered his first-ever battlefield defeat of apparent consequence, and word of it spread swiftly throughout Europe, inflating it to the point where it was claimed that the Emperor himself had been taken prisoner. France's former enemies, Prussia and Russia, took a very sharp interest in these developments and seemed ready to enter the fray from the wings to join with their sometime rival Austria.

But neither the bullet fired from the walls of Ratisbon, nor the shocking reverse at Aspern-Essling, nor even a subsequent failed assassination attempt upon Napoleon in Vienna by an aggrieved Saxon student,[181] determined that the Emperor's ascendancy would come to an abrupt end in 1809. On the night of July 4, forty-five days after its defeat on the Danube, the rested and reinforced Army of Germany crossed swiftly back over the river, thanks to the herculean efforts of the French engineering corps in rapidly constructing bigger and sturdier bridges. A titanic two-day battle, the greatest in European history to date, ensued on the Wagram plateau just beyond the north bank. Over three hundred thousand men were involved representing a multitude of nationalities (the Archduke's imperial Austrian army was just as polyglot as Napoleon's). There were massive casualties on both sides: the French and their various allies suffered 34,000, the Austrians upwards of 43,000.[182] But it was the Austrians who retreated and requested peace terms; it was Napoleon, in his last great and decisive victory, who possessed the field, the Schönbrunn Palace, and the upper hand, not just with Austria but with its suddenly cowering putative allies, Russia and Prussia. Soon the Corsican upstart was also to possess the daughter of the Habsburg Emperor Francis as his second wife, the fertile replacement for Empress Josephine. On the surface, the time did not yet seem ripe for the contingency planning of Fouché and Talleyrand to be triggered into effect.

But now, we shift our attention from the Danube to another river, the Scheldt, a river much closer to the heartland of France than the Danube, and in that summer of 1809 of even greater strategic importance. Here, Joseph Fouché would have the actual opportunity to test out in clever and dramatic fashion his strategy for a succession scenario to Napoleon's imperial rule.

Chapter XI

Excellency

On the Scheldt (meaning "shallow") River, fifty miles upstream from access to the English Channel and the North Sea, lies the great inland port city of Antwerp, one of the largest in Europe, then and now. In 1809, two decades before Belgian independence, it was part of the Kingdom of Holland, at the time a French satellite ruled quite benevolently by Napoleon's brother, Louis Bonaparte. Napoleon had converted Antwerp into France's premier naval base, with a sizable fleet under construction in its massive shipyards, and comprising expansive munitions stockpiles and naval supply depots. As such it constituted "a pistol pointed at the heart of England,"[183] with the Thames estuary just 100 miles across the North Sea from the mouth of the Scheldt. Because of Antwerp's natural and artificial geography, further enhanced by man-made defenses, it presented a significant threat which Britain's Royal Navy had to counter.

Antwerp is at the base of a "Y," with the Scheldt flowing past it and then branching into the Eastern and Western Scheldts, which in turn run roughly parallel to each other and into the North Sea.[184] Between the two branches are a series of islands reclaimed from the sea by dikes. The first island to be encountered by an invasion force attempting to move down either branch of the "Y" towards Antwerp would be dismal Walcheren, made up of flood plains and marshes and feared for the deadly pestilential fevers emanating from its silty, brackish waters. To be stationed in the island's fortified port town of Flessingue or Flushing was considered especially grim punishment duty in the French army, and consequently the small garrison there consisted largely of homesick Irishmen, truculent Spaniards, and former Prussian prisoners who were at this juncture sullenly in the service of the Empire.[185]

The Ministry of Police's daily Bulletin of July 8, 1809, dispatched to the victorious Emperor Napoleon at the Schönbrunn Palace, contained the following note under the heading "Antwerp" (*Anvers* in French): "Details on the formidable expedition prepared in England; naval party commanded by Richard Strachan. . . . It will take action on the coasts of France or of Spain." On July 18, the Bulletin noted that four French prisoners had escaped in a fishing boat and that they had confirmed that an expedition was being prepared against Spain or Holland. Two days later, the Bulletin stated that two more escapees from English custody had provided information on *"l'expédition qui se prépare."* [186] Travel time for special couriers to carry an intelligence report from the Ministry of Police headquarters on the Quai Malaquais to the Schönbrunn ranged from one week to twelve days.[187]

The British expeditionary force that was assembling at the mouth of the Thames and in the fleet anchorage area known as the Downs off the east coast of Kent was "*formidable*" indeed. Forty-two ships of the line, ranging from 44 to 80 guns each, and 220 other warships — frigates, sloops, bomb vessels, brigs, and cutters — were commanded by Admiral Sir Richard "Mad Dick" Strachan, a zealous but cantankerous veteran officer who nevertheless had had limited experience in conducting combined land-sea operations. This would prove unfortunate for the attackers, since Strachan's mission was to force the Scheldt estuary, to put ashore significant ground forces to reduce the forts and batteries lining its islands and its banks, and to proceed to destroy Napoleon's prized naval base at Antwerp and annihilate all the French ships sheltered or under construction there.

Admiral Strachan's British army counterpart for the expedition was John Pitt, the Second Earl of Chatham. The Earl was the older brother of Prime Minister William Pitt the Younger, who had died in office in 1806, and the eldest son of the legendary P.M. William Pitt the Elder. Serving in Tory cabinets rather than on the battlefield, Chatham lacked a combat command background but he most assuredly did possess serious political clout and impeccable connections. His expeditionary force was floating in the choppy Channel in an armada of 352 troop transports, and it was a powerful force indeed for the mission at hand. It was comprised of approximately 44,000 men, including some of Britain's most elite and storied units: the Foot Guards, the Coldstream Guards, the 95th Rifle Corps, the King's German Legion. Also on board was a siege train of 70 cannons, 74 mortars, and an arsenal of Congreve rockets, to provide a land supplement to the thousands of guns which the Royal Navy could bring to bear upon on the defenses of Antwerp.[188]

The Ministry of Police Bulletin for August 1, under the heading "Diverse Events" and the sub-heading "Antwerp," somberly advised the Emperor "The commissioner general of police announces that on 29 July, in the morning, a great military force of eighty sails [this underestimate represented but a fraction of the Royal Navy vessels and requisitioned troop transports actually involved] appeared between Blankenberghe and Ostend. That evening, 90 vessels were within 5 leagues of Flushing. An imminent landing is awaited."[189]

The imposing British expeditionary force nevertheless had two counts against it from the outset. First, the personalities, experience, and capabilities of its co-commanders were poorly matched to each other and therefore to the cooperative task at hand. Second, there was the inescapable fact that the invasion fleet had sailed at least a month too late. Napoleon's victory at Wagram on July 4-5 had already knocked Britain's Austrian ally out of the war, and it had kept other powerful potential allies on the sidelines. On the other hand, the Emperor's overreaching ambitions had led to the stationing of hundreds of thousands of France's finest soldiers in Spain, Austria, and northern Italy. At the end of July, there were only six thousand troops of very poor quality in the general vicinity of Antwerp to defend the great maritime center. But before Admiral Strachan and the Earl of Chatham could burn the French shipyards to the ground and embarrass the Empire, they would have to contend with the cunning decisiveness of France's Minister of Police and acting Minister of the Interior, Joseph Fouché.

The rump ministerial government that held an emergency meeting in Paris on August 1, 1809 to address the growing crisis consisted of Fouché with his twin portfolios, Archchancellor Cambacérès, the Minister for War Henri Clarke, and the Naval Minister, Denis Decrès. Cambacérès had a well-earned reputation for steadfast loyalty to the Emperor, for lawyerly discretion (he often was called upon to mediate the frequent quarrels that flared between Bonaparte family members), and for cautious moderation.[190] By no stretch of the imagination was he a candidate to seek ultimate power, and Napoleon rightfully trusted him although he also periodically castigated him and mocked his homosexuality. Clarke, the son of an Irish expatriate, was an extremely well-organized war minister who meticulously executed the plethora of decrees on armaments, procurements, and provisions which the Emperor incessantly issued. He was not particularly strong-willed,[191] and he had aristocratic leanings and pretensions (he later would rally to the Bourbon cause); he detested Fouché for his radical Jacobin background. Naval Minister Decrès had the extremely difficult task of trying to reconstruct the French navy in the wake of its devastating defeat at Trafalgar. He was charged with building a fleet that could accomplish Napoleon's chimerical vision of triumphing over Britannia's "walls of oak" and thus bringing France's archenemy to its knees. With Strachan's armada bearing down on the Scheldt, Decrès saw all his painstaking work in constructing the great naval base at Antwerp placed at dire risk, and he advocated taking extraordinary measures to protect it. Cambacérès and Clarke, however, clearly were not comfortable making any substantive decisions in the absence of the Emperor, without the protection of his explicit instructions, which they were both so used to receiving and executing to the letter. Cambacérès is said to have exclaimed to Fouché at the quartet's August 1 conference: "I have no wish to lose my head, I can tell you!"[192]

Fouché sided with Naval Minister Decrès. Here was an opportunity indeed. The danger to France's interests was clear and present, and it would be difficult — although certainly not impossible — for the Emperor to second-guess him, at least until after the crisis was resolved. Moreover, it gave Fouché the perfect chance to conduct a dress rehearsal for an assumption of power without it clearly being attributable to him as such. So, with notifications having been separately sent to the Emperor by Clarke and Cambacérès (theirs were coupled with pointed criticisms of Fouché's actions) and by the Minister of Police/Interior, Fouché set about proclaiming a national emergency and calling up vast numbers of National Guard contingents throughout the northern departments of France. His proclamation read: *"Prouvons à l'Europe que si le génie de Napoleon peut donner de l'éclat à la France, sa présence n'est pas nécessaire pour repousser les ennemis."*[193] ("Show Europe that while the genius of Napoleon has given magnificence to France, his presence is not necessary to repulse the enemy.") Here, Fouché artfully managed to praise Napoleon, while simultaneously signaling that the great man was not indispensable, and he did so in tones that echoed the calls to arms by the revolutionary Convention in the 1790's when *La Patrie* was last imperiled by foreign invaders.

Next, Fouché needed to find a military luminary to assume the defense of Antwerp and lead his popular army. A twist of fate enabled him to up the ante of his rehearsal exercise considerably. Napoleon's charismatic former rival, Marshal Jean-Baptiste Bernadotte, a Jacobin transformed into the Prince of Ponte Corvo (a former papal state doled out to him in 1806), had been dismissed from the Army of Germany in the aftermath of the battle of Wagram and sent back to Paris in utter disgrace. Bernadotte's humiliation had happened at precisely the right moment for the roll-out of Fouché's contingency plan.

Marshal Bernadotte, whom we earlier encountered (in Chapter VII) as the Minister of War ousted by Director Sieyès in 1799, came from Gascony in southwestern France; he was a hotheaded commander who had previously espoused pronounced radical beliefs. He had once fought a duel with his own chief of staff, on another occasion he had torn off his epaulettes and furiously flung them like a challenge at his retreating men, and it has even been claimed that he was an inspiration for Alexandre Dumas' musketeer saga.[194] He was a reluctant and resentful member of Napoleon's marshalate, and the animosity between him and the Emperor was mutual, long-term, and on the increase.[195] What had kept Bernadotte in his command, and what had gotten him his princely title, was his in-law status: he was married to the beautiful Désirée Clary, who had been the lover of General Bonaparte prior to Josephine, and Désirée's plainer sister Julie was the wife of Napoleon's brother Joseph, the King of Spain.

The impetuous Bernadotte, who had earlier earned the ire of the Emperor for failures by his army corps to show up where it was expected to be during two earlier campaigns, had perversely snatched a stinging personal defeat from the great victory at Wagram. There, he was in command of a Saxon contingent which performed poorly, recoiling from the Austrians and opening a temporary gap in the French battle lines. That was bad enough, but Marshal Bernadotte, whose loyalties flowed downwards to his men but not upwards to the Emperor or laterally to his fellow marshals, had the temerity to place his own proclamation in the newspapers, fatuously commending his Saxons for bravery and claiming the laurels of Wagram. Napoleon was furious. He promptly relieved Bernadotte of his command and sent him back to France, instructing Minister of War Clarke that "if you have occasion to see the Prince of Ponte Corvo, notify him of my dissatisfaction with the ridiculous order of the day which he had printed in all the newspapers . . . . This is a superficial man who wants wealth, luxuries, titles, but does not wish to undergo the dangers and fatigues of war."[196]

Back in Paris, Fouché sought out the seething, embittered Bernadotte, and encouraged him to redeem his reputation by throwing his hat into the ring as a candidate to lead the defense of Antwerp. For all his egoistic volatility and his current banishment to the Emperor's doghouse, Bernadotte nevertheless had a heroic aura about him, and virtually all of his competitors were currently far from northwestern Europe, stationed several weeks away in Austria or Spain.[197] And he was seemingly enamored with republican virtues and values, which meant that the Minister of Police, to whom he would be beholden, could readily control and exploit him.

However, Minister of War Clarke was horrified that the very man to whom he had been unambiguously instructed to relay the Emperor's opprobrium was now being proposed for the command of an army-in-the-making by the Minister of Police. The aristocratic Clarke also sensed a wonderful opportunity to earn Napoleon's approval while at the same time taking down two erstwhile Jacobins at once — Fouché and Bernadotte. He dashed off an indignant complaint about the disturbing state of affairs to the Schönbrunn.

But Fouché had astutely judged both the situation and the Emperor. Antwerp of was of too great a strategic importance and its defenses were in too great a state of disarray to countenance leadership from anyone without a marshal's baton. And he knew that Napoleon had an ingrained habit of flaring up at his subordinates but also of swiftly re-deploying them again as soon as the situation demanded; Fouché had certainly experienced this trait personally. So he correctly anticipated that Napoleon's series of rapid-fire replies from the Schönbrunn to Cambacérès' and Clarke's complaints about Fouché's extraordinary measures and proclamation, and about his equally extraordinary suggested appointment of the disgraced Prince of Ponte Corvo to oppose the Strachan-Chatham-led invasion of Flanders, would come in the form of stinging rebukes. On August 7, a little over a week after the Emperor had castigated Bernadotte to Clarke, he wrote to Clarke again: "If the English expedition is serious and the Prince of Ponte Corvo is at hand, put the 24th and 25th military divisions under his orders, and send him to direct their movement."[198] The next day he sent a missive to Archchancellor Cambacérès: "You will have received my decree to levy 30,000 national guards. I am upset that in your August 1 council meeting you did not take it upon yourself to call up the national guards . . . ."[199] Again to Cambacérès, on August 10:

> I am distressed that you have made so little use of the powers which I have given you, in these extraordinary circumstances. . . . Don't let the English come to take you in your bed. At the first sound of a descent [upon Antwerp] you

> should have raised 30,000, 40,000, 60,000 national guards, authorized the Minister of War to send the Prince of Ponte Corvo . . . .The attitude which you have taken on this occasion is humiliating and shameful and will encourage the English to attempt similar expeditions.[200]

And the final blow emanating from the Schönbrunn fell upon Clarke, in the form of most unwelcome praise for his rival minister, also on August 10:

> I received your letter . . . . I can't conceive of what it is that you are doing in Paris. . . . When 25,000 English [the actual number being considerably higher] attack our shipyards and menace our provinces, the minister remains inactive! What inconvenience is there in raising 60,000 national guards? What inconvenience is there in sending the Prince of Ponte Corvo to take command at a time when there is no-one else available? . . . . I do not see that M. Fouché has done other than that which he had to, and that he has sensed that it is disadvantageous to remain in dangerous and dishonorable inaction.[201]

Fouché had correctly judged that a crisis response was called for, and he now had the Emperor's imprimatur to implement his mobilization plans along with the assurance that he would not be second-guessed, at least not for as long as the British threat to Antwerp lasted.

On August 15, 1809, on the occasion of the Emperor's fortieth birthday celebrations, at the height of the crisis on the Scheldt, and nineteen years after Louis XVI, under extreme pressure, had announced the abolition of the nobility in France, an imperial decree was issued. Minister of Police Joseph Fouché, the erstwhile regicide scourge of counterrevolutionaries, was now in great favor and he was to receive an aristocratic title. Henceforth, he would take his place amongst the other princes, dukes and barons that the Emperor Napoleon was energetically creating in order (so he thought) to secure the vested loyalties of his military and ministerial entourages. The "Butcher of Lyon" would henceforth be addressed as His Excellency, Joseph Fouché, the Duke of Otranto. Fouché's fiefdom, carved out of the satellite Kingdom of Naples, could be found on imperial maps at the very tip of the heel of the Italian boot, on the strait where the Adriatic and the Ionian Seas meet. Otranto came with an endowment, and the title was hereditary. In addition, the title was accompanied by a rather forbidding and a singularly appropriate coat of arms — in the words of the letters patent accompanying the decree: *"D'azur à la colonne d'or, accolée d'un serpent . . . ."*[202] ("On a field of azure, a column of gold, with a serpent coiled around it . . . .").

www.heraldica.org

The last-cited salvo by Napoleon in the direction of the doubtless squirming Minister Clarke, also contained the following observation: "It is evident that the enemy, sensing the difficulty in taking Flushing, will want to march directly on Antwerp and attempt a quick strike on the fleet there."[203] Had the British commanders right on the scene — in particular, the Earl of Chatham — shared Napoleon's immediate grasp of the situation from Vienna, over 700 miles east of the Scheldt, they would indeed have bypassed the citadel of Flushing on the pestilential island of Walcheren and swiftly moved up the river to attack and destroy the invasion's sole objective at Antwerp, which was very weakly defended in early August. Instead, the invaders took their eyes off the prize and lost precious time in reducing the fortifications around comparatively inconsequential Flushing. Worse, the fevers of Walcheren began to exact a terrible toll upon the British forces, which were crowded together on the dank island, where they drank tainted water, and lacked the necessary sanitary measures. An alarmed British government sent a prominent physician, Sir Gilbert Blane, to investigate and he grimly reported back that two-thirds of the army had become unfit for duty, with a death rate of 250 men a week.[204]

Meanwhile, Marshal Bernadotte arrived to take command and control at Antwerp. (Fouché of course made sure that he had a police agent attached to Bernadotte's staff and reporting back on him.)[205] Bernadotte energetically reorganized the defenses of the port city, and reinforcements were rushed in. On August 18, the Prince of Ponte Corvo had taken over a disorganized, motley garrison of 12,000 men. In less than two weeks he scraped together better than double that number,[206] and his charismatic presence greatly improved morale. At the same time the fighting strength and determination of the invaders, gripped by the Walcheren plague, were plummeting.

By September, within two months of its launch, the British invasion had completely collapsed. In its wake came acrimonious counter-accusations between the well-connected earl and the angry admiral; Chatham unconstitutionally went directly to King George to complain about Mad Dick Strachan without the latter having the chance to defend his conduct.[207] Two senior cabinet members thereupon called each other out to fight a duel and a ministerial crisis blossomed. The government of the Prime Minister the Duke of Portland fell. Almost 15,000 British troops were grievously ill or had died from disease.[208] The curious combination of Minister Fouché, the Duke of Otranto, and Marshal Bernadotte, the Prince of Ponte Corvo, had saved the Empire, or so it seemed.

But quickly and predictably, the imperial castigation that had been directed towards Cambacérès and Clarke began to shift focus as soon as the Antwerp crisis receded. The strutting triumphalist Bernadotte was once again unable to restrain himself from issuing a glowing and self-promoting proclamation. Even though this time it was somewhat more merited than the one he had issued in the wake of Wagram, it immediately reminded Napoleon of his utter distaste for his Gascon in-law. By September 11, still in Vienna, the Emperor was penning the following dispatch to his Minister of Police: "I have been dissatisfied with the order of the day of the Prince of Ponte Corvo . . . . The vanity of this man is excessive. I have ordered the Minister of War to recall him. His talents are mediocre. . . . He all the time gives his ear to the intriguers who inundate the capital."[209]

As long as the British had been proximate to Antwerp, Fouché had been issuing sweeping call-ups of France's National Guard. These levies were not limited to the 60,000 men which Napoleon had implied was a ceiling in his early August directive to Clarke; they were well in excess of 100,000, and they were being drawn from departments all across France, not just from those in the threatened northeast. (Cambacérès commented, with some exaggeration: "All that the Emperor ordered had already been executed by Fouché on his own authority . . . and in place of 30,000, the number determined by the Emperor, he called up 200,000.")[210] Fouché also appointed several of his trusted political allies as senior officers of the guardsmen. To top it off, the Minister of Police/acting Minister of the Interior ordered a grandiose review of the new battalions on the Champ de Mars in Paris, reminiscent of the style of one of the fervid revolutionary spectacles of the National Convention.[211]

Complaints about Fouché soon began to accumulate on the Emperor's desk in the Schönbrunn: renewed ones from Clarke, who saw his authority being further eroded; from General Hulin, the governor of Paris, who complained about finding "the national guard and the *chevau-légers* [lancers] under ordinances and regulations of the police";[212] and from the prefects and mayors of the departments whose labor forces were being stripped for Fouché's army of national defense. Napoleon, with one calculating eye upon his divorce and imminent union with the Emperor Francis's daughter, Marie-Louise, was becoming increasingly uncomfortable with what was happening back on the home front. It smelled of coups and republicanism, with his newly minted Duke of Otranto behind it all.

Chapter XII

Outcast

In the aftermath of the defense of Antwerp, Napoleon initially had ample reason to be pleased with the imperial state of affairs at the close of 1809. Not only had the British invasion threat collapsed ignominiously — and along with it the government of Prime Minister William Cavendish Betinck, the Duke of Portland — but his Minister of Police had raised additional forces which could now be incorporated into the Grande Armée to replace some of the grievous casualties suffered in the wars in Austria and Spain. Also, a significant portion of these new forces were conveniently stationed in the Kingdom of Holland, which under his brother Louis Bonaparte's too-benevolent rule had become a haven for illicit trade with Britain in contravention of the Emperor's sweeping boycott of British commodities known as the "Continental System." With the untrustworthy Bernadotte replaced by a more reliable marshal, Holland could be brought to heel in short order, and expeditiously annexed to France if need be. Finally, Napoleon had taken the steps necessary to make his Empire and French domination of Europe a lasting legacy. He was determined to divorce the non-childbearing Empress Josephine, and as the spoils of his great albeit costly victory on the Danube, he would marry Marie-Louise, the daughter of the Habsburg Emperor Francis (who had at one point been the Holy Roman Emperor, a title and institution which Napoleon had liquidated in 1806 after his victory at Austerlitz). She also happened to be the grand-niece of the martyred Queen of France, Marie-Antoinette. Thus would the Corsican perpetuate and upgrade his own direct bloodline, cement peace with France's long-time enemy, and achieve acceptance by and reconciliation with the crowned heads of Europe in atonement for the sins of the regicides of 1793 and his own extirpation of the Duc d'Enghien in the moat at Versailles.[213]

As a prominent regicide who had just levied an army of national defense in the best Jacobin traditions, the Duke of Otranto could divine that the tide was rapidly shifting away from the legacy of the Revolution and that, with the Empire's power at its zenith, he might himself also soon shift from being indispensable to becoming expendable, as had already happened once before, in 1802. As the Emperor consolidated his monarchical authority and united with one of the world's most renowned royal houses, might there also be some embarrassment in having the former *représentant en mission*, who had voted "*pour la mort*" in the Manège, occupy so prominent a position? Thus, soon after Fouché had received his hereditary dukedom, he was required to relinquish his portfolio as acting Minister of the Interior; Napoleon in absentia had taken due note of the degree to which the second set of ministerial powers had enhanced his head policeman's highly effective and troubling ability to exercise authority. The Ministry of Police was already a powerful enough lever to have placed in the grip of Fouché. Napoleon ordered the Duke of Otranto to concentrate on using his remaining ministry's Third Division to commence shaping public opinion in a manner favorable to the forthcoming "Austrian marriage."

Fouché, on the other hand and as usual, had his own ideas and agenda. He clearly viewed himself as by far the most astute member of the imperial government, and he had had his eye on the portfolio of the Ministry of Foreign Affairs, held by Jean-Baptiste Champagny, a loyal servant of the Emperor, ever since the ouster of Talleyrand. Having successfully tried his hand at running a war, Fouché would now turn his talents to achieving peace and prosperity. He would have the audacity to bypass Napoleon and Champagny and engage in direct, unauthorized diplomacy in a rogue attempt to reach an accommodation with France's ancestral enemy, Britain.

To effect his initiative, in November 1809 Fouché turned to an Irish royalist officer and prisoner of war, François Fagan, whom he had converted into an agent of the *haute police.*[214] Fouché sent Fagan to London, where the secret emissary used his connections to obtain an audience with the Marquess of Wellesley, the former Viceroy of India and the older brother of the future Duke of Wellington. As part of the political fallout from the failure of the Walcheren expedition, Wellesley had become Secretary of State for Foreign Affairs only a month before, joining the cabinet of Britain's latest Prime Minister, Spencer Perceval. Colonel Fagan's mission was to sound out the new government's attitude towards a comprehensive peace settlement. Wellesley, just becoming acclimated to his position but sensing the strangeness of this non-credentialed approach, was neither dismissive nor encouraging, merely noncommittal.[215]

Meanwhile, Napoleon had independently decided upon opening his own line of clandestine communication with the Perceval government. He was determined that his diplomacy would be undertaken from a clear position of strength, building upon France's victories at Antwerp and over Britain's sole Coalition partner at Wagram. The Emperor desired to signal to Foreign Minister Wellesley that he would soon incorporate his brother's Kingdom of Holland into France and, with forces of the *Grande Armée* stationed along the coastline, put an abrupt end to the serious breach in the Continental System which venal Dutch customs agents and hordes of smugglers had opened while King Louis Bonaparte looked the other way. Napoleon may well have been interested in determining whether there might be an attractive incentive for staying his hand on the threatened annexation, but his idea of a timely diplomatic approach to Britain was much more along the lines of launching an ultimatum at his adversary rather than in undertaking a serious and sweeping peace initiative.

The Emperor so informed his younger brother Louis, whom he had been badgering for several years to eliminate the illegal trade which had transformed Holland, in Napoleon's words, into "an English province."[216] By late 1809, Napoleon had escalated these demands into personal insults and threats, telling Louis that "in ascending the throne of Holland, [you] have forgotten you are French" and that "the merger of Holland with France can happen voluntarily, or it can happen by force."[217]

Louis Bonaparte was a highly complex and rather tormented individual who was burdened by ill health, by an unhappy marriage to Josephine's daughter by her first marriage, Hortense (he was estranged from her and involved in an exhausting custody battle over their two sons, as to whom there were paternity questions), as well as by fear and resentment of his bullying brother. Napoleon had put him on the throne in Amsterdam to subjugate the Dutch and, instead, Louis immediately *became* Dutch, doing everything in his power to administer the country in a way that furthered the autonomy and best interests of his subjects rather than the imperial agenda of France. Those subjects had been initially suspicious and resigned to exploitative misrule, but the enthusiasm with which "goede Lodewijk" immersed himself in administrative reforms and local customs very quickly won over the hearts and minds of the indigenous political and business leadership and the Dutch people at large.[218] In direct ratio to the good works and concomitant rise in popularity of Louis, Napoleon's anger with his sibling grew, and he increasingly came to view him as both weak and disloyal.

Louis contrarily saw Napoleon's authorization to convey the annexation threat to Britain's new foreign minister as a last-ditch opportunity to save the autonomy of his beloved kingdom, which was already ominously swarming with French army and gendarmerie units post-Walcheren. Perhaps, Louis thought, Britain could somehow be brought to the bargaining table, and perhaps his brother's ultimatum could be stayed and tempered into a genuine, meaningful dialogue as to the possibilities for a grand accommodation, an accommodation which would redound to the benefit of not just the trading genius of Holland but to the peace and prosperity of Europe in general. The Minister of Police, who kept in close touch with the beleaguered Louis and always lent him a sympathetic ear, was ready with the suggestion of an individual who would make the perfect emissary.

This time Fouché's choice was not to be the ineffective Colonel Fagan, the POW he had turned into a double agent, but rather a sophisticated man of business with impeccable commercial and political connections on both sides of the North Sea, Pierre-César Labouchère, originally from Fouché's home city of Nantes. Labouchère had built an immense fortune as a member of the trading firm of Hope and Company in Amsterdam. He demonstrated his negotiating skills early in his career, when it had been made clear to him that he was not on the partnership track at Hope. When his request for the hand of the Englishwoman he was courting was summarily rejected by her father, the legendary mercantile tycoon Sir Francis Baring, Labouchère inquired of Baring whether the response would be different if he were in fact a partner in the prestigious firm of Hope. He received an affirmative answer from Sir Francis, and the enterprising Labouchère thereupon scrambled back over to Holland to advise his employer that if he was named a principal, Hope of Amsterdam and Baring of London would thenceforth be allied. Partnership and marriage ensued quickly and simultaneously.[219] Here was a man with the skills to adroitly represent Louis Bonaparte's desire for a Dutch commercial renaissance and Joseph Fouché's plans to deliver a resounding diplomatic coup to parallel his military triumph! Louis advised Napoleon of Labouchère's role, but what was kept hidden from the Emperor was the broadening of discussions well beyond the Emperor's paramount intention of threatening to remove the remnants of Dutch sovereignty unless there was an immediately forthcoming and attractive quid pro quo from across the Channel.

The doors to the Whitehall offices of the Marquess of Wellesley were always wide open to Sir Francis; the powerful duo knew each other well from their mutual time in India. Now they were also open as well to Baring's son-in-law Labouchère, who journeyed over to London in February under a special passport. But once again, as he had done with the initial probe by Fagan, the cautious Wellesley played the game of back-channel diplomacy in a non-discouraging but also noncommittal fashion, noting that any peace accord would have to be comprehensive and cover such flashpoints as Spain, Naples, Malta, and the release of George III's seized Hanoverian holdings, in addition to arriving at terms for the resumption of the cross-Channel commerce which had been frozen since the collapse of an earlier Anglo-French accord in 1804.

The Labouchère mission soon became more complicated, and the particular tool used by Fouché to try to both remain abreast of and shape the diplomacy would lead to his downfall. The next agent he involved in the matter was an incarcerated financier named Gabriel-Juilien Ouvrard. This notorious risk-taker, who had made a fortune speculating in military and naval supplies, had until recently been languishing in the French prison of Sainte Pélagie after defaulting on astronomical debts he had incurred using the French Treasury's funds. He was also very well acquainted with the House of Hope in general and with Pierre-César Labouchère in particular. Fouché had Ouvrard brought before him. The Minister of Police told the financier that he would give him a passport to travel to Amsterdam if he would make contact with Labouchère, report back directly to Fouché on the progress of the talks with Wellesley, and open his own separate and direct line of communications via his commercial connections with the British as well. Ouvrard may very likely have thought that Fouché was acting with the Emperor's authority (which would not have been unreasonable under the circumstances); he most certainly sensed an opportunity to clear his slate of debts with the Treasury as an insider poised to profit from any ensuing peace, and at the very least he saw the mission as a welcome escape from his immediate troubles. In the released prisoner's words, Fouché "would act to prevent my total ruin . . . he would put an end to persecutions which had lasted ten years, he would assure my family's future."[220] Off to Amsterdam Ouvrard went, clutching the precious passport to the Kingdom of Holland personally issued by the Minister of Police, and seeking out the authorized emissary Labouchère.

But the scheme backfired badly when Labouchère subsequently informed Louis Bonaparte of his resulting conversation with Ouvrard in which the latter, acting in concert with Fouché's instructions, encouraged an expansive and conciliatory approach to the discussions with the British Foreign Minister. In early May of 1810, King Louis in turn naively and carelessly informed the Emperor of the state of affairs; Napoleon was on a state visit to Holland with his new Empress (in the pithy words of Ouvrard, "to show off the daughter of the Caesars in the capital of the ancient Austrian province").[221] To compound the problem for Fouché and for himself, Louis spoke favorably to his brother of a proposed diplomatic rapprochement with Britain, when what Napoleon had wanted was a warning salvo fired at the newly formed government in London.[222] The involvement of the high-profile prisoner Ouvrard led the Emperor to quickly sense that something insidious had been going on without his authorization or knowledge. He pointedly told his unreliable brother that all discussions with Wellesley were henceforth terminated, and he demanded that Labouchère (whom Napoleon later came to understand was innocent in the matter, or at least only acting in accordance with the apparent authority vested in Fouché) turn over every piece of correspondence in his possession respecting the *sub rosa* negotiations.

On his return to Paris on June 1, in a withering confrontation reminiscent of that to which he had subjected Talleyrand two years earlier, the Emperor directed his Minister of Police to arrest Ouvrard immediately and turn over all communications relating to the Labouchère mission. Fouché obdurately resisted and Napoleon thereupon lost all patience with his Duke of Otranto. He reportedly exclaimed to Fouché before a gathering of ministers at the Palace of Saint-Cloud: "You think yourself very deep, but in truth you are nothing of the kind; it is Talleyrand who is deep and on this occasion he has made sport of you . . . . You have been nothing but his tool."[223] He stripped Fouché on the spot of his remaining ministry portfolio and sent his blindly loyal aide, the cavalry commander and head of the elite gendarmes (the same officer who had seen to the execution of the Duc d'Enghien), General Savary, the Duke of Rovigo, to carry out the mission of taking the hapless Ouvrard back into custody.

In his *Mémoires*, Ouvrard records a curious incident. He states that just before he was arrested by Savary, he was approached by Talleyrand, who as an inveterate speculator himself, knew Ouvrard very well. According to Ouvrard, the fallen former Foreign Minister cryptically informed him, "You were spoken about today at Saint-Cloud; come to dinner at my place tonight, perhaps I know something."[224] Counselor Pasquier, in similarly cryptic fashion, refers to the involvement of Talleyrand in the Ouvrard/Labouchère affair, and he notes the long-time involvement of Talleyrand with Ouvrard in dealings on the Paris exchange. [225] Given the nature of the Emperor's biting remarks to Fouché at Saint-Cloud, therefore, it may well have been the case that Fouché's great ministerial rival had evened the score for his own 1808 downfall.

Napoleon named his unswervingly loyal cavalryman, the Duke of Rovigo, as his new Minister of Police. This came as a surprise to all, not the least to a senator who had rushed to Saint-Cloud under the misimpression that the coveted position was his, and even to Savary himself, who commented in his *Mémoires*: "When this appointment was made known through the next day's *Moniteur*, no one would give credit to it. Had the Emperor nominated to those functions the ambassador of Persia then in Paris, the circumstance would not have created greater apprehension."[226] Savary would quickly come to be seen as a particularly heavy-handed and unsubtle police minister, perhaps best known for further expanding and robustly utilizing the French prison system, but not very well regarded for his ability to gather and interpret intelligence. In 1812, with the Emperor far from Paris on the retreat from Russia, Minister of Police Savary would actually be captured in his own home and held prisoner by the operatives of a rogue French officer named Malet, who had been a mental patient and who was in the course of staging a phony but briefly convincing *coup d'état*. Savary's image and reputation would suffer commensurately.

But Savary's rough tenure at the Ministry of Police was not entirely his own fault, given how the transition took place. He writes aggrievedly in his memoirs that while "I had flattered myself that my predecessor would leave me some documents calculated to guide my first steps in this new career," the Duke of Otranto, instead of cooperating with the Duke of Rovigo in a smooth succession displayed "so much unwillingness . . . to put me in possession of information which so deeply concerned the welfare of the state."[227] Fouché's credo was that information was power, and he would obstinately withhold it from not only Savary but from the Emperor as well.

In the immediate aftermath of the show-down between Napoleon and Fouché at Saint-Cloud, the Duke of Otranto's dismissal was not initially stage-managed as a complete disgrace: the Emperor, in keeping with his entrenched philosophy of not severing all ties to those who might in the future somehow prove useful, offered Fouché the consolation position of the governorship of Rome, the second city of the Empire and a particularly sensitive post, given that Napoleon was then holding Pope Pius VII under house arrest. However, the Emperor soon learned of the earlier mission on which Fouché had sent Colonel Fagan to Whitehall, which had predated any authorization of any kind of diplomatic initiative.[228] (Here again, might the informant have been Talleyrand?) It also suddenly occurred to Napoleon that his ex-Minister had in his possession bundles of highly sensitive and potentially embarrassing letters pertaining to the scandalous family affairs of the feuding Bonapartes. He promptly dispatched his long-term military chief of staff, Marshal Louis-Alexandre Berthier, along with the man who had brokered Fouché's introduction to General Bonaparte eleven years earlier, Pierre-Francois Réal of the Ministry of Police (no doubt chafing that Savary had been appointed to the top position in his stead). These two senior emissaries, accompanied by a detail of gendarmes, were instructed to demand that Fouché immediately hand over all correspondence pertaining to the Emperor's spouses, siblings, and in-laws. Berthier and Réal found the Duke of Otranto at his magnificent Chateau de Ferrières, located in the estates of Pont-Carré, a forested region to the east of Paris; there, they delivered their ultimatum. But Fouché brazenly rebuffed the delegation, unconvincingly insisting that he had already burned everything that the Emperor now demanded. As Ouvrard — not an eyewitness, since he was undergoing close interrogation in the first of three prisons to which he would be consigned by Savary over the next several years — described it, *"On avait traité avec Fouché de puissance à puissance par des ambassadeurs; les ambassadeurs n'obtinerent rien; ils revinrent de Pont Carré, les mains vides, announcer à l'empereur un refus que plus d'un roi n'aurait pas osé se permettre."* [229] ("Fouché had been treated as though on a power-to-power basis through ambassadors; the ambassadors obtained nothing; they came back from Pont Carré, their hands empty, to announce to the Emperor a refusal greater than a king could have dared to permit.") The fig leaf of Fouché's Roman governorship was immediately stripped away, and he was directed to remain in internal exile at his senatorial seat in Aix. Instead, the Duke of Otranto chose to flee to Italy. There he would seek the protection of yet another independent-minded Bonaparte sibling.

As of midsummer 1810, Fouché was not the only prominent figure of the Empire who had taken to flight. Napoleon had continued to insert troops into Holland, annex regions of the Kingdom, and strip away its remaining vestiges of sovereignty, including making demands for the wholesale replacement of Dutch government officials by Frenchmen. On May 20 the Emperor wrote his obstinate, morose brother: "Your government wants to be paternal, it is nothing but weak . . . . Love France, love my glory, that is how to serve as King of Holland . . . Return from your mistaken route . . . or your people will chase you out and you will leave Holland the object of derision and of pity by the Dutch"; he signed it, "Your affectionate brother, Napoleon." Imperial patience swiftly came to an end in this instance as well. Just three days later Napoleon again wrote to Louis, in far more frigid tones: "Do not write me with any more of your trite phrases; for three years you have repeated them, and each time proved them false. This is the last letter in my life that I will write you." ("Your affectionate brother" was dropped from the closing this time.)[230]

French troops converged on Amsterdam and for a brief and stunning moment it appeared as though one Bonaparte would actually be laying siege to the capital of another, a Corsican vendetta played out on a Continental stage. But Louis did not wish to bring down any further sufferings upon his Dutch subjects beyond their inevitable servitude to his elder brother's imperial schemes. He abdicated and fled the capital on July 1, forsaking his adopted and cherished land of polders, dykes, and windmills for Bohemia, where he would place himself under the protection of Napoleon's new father-in-law, Emperor Francis of Austria, before moving on to the comparative safety of Switzerland.[231]

General Savary, as the successor to the Ministry of Police portfolio, greatly relished what had befallen his uncooperative predecessor. As an ardent loyalist of the Emperor, he devotes considerable space in his *Memoirs* to inveighing against Fouché's treacherous conduct. However, he also provides a credible assessment of what had propelled the Duke of Otranto along the road to his downfall and disgrace. Specifically referring to the influence which Minister Fouché had exerted over Louis Bonaparte, Savary states: ". . . [T]he minister of police wished to interfere, more or less, in every business, and kept upon terms with every party." And he further notes,

> I soon had occasion to satisfy myself that the administration of police was never carried on in the Emperor's interest; that it had been made available as a means of acquiring his confidence, and at the same time abusing it, and that it was a dangerous weapon in the hands of a disturber of the public tranquility, who made it his whole duty to follow the stream of fortune.[232]

One can readily question, however, which of the two antagonists had become the greater disturber of the "public tranquility" by 1810: the uncontrollable police minister with his unauthorized peace-mission gambit, or the Emperor who was still engaged in a disastrous war in the Iberian peninsula and who would be soon planning the even more disastrous invasion of the realms of the Czar. It is interesting to consider the thoughts of the speculator Ouvrard on the matter; on the one hand, as a frequenter of the Empire's prison system, he was not a particular partisan of Napoleon but, on the other, he may justifiably have felt himself to have been the dupe of Fouché and perhaps of Talleyrand as well. He wrote: "Napoleon seemed to believe his Minister thought him not entirely necessary . . . . He was deeply wounded when the English journals consistently represented him as acting in accordance with the views and ideas of Fouché." [233] By the summer of 1810, the Duke of Otranto may have possessed a better geopolitical compass than the Emperor of France, but the former was not — quite yet — in the position to act as captain and navigator.

Chapter XIII

Subverter

The first order of business for Fouché was, as always, self-preservation. He had defied an already angry Emperor, and his archenemy, Savary, the Duke of Rovigo, had taken command of the fearsome powers of the Ministry of Police, although it was a ministry that was yet to be purged of Fouché's hand-picked lieutenants, some of whom would prove difficult for Savary to root out. The Duke of Otranto had decided upon the prudent course of action by fleeing France, where at the very least he would have been subjected to the most intense and invasive levels of surveillance. In Italy he could avail himself of the good offices of yet another of Napoleon's independent-minded and restive siblings: Élisa Bonaparte, the Grand Duchess of Tuscany. Endeavoring to stay one step ahead of the spreading news of his demise, Fouché issued himself a passport for Florence and, accompanied by his oldest son and three servants, he commenced a zig-zag series of evasive movements intended to throw off any pursuit, movements that would bring him as a supplicant to Élisa's *Palazzo della Crocetta.*

The relationship between the suddenly ex-Minister of Police and Napoleon's oldest sister had not started out particularly well during the early years of the Consulate. Élisa had been very close to her brother Lucien, the clan member who had decisively helped Napoleon when the coup of 18-19 Brumaire teetered on the verge of failure in the Palace of

Saint-Cloud. (Lucien, who had once espoused ardent Jacobin beliefs and aligned himself with Robespierre, had subsequently opposed Napoleon's assumption of imperial power, and opted for self-imposed exile in Italy; at the time of Fouché's flight he was being held in Britain as a well-treated and highly regarded prisoner, having been captured at sea by the Royal Navy.)

But Élisa's initial distaste for the behind-the-scenes machinations of the Minister of Police, who had used Lucien's seditious anti-imperialism to undermine him, was soon transformed into a sense of obligation. Fouché had helped to cover up a variety of Élisa's romantic affairs (while also routinely filing away the details) in which she had indulged herself throughout the course of the Consulate, cuckolding her unprepossessing husband, Félix Baiocchi, an undistinguished junior army officer whom she had married in 1797 despite the opposition of Napoleon. And Fouché, intent upon winning over Élisa, provided her a service that went well beyond sweeping adultery under the opulent carpets of the Tuileries: he apparently suggested to Napoleon that the best way to end this particular strain of Bonaparte family embarrassments and to take advantage of Élisa's innate drive and intelligence was to give her a fiefdom, one carved out of what was once ostensibly supposed to have been the Republic of Italy but which was now one of the spoils of conquest to be doled out as the Emperor saw fit.[234]

In 1805, Élisa and Félix were consequently named the Princess and Prince of Piombino on the west coast of Italy opposite the island of Elba. This starter principality was a part of Tuscany; by the time of Fouché's 1810 odyssey, Élisa and Félix had been promoted to rulers of the entire province. The real power was vested in Grand Duchess Élisa, who shared her brother Louis' love of administrative detail and public works, coupled with a penchant for making money (she oversaw the operations of the immense Carrera marble quarries, which by appointment to the Empire supplied the raw materials for its proliferating buildings and sculptures). Also like Louis, Élisa chafed under the flood of restrictive commands and confiscatory demands that emanated from Paris; in 1809, Napoleon felt the need to admonish her: "You are a subject, and like all the French you are obligated to obey the orders of the Ministers."[235]

It was time for the Duke of Otranto, *in extremis*, to draw upon his open account with Élisa. But it was only the complacent Prince Félix whom he encountered at the Florentine *palazzo* in August 1810; Élisa had already left for France to attend the command performance of her imperial brother's birthday celebrations. So, Fouché was forced to correspond with her rather than to plead his case in person, and this is what he wrote the absent ruler of Tuscany on August 8:

> I have never demanded any favor of the Emperor, I ask him one today through your offices. At the approach of his birthday, that His Majesty forget the errors with which he reproaches me and that he permits me to be re-united with my wife and children; in whatever place that may be, I will be truly grateful.[236]

Fouché — who was likely transporting with him at least a sampling of the incriminating Bonaparte family papers which he had previously claimed to have burned — sensed that it was premature to play upon any nascent disloyalty on the part of the Grand Duchess towards her older brother. Instead, the Duke of Otranto further protested his loyalty and innocence in a letter to Élisa on August 23, asserting that he had been "shaken to the depths of his very soul" to be treated by the Emperor as though he were "a disloyal minister" and dramatically exclaiming, "What a triumph for the enemies of the Emperor!"[237]

While Fouché awaited the results of Élisa's hoped-for intercession, he crisscrossed the western part of Italy, popping up in Livorno, Pisa, Piombino, and Naples in addition to Florence, thereby aiming to avoid surveillance and harassment by police agents who were by now reporting back to Savary on him. At one point he may have even contemplated fleeing to the United States to seek asylum, but he claimed that the Royal Navy and a bout of seasickness barred his way.[238] However, this voyage not taken may have been no more than a smokescreen he used to cover his movements, as he rapidly traveled from one refuge to another.

Weeks later, Fouché received word that Napoleon had relented to the entreaties of his sister Élisa and of Madame Fouché, for whom the

Grand Duchess had secured a personal audience with the Emperor. (The homely Jeanne Fouché, to whom by all accounts her otherwise famously duplicitous husband was quite devoted, was apparently ailing; travel was difficult for her and she would die in two years' time at the age of 49.) The quasi-pardon may have been obtained not only by the pleas of the two women, but also due to Fouché's selective disgorgement of portions of his cache of scandalous Bonaparte papers.[239] Napoleon permitted the ex-minister and his family to henceforth reside in his former senatorial seat, Aix-en-Provence; this dispensation was sweetened further by a blanket authorization permitting the Duke of Otranto to travel in Italy, including to the Kingdom of Naples, under the rule of Joachim and Caroline Murat. One year later, in 1811, Fouché received imperial permission also to reside at his Chateau de Ferrières, in the estates of Pont-Carré, where he had so brazenly defied the Emperor's emissaries.[240]

Fouché immediately expressed his gratitude to the Grand Duchess of Tuscany, writing "[t]hat which touches me the most is the great delicacy with which you have always accompanied the consolations you have bestowed upon me. I pray Your Highness to believe that she will never have a truer and more devoted servant than the Duke of Otranto."[241]

In less than three years, Élisa would lose all of her Tuscan domains and become first a fugitive and then a prisoner, thanks in great measure to the intrigues of her "devoted servant" with her unscrupulous sister Caroline and Caroline's husband, the supremely egotistical King of Naples, Joachim Murat.

We have already noted Napoleon's fatal penchant for rarely placing anyone who acted against his interests in permanent confinement or exile, based upon his supreme self-confidence in his ability to control and intimidate others, as well as upon his belief that they might ultimately continue to serve some useful purpose; we have seen it with Bernadotte, with Talleyrand, and with Fouché before, in 1804. Now, once again, while still far from creeping back into the inner circle, Fouché adroitly navigated the transition from disgraced minister, to semi-disgraced returnee, to occasional informal counselor (at one point he reportedly advised against the calamitous invasion of Russia),[242] to official representative of the Empire. In July 1813, after the previous governor had gone mad, Napoleon named the Duke of Otranto to the post of Governor-General of the Illyrian Provinces, thereby signaling Fouché's gradual, albeit incomplete and tenuous, revival of fortune.

In deciding upon this new assignment, the Emperor was no doubt partly motivated by the advantages of putting a goodly distance between Fouché and the conspiracies and intrigues of Paris.[243] Also, he clearly thought it useful to employ the Duke of Otranto's diplomatic and surveillance skills in order to protect a new and important buffer zone for the French Empire. The Illyrian Provinces, stretching along the eastern coastline of the Adriatic Sea, had been severed by Napoleon from Austria via the 1809 Treaty of Schönbrunn after the Habsburgs' defeat at Wagram; the Provinces served to keep the Austrians geographically separated from the Kingdom of Italy. The Kingdom, in turn, was ruled by Napoleon's stepson, the Viceroy Eugène de Beauharnais, and it encompassed the northeastern part of the Italian peninsula. (Much of the rest of Italy was then constituted by the Grand Duchy of Tuscany, Élisa's realm, stretching from Rome to Turin in the northwest, and by the Murats' Kingdom of Naples to the south.) After the destruction of the *Grande Armée* on the snowy steppes in 1812, a powerful Sixth Coalition had been formed against the Emperor, with Austria once again rejoining the crusade against Bonaparte, and this time in league with Russia, Prussia, Sweden, and Great Britain. With Napoleon and his hastily assembled replacement forces confronting the massive and converging armies of the first four of these five nations on the plains of Germany, and with the loyalties of his own allies in the Confederation of the Rhine beginning to waver, he desperately needed stability on his southern flank. To deliver it, the Emperor depended upon the allegiance of three men: the Viceroy Eugène, Joseph Fouché, and King Joachim Murat. Only the first of them would prove trustworthy.

Fouché's tenure in the Illyrian Provinces proved to be very brief. By October 1813, Austrian troops were pouring over the border to reclaim their lost territories, and Croatian troops in the French garrison switched sides, a phenomenon which would be repeated in the coming weeks and months by other erstwhile allies who could readily sense and adjust to the new direction of events. However, this evanescent posting serves to provide the historian with a striking picture of the Duke of Otranto, at age 54 and recently widowed. The intimate portrait comes to us courtesy of a chronicler who worked directly for the new Governor-General of Illyria: the French writer Jean-Charles Nodier.

Nodier would later become known as a prominent romantic novelist and fancier of the occult, writing fables in a Gothic vein which featured vampires and demons. However, at this stage of his career, he owed his very freedom to Fouché. In 1803, Nodier had penned a vituperative anti-Napoleon poem, "La Napoléone," on the occasion of Bonaparte's return from Egypt, and it became immensely popular with émigrés and Jacobins alike:

> Sychophant spewn from the walls of Alexandria
> To the opprobrium of France and the wrath of Europe
> Why did our vessels and our ports receive the renegade?
> From betrayed France he earned a haven and she a set of chains.[244]

The understandably furious target of this diatribe ordered Fouché to use his ministry's Third Division to roll up the distribution network for "La Napoléone"; the ensuing heat induced the author to turn himself in, and Nodier thereupon became an inmate at the prison of Sainte Pélagie.

But Nodier was fortunate in that his father had once been an Oratorian instructor. That old-school tie continued to count for something with Fouché, who listened patiently to the agitated parent's proffered excuse that young Charles had been under the influence of opium when he wrote his screed. Fouché's wise counsel to Nodier *père* was to have his son write a *pro*-Napoleon poem while in his jail cell; Charles complied and Fouché slipped the paean of praise to the First Consul, noting without saying more that its author was being held at Sainte Pélagie. Napoleon thereupon gave his assent to the writer's release, apparently unconscious of the fact that the prisoner was actually the same poet who had earlier written about him "Your name is anathema, symbol of hate to all."[245]

By happenstance, in 1813 Fouché and Nodier were reunited in the Illyrian capital of Laybach (now Ljubljana in Slovenia); Nodier was the editor of the *Télégraphe Officiel*, the local imperial propaganda organ published in multiple languages. Consistent with Fouché's previous hands-on oversight of the Parisian press from his Quai Malaquais headquarters, the Duke of Otranto took a keen, micro-managerial interest in using the Laybach journal to shape public opinion. (It is also likely that Nodier's personal antipathy for Bonaparte was not viewed as a negative by his new boss.) Nodier's posting in turn gave him the opportunity to observe Fouché at close quarters and on an ongoing basis. He provided us with this compelling physical description of the Duke of Otranto in his work, *Souvenirs de la Révolution et de l'Empire*, which also gives the reader a hint of its author's ability to depict the grotesque and otherworldly:

> His face was pale with a shade that was unique to him, and which I have difficulty defining. This was not a pallor which betrayed the permanent effects of worry repressed with effort; it was not an unhealthy, wan color which reveals poor blood and a sickly constitution. It was a frigid shade, but living, like that which time confers on monuments. The power of his well-set eyes prevails . . . over every other impression that his features first produce. They were very clear blue, but always lacking that light which animates passions . . . They [have a] curious fixity, striking and deep, but at the same time lifeless . . . I often told the Duke of Otranto of flattering accounts and unexpected events; I have been near him, and alone with him, at the arrival of a message worse than bleak, and I have never seen him contradict himself with any flash of animation from the impassive immobility of his glassy eyes. For me, I ask myself by what incredible operation of will can one extinguish his soul, to conceal from his own pupil its lively transparency, to fit his expression into an invisible container, like the retractable claw of a cat.[246]

Assuming the accuracy of Nodier's portrait, had the two men not already parted company by October 1813 the editor of the Illyrian *Télégraphe* would have had yet another opportunity to observe Fouché's impassive reaction to shockingly bad news for the future of the Empire and its loyal officials. During a titanic three-day battle centering on the city of Leipzig and the plains of Saxony surrounding it, involving well over half a million combatants, Napoleon's army had suffered a catastrophic defeat at the hands of the Allies and was in full retreat westward, back across the Rhine. The Bavarians and the Saxons had switched sides, ex-Marshal and now, improbably, *King* Bernadotte was leading the Swedes against the Emperor, and mighty Russian, Prussian and Austrian armies were advancing along the entire eastern borders of France, Switzerland, and Italy. Wellington was pushing into France through the Pyrenees from the southwest. The final drama was about to unfold. It was high time for Joseph Fouché to extract himself from the lost Provinces of Illyria, and to start backing the winning side.

In the aftermath of the Battle of Leipzig, the Habsburg court emissaries at the Austrian headquarters tent must have been astonished at the sight of the premier cavalryman of the era cantering up to them, resplendent in his ostrich-plumed *czapka*, with his Mameluke scimitar hanging at his side, and mounted upon his charger with its trademark tiger-skin saddle blanket. Joachim Murat, the flamboyant King of Naples, had decided to detach himself from the fast-retreating *Grande Armée*, and before his return to Italy, to make a brief detour to parley under a flag of truce with the Austrian enemy to determine how he could best fit into the new European order, the order he plainly saw would soon be created by the victorious Allied armies of the Sixth Coalition. At the same time, back in Naples, his wife, Queen Caroline Bonaparte, was also engaged in clandestine communications with Austrian representatives as to how she and her husband might abandon her brother and thereby manage to hold onto their suddenly unsteady thrones.

We have earlier noted that the Murats were supremely ungrateful to Napoleon for his grant to them of the southern portion of Italy (excluding Sicily, which was ruled by a Bourbon king under the protection of a British fleet). Furthermore, they had been involved in the succession-plot scheming of 1808-09 with Fouché and Talleyrand, the plot which had been brought to the attention of the Emperor thanks to his son-in-law Eugène, and the disclosure of which had caused the shocking downfall of the Prince of Benevento. Napoleon understandably trusted neither his sister Caroline nor her horseman husband, but he nevertheless committed a stunning misjudgment when he selected Joseph Fouché as the man to keep the two of them in line. He knew that the Duke of Otranto had counseled the Murats over the years, which might have led him to believe he would make productive use of his leverage, but he also knew that the Duke had conspired with them, and he furthermore knew far too well that his emissary to Naples had once already engaged in unauthorized correspondence with the enemy. Yet Napoleon nevertheless entrusted him with the highly sensitive mission of preserving their allegiance.

What was at stake strategically was the Emperor's ability to defend northern Italy along the natural boundary of the Po River and the Alpine approaches of France by fielding a very substantial combined army of Neapolitan forces and the Army of Italy, the former led by Murat, and the latter by the now Viceroy Eugène, two of the ablest combat commanders that France possessed. But if the Murats struck a deal with Austria to join the Coalition, or even simply dropped out of the war, Eugène would sooner or later be overwhelmed, Italy would be lost, and the southern approaches to France's heartland would be left wide open.

Napoleon's instructions reached Fouché in Bologna on November 15, 1813. The Duke of Otranto was ordered to act as commissioner-general for Italy, with the task of encouraging the Viceroy, the King and Queen of Naples, and the Grand Duchess of Tuscany to work together for the sake of the Empire. The mission conferred upon him was clear: "You will make the King understand the importance of sending 25,000 men to the Po. You will also make the Queen understand it, and you will do everything possible so that . . . no-one is led astray by the false promises of Austria and by the honeyed words of Metternich."[247] Assuming a veneer of dutifulness, Fouché informed Murat that he was on his way to the Royal Palace in Naples to see him on official business of the Empire. For the record, he masked his real intentions with a self-serving message, sent to Murat from Parma on November 21: "Our fortunes, Sire, however widely we may be sundered in terms of rank, have but one foundation.

We both owe them to the Emperor. On him and on the continuance of his prosperity they both depend."[248]

On November 30, Napoleon's commissioner-general arrived in Naples to commence a series of discussions with the Murats in which prolonging Napoleon's prosperity was not seriously considered. The precise details of these talks remain unclear, but their general outlines do not. Joachim and Caroline were considering three options. The least favored was to continue to adhere to the fading fortunes of imperial France. The two being carefully weighed were for the Kingdom of Naples to join the Sixth Coalition and treacherously take the field with the Austrians against Eugène's French forces in northern Italy, or for Murat to declare *all* of Italy to be independent (but under his rule, of course) and neutral - to cast out all "foreign" influences, be they Habsburg, Bourbon, British, or Bonapartist (excepting Caroline, of course) and to win for this newly united kingdom an influential seat in postwar Europe. It appears that Fouché counseled the King to take the latter approach, for when he left the Royal Palace of Naples he wrote the following to Murat: "Your conduct in this matter will be measured, as with everything in this world, by its success. If you can contribute to the general arrival of peace, if your name acquires enough weight in the balance of European affairs to raise the dignity of thrones and the independence of nations, the world will benefit." He prudently added, "Maintain a strong army, it will be your sole guarantee."[249] And Fouché would, after the ultimate triumph of the Allies in Italy, complain to the French diplomat the Marquis de Caulaincourt, "If the King of Naples had listened to me, he would be laying down the law to the coalition instead of being compelled to take his orders from them. Moreover, he would have achieved a lofty ambition . . .".[250] The idea of a unified and independent Italy with himself serving as the chief advisor to and manipulator of the Murats likely held much attraction for the Duke of Otranto. In any event, his conversations with the royal couple clearly took a very different direction from that which the Emperor had charged him to pursue.

On December 16, Murat wrote Napoleon a plaintive letter, beseeching him to acknowledge the independence of Italy and calling upon him to make peace at all costs, for the good of Europe. This went unanswered.

On January 15, Murat wrote him again: "Sire, I have just concluded a treaty with Austria," adding with breathtaking naiveté and some degree of insolence as well, "I need to learn you are still my friend, for I shall always be yours."[251] Seemingly, two decades of comradeship on bloody battlefields from Alexandria to Moscow caused more conflicting albeit superficial emotions in Murat than did two decades of imperial government service in Fouché.

In seeking a safe harbor, Murat had chosen to ride the whirlwind or rather, using Queen Caroline's metaphor, he was "walking on the edge of a precipice."[252] He made territorial demands upon his new and mistrustful Austrian and British allies which they were unwilling to honor or fulfill, especially because he evaded complying with their demands that he immediately join them in attacking Viceroy Eugène's Army of Italy, situated along the banks of the Po River. Prince Metternich wrote disparagingly of his new ally to the Austrian ambassador to Naples, "We might just as well recognize him as an outright enemy."[253] And Napoleon, as he desperately struggled to beat back the Allied armies swarming into France itself, wrote to his duplicitous emissary Fouché on February 13, 1814: "I have received your different letters . . . The conduct of the King of Naples and that of his Queen has no name. I hope to live long enough to avenge myself and France upon such an outrage and such frightening ingratitude. Go through Lyon or Marseilles depending upon which route you take and come back to Paris."[254]

Murat, hopelessly out of his depth, was now isolated and friendless. The beleaguered Emperor remained in apparent ignorance of what had actually transpired during the Duke of Otranto's mission to Naples. Napoleon did however urge Eugène to reach some sort of temporary accommodation with Murat, stating: "Later on we can do as we wish, for after such ingratitude . . . no obligation is binding."[255]

Fouché, having pocketed a 170,000 franc consulting fee from the King of Naples,[256] opted to take the return route to Paris through Lyon. However, before we accompany him on his return to the second city of France and the scene of his earlier crimes, it is worth noting one other bit of collateral damage which the Murats' suborned betrayal inflicted upon French interests in Italy in early 1814. As the Neapolitan army moved northward to do the bidding of the Sixth Coalition — or perhaps still to declare Italian independence — it forced Grand Duchess Élisa to vacate her throne in Florence. Murat initially permitted his pregnant sister-in-law to act as the ruler of the small principality of Lucca within Tuscany, and she promptly followed his lead by also breaking relations with France. She wrote to her older brother in February: "Surrounded by powerful enemies, menaced by land and by sea, betrayed by the King of Naples who deserted your cause, I remain alone in the midst of numerous armies . . . without money, without troops, without munitions: in these desperate circumstances, what more can I do for Your Majesty? . . . [I]t is time that I look after my own interests."[257]

But Élisa soon had to give up the remnants of her vanishing power in tiny Lucca, as the Austrians and British pressed to eliminate a Bonaparte sibling occupying even a diminutive throne located in their respective spheres of influence. She would give birth contemporaneously with her political downfall. One of her former courtesans sardonically noted that the blessed event coincided with the very "moment when she ceased to have need of an heir."[258] Rather than acting as Élisa Bonaparte's "devoted servant," the Duke of Otranto had unconcernedly set in motion her demise.

Leaving the dethroned and dispossessed Élisa in his wake, Murat slowly moved his Neapolitan army north towards the Po. He again simultaneously flirted with the tempting option of declaring a unified and independent Italy, but he eventually and reluctantly engaged the French Army of Italy on April 13 at Piacenza on the Taro River, a tributary of the Po, nevertheless allowing it to disengage and withdraw. He had thereby irreversibly alienated both his old comrades and his new partners at one stroke. Shortly thereafter, the Allies would advise Viceroy Eugène of the fall of Paris, and under the terms of a military convention he entered into with the Austrians, the French troops of the undefeated Army of Italy would ultimately be able to return home with their honor intact.[259]

Joseph Fouché had declined to pursue the mission given him to attempt to coordinate on behalf of the French Empire the actions of the Kingdom of Naples with those of Eugène's Italy and Élisa's Grand Duchy of Tuscany; the Kingdom of Naples was soon to find itself completely expendable to the interests of the Sixth Coalition. (In a year's time, the by-then-ridiculous Joachim Murat would be hauled before a Bourbon firing squad in Calabria; one can well envision an alternative outcome of a more steadfast Murat commanding the Emperor's cavalry at Waterloo and thereby making a decisive difference.) Fouché's mutinous, deliberate decision had directly led to the toppling of all three thrones and to the imminent collapse of Napoleon's southern flank.

After the tribulations of 1793, that portion of the people of the city of Lyon who had survived the terrible siege by the forces of the Convention and the aftermath of the gruesome reprisals administered by Fouché and Collot d'Herbois, came to enjoy a renaissance under the Consulate and the Empire. Napoleon rapidly rebuilt the demolished city center, making it once again worthy of its name, the Place Bellecoeur, and he restored France's second city's reputation as a wellspring for the fine arts and commerce, elevating it from the prostrate *"Ville Affranchie"* to a prosperous imperial showcase. But in early 1814, Lyon was menaced once again: this time not by fellow Frenchmen, but by one of the multiple Allied armies swarming across the frontiers of France, an Austrian army on the march across the nearby border with Switzerland, heading directly towards the great city on the Rhône and Saône Rivers.

Napoleon's choice to lead the defense of Lyon against the coming onslaught was Marshal Charles-Pierre Augereau, Duke of Castiglione, his imperial title having been chosen to honor a great victory he had helped engineer for General Bonaparte during the first campaign in Italy in 1796. Augereau was a man of very humble origins and Jacobin leanings who had served as a mercenary in the Russian, Prussian, and Neapolitan armies before the wars of the Revolution. He had once been a fencing master and had dueled repeatedly with fellow officers. His temper was fierce and his bravery was undisputed: at the battle of Eylau in 1807 he rode into the vortex of the great clash with the Russians during a blinding snowstorm while strapped to his horse in order to keep himself from succumbing to wounds and falling to the ground. As was the case with a large number of the members of Napoleon's increasingly disillusioned marshalate after 1812, Augereau experienced growing feelings of ambivalence about his leader and the destructive course he appeared determined to pursue, and this ambivalence provided fertile ground for his subversion. In 1813, as the tide was clearly turning, he reportedly commented to Fouché: "Our great days are over . . . He [the Emperor] will not make peace; he will get himself surrounded by 500,000 men."[260]

Napoleon initially gave Marshal Augereau a "shadow force," existing on paper but not in reality, with which to defend Lyon. Nevertheless, at age 57 the battle-scarred Augereau threw himself into making preparations with much of the youthful vigor of his days with the Army of the Alps in 1796. He started by rallying the Lyonnais with a ringing proclamation in late January:

> The love of your city has always been your distinctive characteristic. To this noble motive is joined the honor of the French name, and the recognition that you owe to your august sovereign, whose first care, upon taking the throne, was to heal your wounds and raise back up your buildings. You have always been, as you know, the objects of his solicitude.[261]

He soon was able to scrape together a fairly significant force by gathering up volunteers, by getting some veteran units diverted to him and away from the defense of the border with Spain, and by stripping the neighboring depots, garrisons and rear echelons. His makeshift army initially repelled a sizable advance column of Austrians, who fell back towards Switzerland until they were massively reinforced and ready to resume their invasion of France.

On March 13, 1814, as the newly bolstered Austrian forces again threatened Lyon, Joseph Fouché entered the city, having come westward by way of Turin and over the Alps. It is unclear whether he evaded the Austrian lines or whether he was in fact *permitted to pass through them* in order to get there.

By mid-March, the French defenders of Lyon were stretched exceedingly thin, having to defend the heights surrounding the city and being outnumbered by their foes by over two-to-one in manpower and five-to-one in artillery. During the evening of March 20 they suffered a significant reverse at the Battle of Limonest, on the northern outskirts overlooking the Saône, a battle from which Marshal Augereau was curiously and uncharacteristically absent. But the French commander-in-chief did reappear later that very same evening at a council of war which included the civilian authorities of Lyon, the leader of whom would later be awarded honors by the victorious Habsburgs. Augereau put two options before the council: engage in relentless street-to-street and house-to-house fighting against the enemy, or declare Lyon an open city and spare it a second devastating siege and investiture.[262] Counseled strongly to choose the latter, Augereau quickly acceded. In the dead of night, he and his army slipped out of the city and fell back upon Valence, sixty miles to the southwest. Thus the front to Napoleon's south, already greatly weakened by the defection of Murat and the consequent pressure brought to bear on Viceroy Eugène, finally and completely collapsed, despite Minister of War Clarke's admonition to Augereau to make the enemy "buy French soil as dearly as possible."[263]

However, Pierre Augereau was by now finished with buying time for the Emperor and defending French soil with the blood of his own men and that of the citizenry of Lyon. He issued his final proclamation as a Marshal of France, this time from his lines before Valence, on April 16 1814: "The Senate, interpreting the national will to throw off the tyrannical yoke of Napoleon Bonaparte, has pronounced on April 2 his downfall . . . A new constitutional monarchy, strong and liberal, and descending from our ancient kings, replaces Bonaparte and his despotism." He bitterly pronounced that the by then ex-Emperor, who had elevated him from an inconsequential career as a soldier-of-fortune to the absolute heights of imperial command, had "immolated thousands of victims to his cruel ambition [but] has never mourned the death of a soldier."[264]

So, precisely what had the peripatetic Duke of Otranto, a man never without his own agenda, been seeking to accomplish during his visit to Lyon from March 13 until March 19, the day before commander-in-chief Marshal Augereau's non-appearance at Limonest and his withdrawal of his army in the face of the enemy all the way to Valence?

We will soon see that Fouché's archenemy Savary has a pointed and specific accusation to make. But before we assess that hostile source's hearsay assertion, another prominent witness, Jean-Antoine Chaptal, has shed light upon the matter. Chaptal was a very talented industrial chemist, a prominent lecturer, and the author of many learned papers. He had been able to survive the Jacobin purges of the Revolution by being very good at manufacturing vast quantities of gunpowder, operations which he oversaw at the great works at Grenelle. Unsurprisingly, his talent for producing munitions quickly came to the attention of that greatest of customers for his wares: the First Consul, who conferred on him the title of Comte Chaptal de Chanteloup, and who appointed him his Minister of the Interior. Chaptal served in that role from 1801 until 1804, when he resigned after a serio-comic conflict with his employer over the affections of a prepossessing actress in the Comédie Francaise, whom Napoleon also happened to fancy at the time.[265] During his term as Minister, Chaptal energetically pursued sweeping industrial, agricultural, health care, and public works initiatives, and it is certainly possible that he may have occasionally clashed with the Ministry of Police, especially with respect to the administration of the French prison system. And despite his 1804 temporary rupture with Napoleon, Chaptal seems not to have been prepared to abandon his benefactor ten years later: the Emperor had sent him to Lyon as a special commissioner to see to it that the second city had all the ordnance and provisions that could possibly be commandeered for its defense against the Austrians. Allowing for all of this, Chaptal's account of his March 1814 encounter with Fouché does not seem to have been shaped by the type of bitter vendetta in which Savary was engaged against his Ministry of Police predecessor and nemesis.

Chaptal writes in his memoirs that several days after his own arrival in Lyon in mid-March, he was visited by the Duke of Otranto. He asserts that Fouché described his recent past actions in Italy as follows:

> I was in Illyria, in the role of governor, when I received a letter from the Emperor which ordered me to proceed to Naples to convince King Murat not to desert his cause and especially not to bring his troops over to the Austrians. I thus left for Naples. I told the King that the Emperor was lost and that nothing remained to him but a doorway to safety, which was to ally himself to the four great powers, and that Austria, which had already invaded part of Italy furnished him the means. The Queen gave into my reasoning; Murat resisted until the next day, but finally he consented to everything and promised he would send his army to join that of Austria. I left for Rome, where I remained until Murat did it.[266]

This account will immediately be seen as contradicting Fouché's claims to the Marquis de Caulaincourt that he counseled the Murats to strive for a strong army and an independent Italy. One can only speculate whether Chaptal's version of Fouché's remarks was wholly manufactured, or whether — and perhaps this explanation is more convincing — Fouché was disposed to relate varying accounts of his actions to different audiences at different times. Chaptal continues with this recounting of Fouché's disclosures about his current mission:

> Sure of success as to this, I came to Lyon to take over the army which Augereau commanded and make it march against the Emperor. I am in correspondence with [Austrian Minister of State] Metternich; he and the three sovereigns are awaiting at Dijon the outcome of my enterprise. The revolution will be short. We have organized a regency with Marie-Louise presiding. *We have decided on our proclamations to the French people,*

> *our letters to the generals* [emphasis added]. All is ready. I have always hated the Emperor.[267]

(This putative line of communication with Metternich could well account for Fouché's ability to have entered Lyon from the direction of the advancing Austrian force.)

Chaptal asserts that he advised the Duke of Otranto that his subversive scheme would fail, that the army defending Lyon was loyal to Napoleon, and that it lacked confidence in Augereau. He also states that he expressed shock at the role played by Fouché in Italy, and that his visitor coldly replied, "My role was easy: I wrote to one [Metternich] that I would detach Murat from the Emperor; to the other [Napoleon], that all my efforts were vain and that Murat had gone to join Austria."[268]

Chaptal concludes that Fouché's scheme to alienate the defenders of Lyon in fact failed. But the evidence points the other way: Augereau's hold over his men was stronger than Chaptal thought, and the disillusioned commander was able both to absent himself from the Limonest battlefield (he, the man who had led from the front in so many prior engagements) and to abandon the city to enemy occupation. In addition, there is this tantalizing albeit opaque reference in a dispatch written by Metternich to Emperor Francis on April 11: "Tomorrow, with Prince Schwarzenberg and the French Marshals, we shall determine on the best way of carrying out Napoleon's immediate removal. This will depend on the answer we expect from Augereau's army."[269] Was Fouché acting as the indispensable go-between with Austria? Finally, there was the manner in which that expected answer was embodied in Marshal Augereau's proclamation of April 16. This is where the account of Savary, the Duke of Rovigo, which focuses upon a curious and perhaps coincidental meeting, comes into play.

After the Emperor abdicated his powers on April 6, 1814 at Fontainebleau, a decision forced by the crushing weight of the Allied invasion and by a restive cohort of his own marshals and his brother Joseph,[270] he journeyed south in a carriage-convoy to embark for his Elban exile. His personal carriage, along with thirteen other baggage vehicles, was escorted by a cavalry detail officered by four commissioners selected from each of the primary Allies: a Briton, an Austrian, a Russian, and a Prussian. On the morning of April 24, near Valence, Bonaparte and his entourage happened to encounter Marshal Augereau along the roadway, seemingly by chance, although Augereau may in fact have been tipped off by a member of the advance party that the convoy was approaching. [271] A variety of sources state that Napoleon immediately upbraided Augereau for abandoning Lyon, that the latter awkwardly attempted to defend himself and expressed regret over the Emperor's downfall, and that Augereau thereupon asked for and received permission to embrace his former brother-in-arms in farewell. It is said that only later in his journey did Napoleon learn of Augereau's vituperative proclamation of April 16, when he saw it published in a journal. He was absolutely furious, and for the rest of his life he harbored a profound contempt for the Marshal's betrayal.[272] But Savary, in his score-settling memoirs, after recounting the foregoing version of the meeting, actually attempts to exonerate Augereau and to place the blame for his apparently disloyal actions elsewhere:

> They [Napoleon and Augereau] had scarcely parted, when the Emperor was overtaken by his valet. Amongst the public papers which the latter brought with him was the *Moniteur*, containing the same proclamation issued by the same Marshal Augereau to his army, on announcing to it the return of the House of Bourbon [in the person of Louis XVIII]. It was replete with invectives against the Emperor, whom he dared to accuse of cowardice. Nevertheless he had come to embrace him. This may be easily explained; for all those who have known the Marshal are aware of his being incapable of publishing such a document. I was informed by the person who drew up the proclamation addressed by Augereau to the troops under his command, on the occasion of the return from the island of Elba, that Fouché composed the first-named proclamation.[273]

Initially, in sifting through this, one can readily dismiss the Duke of Rovigo's supposed belief that Augereau's behavior at his unplanned meeting with Napoleon demonstrated his steadfast loyalty. Perhaps the Marshal indeed exhibited some vestiges of remorse in the meeting on the Valence road, but an eyewitness account completely contradicts those of Savary and other sources which may well have drawn upon Savary's version of what occurred. That account comes from one of the four escorting Allied commissioners, the Graf von Waldburg of Prussia. He states that Augereau lashed out at Bonaparte with a series of "bitter reproaches on his insatiable ambition, to which he had sacrificed everything, even the happiness of all of France." Napoleon, tired of being subjected to this harangue, retreated back into the carriage, whereupon "Augereau, his hands behind his back, did not take his hat off, and only . . . made a contemptuous gesture with his hand in bidding him adieu." The Prussian witness further observed that Augereau thereupon turned and addressed himself and the other Allied commissioners who were present at the scene with "un salut très-gracieux."[274]

Also, *contra* Savary, the historical record shows that the next day, on April 25, Augereau rode back into Lyon to a hero's welcome, as cheers of *"Vive le saveur de notre ville!"* resounded from adoring crowds, and that he received the salutes of an Austrian honor guard drawn up by the Prince of Hesse-Homburg. At a banquet in his honor that evening, he toasted "Louis XVIII, our beloved monarch, the king and father of all Frenchmen." Further acclaims and awards awaited him in Paris, at the court of the new Bourbon King of France.[275]

But even if Augereau (who died in 1816 and left no account of whatever conversations he may have had with Fouché in March of 1814) was not an unwilling turncoat, Savary's version does provide some corroboration that Fouché's visit to Lyon at least expedited the process of the Marshal's betrayal, as well as corroboration for Chaptal's assertion that the Duke of Otranto had advised him that he had already drawn up the requisite proclamations denouncing the Emperor and proclaiming the end of his regime. Augereau may have already become unsteady in his allegiance, as had Bernadotte, Murat, and a cabal of other of Napoleon's marshals. But, in Lyon as in Naples, Joseph Fouché had both the opportunity and the motivation to deliver the decisive push.

Part III

Restoration

Chapter XIV

Lazarus

In the middle of January, 1815, Louis XVI and Marie-Antoinette returned to the land of the living, coming up out of the cold, hard soil of the Cemetery of the Madeleine in Paris. Once constituting the beautiful and expansive gardens of a Benedictine convent, the Madeleine's makeshift graveyard served as a defiled dumping ground during the Terror for victims of the guillotine, as well as for the bodies of the hundreds of Swiss Guards massacred while doggedly defending Louis and his family in the Tuileries Palace. Most of the corpses had been flung into a giant trench. Louis XVIII, soon after he assumed the throne in the spring of 1814, had ordered that his older brother's and sister-in-law's royal remains, complete with their respective severed heads, be located, exhumed, and re-interred after a solemn requiem mass. An investigation was launched to find the martyred monarchs' grave sites, and eyewitnesses to the casual and disrespectful disposal of the two bodies led Bourbon investigators to an area of the Cemetery of the Madeleine marked by a pair of weeping willow trees situated alongside a stone wall with a door that opened onto the Rue d'Anjou-Sainte Honoré. Thus it was that, at the commencement of the momentous year 1815, a group of witnesses assembled to supervise the excavation at the Madeleine: le Comte de Blacas, Louis XVIII's most-trusted advisor, was there, as was Chancellor Dambray, the arch-royalist le Bailly de Crussol, Peer of France, and the Bishop of Nancy, accompanied by other clergymen and His Majesty's surgeon.[276] Also present at the scene, or at least asserting that he was present, was the masterful author Chateaubriand, an unrepentant distorter of history who constantly sought to establish the centrality of his own role in human affairs and who served as a supremely eloquent advocate of Bourbon legitimacy. He subsequently insisted in his *Mémoires d'outre tombe* ("Memoirs from beyond the grave") that "in the midst of the bones, I recognized the Queen's head by the smile which that head had given me at Versailles." [277]

Unreliable as Chateaubriand's positive identification may have been, given that Marie-Antoinette's body had been underground for twenty-two years in an open coffin covered with quicklime, the royal witnesses were nevertheless satisfied that the skeletal detritus extracted from adjacent spots in the Cemetery of the Madeleine was indeed that of the King and Queen of France.[278] The task at hand was to convey them for Christian burial at the ancient and sacred resting place of royalty, the once-hallowed Abbey of Saint-Denis on the outskirts of Paris. In 1815 Saint-Denis was, however, shockingly bereft of the mortal remains of France's great monarchs. Before the Revolution, it was replete with those remains, which dated all the way back to those of the Capetian kings of the tenth and eleventh centuries. But the Abbey's tombs had been savagely ransacked by revolutionaries in 1793, and the bones of Henry IV, Louis XIII, the Sun King Louis XIV, Louis XV, Anne of Austria, and Marie de Medici, among many others, had been carted away and unceremoniously tossed by the Jacobin mob into a common trench.[279]

The funeral cortege of Louis XVI and Marie-Antoinette left the excavation site at the Cemetery of the Madeleine and turned onto the Rue d'Anjou-Sainte Honoré on the frosty morning of January 21. Perhaps coincidentally, perhaps not, until the procession exited from the city walls of Paris it precisely retraced in reverse the route taken by the doomed King Louis on his way to the guillotine at the Place de la Révolution twenty-two years before to the very day. Along the somber route, cannons were fired at one-minute intervals, drums covered in black fabric were solemnly beaten, and the fluttering white *fleur-de-lys* flags of the Bourbons bore badges of mourning and ribbons of black crepe.

The Parisian onlookers, however, seemed sullen and undemonstrative, at least until a horse drawing one of the funeral carriages stumbled on the Boulevard des Italiens and the black plumes on the top of the carriage became entangled with an overhanging street lamp. Derisive laughter began to well up, "the people broke out in sarcasms upon the funeral pomp," and cries of *"à la lanterne,"* a grotesque reference to past extemporaneous lynchings from lampposts by revolutionary mobs could be heard.[280] But the real damage to the Bourbon cause that day was not attributable to the mishap of the cortege but rather occurred at the ensuing memorial service at Saint-Denis, with the dead King's sister, the Duchess of Angoulême, his youngest brother, the Comte d'Artois, and d'Artois' two sons, the Dukes of Angoulême and of Berry, in attendance: the presiding clergyman, the bitter Bishop of Troyes, threateningly called from the pulpit for present-day revenge against the multitudinous past crimes of the Jacobins and their regicide leaders. Paris and all the non-royalist-leaning regions of France were swept by fears that a royalist day of reckoning, another Saint Bartholomew's Massacre, was now imminent, fears that were magnified by repetitions of and variations on the Bishop's diatribe by embittered clergymen in cathedrals and churches across the country on the proclaimed national day of mourning.[281] This pervasive paranoia was coupled with growing contempt for the arrogant and ostentatious House of Bourbon — particularly for those in the line of succession to Louis XVIII — contempt mixed with anger over the regime's powerful symbolic abnegation of what many revered as the hard-won liberties gained by the Revolution.

The royalist Chateaubriand watched the funeral cortege "with a fatal presentiment"; he referred to the prospect of an "annual reproach which a repeated funeral ceremony seemed to make to the nation," and ominously observed that "evil tempts more than good; when wishing to perpetuate the sorrow, one often perpetuates only the example."[282] Just at the time the bodies of its martyred royal couple were finally being reclaimed, the Bourbon Restoration itself was in growing jeopardy. It had only two more months to live, in its first incarnation.

Of all the citizens of troubled France, it would turn out to be the regicide Fouché who would enable Louis XVIII and his family to gain a second chance.

⚜

It initially was with hope and relief in many quarters, not with fear and resentment, that Louis XVIII's ascension to the throne in May of 1814 had been greeted by a war-weary French populace. Louis had arrived at the Tuileries as a constitutional and not as an absolute monarch, although his insistence that he granted the Constitution (*"la Charte"*) rather than having it imposed upon him by the French people was an early indicator that his good intentions and innate liberality would be often and disastrously trumped by his insistence upon retrograde symbolism; the re-interment ceremonies of 21 January were just the latest and most extreme evidence of this flaw. For example, he asserted that he was actually in the *nineteenth* [283] and not the first year of his reign, as though the Revolution, the Directory, the Consulate, and the Empire had never existed. And that icon of the Republic, the tricolor, which had proudly flown in the vanguard of hundreds of French victories from Valmy to Wagram, was replaced by archaic white standards, lilies, and cockades.

But the reality of the new regime, in its early stages at least, was that the *Charte* did in fact provide for individual rights, for equality before the law including theoretical non-exemption of the aristocracy from taxation, and for a free press and religious freedom as well. There was a two-chamber legislature. Under the *Charte*, there was to be no vengeance, no re-appropriation of confiscated properties by the returning émigrés. Importantly too, the Allied occupiers had swiftly left French soil with their mission accomplished; they did not exact reparations, as they fervently wished to see the Bourbons succeed and the twin plagues of Jacobinism and Bonapartism to disappear, completely and forever.

Positioned atop the new order was the rotund, waddling, benevolent figure of the King himself, returned from his peripatetic exile in five different countries. A French populace initially eager for peace and a return of prosperity affectionately referred to him as *"Louis le Désiré"* ("the Desired One"). At age 59, Louis XVIII was a curious amalgam of common sense and generous instincts, of self-preserving pacifism and limited ambition, of a strong sense of selfish entitlement and chronic lassitude. His prodigious appetite led wags to refer to *Sa Sereine Majesté Louis Dix-Huit* as *"Louis Dix Huîtres"* ("Louis Ten Oysters"), with that number actually underestimating his per-sitting shellfish capacity by at least ninety percent.[284] A telling anecdote illustrating Louis' imperturbable outlook, which could alternately work for him and against him, concerns an instance when Marshal Marmont tried to warn him away from attending the theatre because of a rumored imminent assassination plot. Louis' reported response was: "My dear Marshal, your business is to protect me, mine is to go amuse myself at the *comédie*."[285] He was enamored of the appearance of authority more than its actual exercise. For example, it was very important that the *Charte* be granted by him to the people of France rather than have it imposed upon him by them; the liberality of its terms was not nearly as much of a concern for the King as it was for his much more conservative younger brother, the Comte d'Artois, and d'Artois' two sons, who collectively and serially constituted the immediate line of succession to the childless Louis.[286] At one point one of Louis' offended nephews asked him how he could possibly read the scurrilous popular press which flourished under the *Charte*; Louis pithily responded that it was entertaining and that it "tells me what you won't."[287]

The very closeness of Marshal Marmont to His Majesty was also indicative. Marmont had been part of Napoleon's marshalate; like almost all of them, he had been welcomed by Louis into the service of the restored Bourbon throne. Early on, Chateaubriand had noted how "MacDonald, Ney, Moncey, Sérurier, Brune, the Prince of Neuchâtel [Berthier], all the generals . . . received the most affectionate words from the King" on his return to France in 1814.[288] And not only were Napoleon's former top commanders the beneficiaries of Louis' largesse: twelve of the King's sixteen ministers had played important government roles during the interregnum from Revolution to Empire, and heading up the list was Louis' foreign minister, France's ambassador to the Congress of Vienna and influential counselor, Prince Charles-Maurice de Talleyrand, who had acted as the catalyst for Louis' return to the throne in 1814. The presence of some ex-revolutionaries and Bonapartists at the Tuileries Palace was quite tolerable and even pleasing to Louis; he drew the line sharply, however, at reconciling with regicides, let alone hiring them. Joseph Fouché and those like-voting delegates in the Convention of 1792 who had survived were distinctly unwelcome within the broad, bright circle of amnesty and forgiveness drawn by the King. The Prime Minister of England at the time, Lord Liverpool, would later ruefully note that "It was unfortunate that the King did not employ Fouché; but considering him as a regicide, it is impossible not to enter into Louis XVIII's feeling with regard to him."[289]

But there was one critical constituency who did not see Louis as the "desired one," or the return of the Bourbons as benign: the proud but humiliated veterans of the French army. Resentful of the loss of hard-won conquests, of apparent slights to the coveted Order of the Legion of Honor, of obese Louis' reliance on Allied bayonets to reclaim the throne, of reductions in pay and pensions while the King assiduously built himself a new *Maison Militaire* bodyguard comprised of soft and callow aristocrats and well-compensated Swiss mercenaries, many of the officers and men of the erstwhile *Grande Armée* bridled and chafed at the new order. Again, it is Chateaubriand who recorded the cracks which began to appear in the façade of the First Restoration: he witnessed Louis, en route to attend Mass in Paris, pass a regiment of "the old foot guards" (presumably beforehand a unit of Napoleon's elite Imperial Guard) arrayed along the Pont Neuf to Nôtre Dame, and he recounts that "I do not believe that human faces ever wore so threatening and so terrible an expression . . . Some, moving the skin of their foreheads, brought down their great bear-skin busbies over their eyes, as though to keep them from seeing; others lowered the corners of their mouth [sic] in angry scorn; others again showed their teeth through their mustachios, like tigers."[290] This was not an isolated event or an atypical unit. Throughout ostensibly Bourbon France, army garrisons celebrated the birthday of Napoleon on August 15, 1814 with cannonades and cries of *"Vive l'Empereur,"* they mocked Louis as the "*gros cochon*" and showed open contempt for members of his royal family when they made periodic awkward inspection tours, and they hid tricolor cockades in their knapsacks, waiting expectantly for the day when *"il reviendra,"* the day when their own "desired one" would return from his exile in Elba.

It was precisely that possibility, the return of Napoleon Bonaparte, that gravely concerned Joseph Fouché, as he endured his own sort of self-imposed exile on his estate of Chateau de Ferrières, an exile punctuated by occasional fact-gathering forays to his residence on the Rue Cerruti in nearby Paris. Fouché could afford to be patient. He sensed that the relief and acclaim that had greeted Louis and his royal kin in May 1814 would dissipate and that the Restoration which had spurned his offers of services would rapidly wear out its welcome. Not only was the army a serious problem for the Bourbon dynasty, but so was that huge proportion of the population who valued their cherished individual rights and liberties and therefore justifiably feared that the unhealthy Louis' ultra-conservative and vengeful successors would tear up the *Charte* at the first opportunity. Even the returned émigrés were becoming restive because their moderate ruler was not acting to restore their confiscated properties (although the Comte d'Artois and his sons strongly advocated that he do so). And, importantly, there were some signals from delegates to the Congress of Vienna that the former Allies themselves were losing confidence in Louis' ability to stay in control. In short, the situation was becoming ripe with the types of possibilities and opportunities which Fouché could exploit to maneuver himself back from the moribund periphery and onto center stage for the first time since 1810. Only an impulsive return to the mainland by the Corsican exile from his tiny island kingdom in the Mediterranean could seriously disrupt the various plots that were forming in the fertile mind of the Duke of Otranto.

Those signals from the Congress at Vienna included communications between Fouché and his longtime rival and sometimes ally of convenience Foreign Minister Talleyrand, France's delegate to the Congress, who could also deduce that the Bourbon base was being rapidly eroded. They included intelligence regarding serious disenchantment with the Bourbons on the part of Czar Alexander, who considered them unfit to rule ("the burden of a crown is not for such men").[291] Most tellingly, they appear to have included a direct inquiry sent to Fouché by Prince Metternich, with whom, as we have seen, Fouché very likely conspired in early 1814 to bring about the collapse of Napoleon's southern flank. According to Savary (and in this case there *is* separate substantiation for his account), Fouché claimed to him that he had in late 1814 received a letter from Metternich which he said posed three questions about the delicate political situation in France and which asked for him to assess possible alternative scenarios. The trio of inquiries from the Habsburg Empire's leading diplomat was as follows:

> In the case the Emperor should re-appear in France, what might be the result of such an event? Should the King of Rome [Napoleon's three-year-old son by Marie-Louise, who was then under the protection and close watch of his grandfather, Austria's Emperor Francis I] be brought to the frontier, and supported by a corps of Austrian troops, what might this lead to? . . .[I]f neither occurrence should take place, and if the movement springing from the population should assume a national character, what direction would it take?[292]

Again according to Savary, Fouché asserted that he responded as follows to the first query, "If the Emperor re-appeared on the frontier, all would depend upon the conduct of the first regiment sent against him: should it go over to his side, the whole army would follow its example." To the second question, which may have been something of a red herring, his reply was "If the King of Rome presented himself at the frontier . . . all parties would instantly join him." And finally, as to what would happen in the absence of the first two scenarios, Fouché predicted that if "the revolutionary movement proceeded from the interior [i.e., spontaneously], it would be effected on behalf of the Duke of Orléans."[293]

Taking the second scenario first, the Habsburg Emperor Francis was not about to permit his grandson, the child styled by Napoleon as "the King of Rome," to be taken across the Swiss border and placed on the throne of France, certainly not while his Corsican father was alive and potentially a candidate to escape or even be recalled from exile. Furthermore, the child's mother was not the least bit inclined to return with her son and rule as regent. The pliable Marie-Louise was far happier playing her role as the duchess of picturesque Parma, and luxuriating in the arms of the protector and escort assigned to her by Metternich, the dashing, one-eyed Count von Neipperg, with whom she would have several children, later legitimized after Napoleon died in 1821.

The last-posited scenario, concerning potential adherence to the Duke of Orléans, stemmed from the highly unusual background and appeal of the title-holder, Louis-Philippe, who would later in fact become France's last king after the 1830 "July Revolution." The Duke was a member of the so-called cadet (junior) branch of the Bourbon dynasty, which would assume the throne legitimately if the senior branch of the House of Bourbon were to die out (which in 1791 it had seemed in imminent danger of doing). At the onset of the Revolution, the very liberal-minded Louis-Philippe and his father had dropped their royal titles and, swimming with the tide, each respectively had taken the name "Philippe Égalité." The father was a delegate to the Convention and, at the conclusion of the trial of Louis XVI, he had shockingly voted "*pour la mort*" as the fate of his cousin hung in the balance; at the height of the Terror he replicated the trip made by his condemned cousin to the Place de la Révolution and then on to the Cemetery of the Madeleine. The regicide's son had joined the Jacobin Club and served valiantly as a very young lieutenant-general at the great victory of Valmy and in other pivotal military engagements of the French Revolutionary period, before seeking refuge in America in order to avoid sharing his father's fate. He subsequently reverted to his royal title. While this astonishing background understandably made the House of Orléans rather an anathema to their blood relatives in the senior branch of the Bourbon family, Louis-Philippe nevertheless remained very much a *prince du sang*, as well as a liberal-minded individual who had served bravely as a combat commander under the tricolor against France's foreign enemies; furthermore, while he had avoided any involvement in the Terror, his father's regicidal brand obviously made the House of Orléans quite reassuring to Fouché. But one serious problem with the Duke of Orléans' supposed candidacy as a replacement constitutional monarch who could potentially win over the allegiance of the army was that at present he did not want to orchestrate or be the beneficiary of a coup d'état against Louis XVIII; it appears that he was approached very cautiously by Talleyrand at the instigation of Fouché in this regard, but rejected the overture.[294]

The other serious problem with the Duke of Orléans was that his growing popularity in many circles, both within France and abroad, threatened to precipitate the occurrence of the dreaded first scenario considered by Metternich and Fouché: the escape and return of Napoleon from the island of Elba. This had been an eventuality that had worried Fouché greatly, and he had tried to address it in a number of ways. He actually wrote Napoleon directly in 1814, with false sycophancy suggesting that he remove himself across the Atlantic:

> It will be said that the rock of Elba is the fulcrum on which you position the levers with which you seek again to raise the world . . . It would be more glorious and more consoling for you to live as a simple citizen; and today the safest and most convenient asylum for a man such as yourself is the United States of America.[295]

In addition, Fouché sent the Comte d'Artois unsolicited, worried notes about Bonaparte's proximity to the French mainland, he unsuccessfully urged the Bourbons' Minister of Police Antoine d'André to increase the surveillance of Elba and to strengthen naval patrols, and he accurately predicted to Louis' trusted advisor Blacas that unless royalist security was stepped up, "the spring will bring Napoleon again with the swallows and the violets."[296] This supremely sage advice went unheeded.

Seismic faults soon opened. As noted, much of the army had resented Louis XVIII and his entourage from the very beginning of the Restoration. The January 21 commemorative ceremonies apparently signaled an imminent return to absolutism and triggered deep distrust amongst the middle and lower classes. These hostile sentiments in turn began to fuel the perception that the Duke of Orléans was an attractive, viable alternative to the status quo. From his diminutive Mediterranean palace in Portoferraio, Napoleon, who was avidly reading the popular press, sensed that a serious rival had suddenly appeared in the wings; he would later comment to his secretary Baron Méneval that, "in returning from the Island of Elba, it was not Louis XVIII — for this prince could not have kept himself on the throne for another six months — whom he had dethroned, but the Duke of Orléans, that he was sorry for this, because this prince was the only Frenchman in his family."[297]

So it was that Napoleon Bonaparte, angered by the Bourbons' self-destructive failure to pay him the guaranteed stipend necessary to maintain him and his truncated household on Elba, despairing over the loss of his adulterous second wife and barely known young son, and justifiably fearful that teams of assassins would be dispatched by his enemies to his island kingdom, resolved to cross yet another Rubicon.[298] On February 28, 1815, evading the Royal Navy and accompanied by the minuscule force of just over a thousand elite troops which the Allies had permitted him to retain, the Emperor landed at Golfe-Juan on France's southern coast, not far from the spot where he had disembarked on his fateful return from Egypt sixteen years before.

Up to this point Fouché had been a marginalized Cassandra, but now he too would seize the opportunity and the moment.

⚜

The first regiment Napoleon encountered, the 7th Regiment of the Line at Grenoble under a Colonel La Bédoyère, tore off their white cockades and enthusiastically defected; as Fouché had accurately predicted in his response to Prince Metternich's opening question, its action set off a domino effect within the French army. All eyes were on the unfolding drama as the Emperor rapidly gathered strength and moved north towards Lyon, towards a showdown with "the Bravest of the Brave," Marshal Michel Ney, who had famously sworn to his new master Louis XVIII that he would bring Bonaparte back to Paris in an iron cage. But at the same time, unnoticed by many, something quite shadowy and peculiar was going on to the north of Paris.

Ever since the events surrounding the re-interment ceremonies of January 21, Fouché had been actively lining up participants in a possible coup d'état, one which could topple the Bourbons and pre-empt Napoleon's return. At the center was a trio of active generals whom Fouché had suborned: Lallemand; Lefebvre-Desnöettes; and Drouet, Comte d'Erlon. According to his scheme, the last-named, on a pre-arranged signal, was to lead the troops of the Lille garrison southward towards Paris, gathering forces on the way. There, they would be joined by the National Guard, over whose commanders' loyalties Fouché had retained considerable influence ever since the defense of Antwerp. The plan was that they would surround the Tuileries, with assistance from the citizens of the *faubourgs*. Louis would be forced to flee, and the Duke of Orléans, who had requested his own command with which to oppose Napoleon but been denied it by his untrusting relatives, could then be called upon to take the throne.[299]

On March 6, just as the word of Napoleon's landing and initial progress was reaching Paris, Fouché, without any formal political authority whatsoever, activated the plot which came to be known as the "Conspiracy of the North." At his go-ahead signal, General Lallemand instructed Generals d'Erlon and Lefebvre-Desnöettes to lead the sixteenth military division out of its barracks and on the road to Compiègne outside Paris. As was the case with Wehrmacht units in "Operation Valkyrie," the failed coup that aimed to take control of the Third Reich in July 1944 in connection with the attempted assassination of Hitler, it is not entirely clear just how knowledgeable the French troops or even their commanders were of their ultimate objectives. However, former prefect of police Pasquier subsequently asked one of the participants in the plot, Count Lavalette, if the aim was not simply to rally the troops to Napoleon's side:

> Pasquier: "Were not all these generals about to go and throw themselves into the arms of Napoleon?"
> Lavellette: "Not one bit of it, and it is even the news of his landing and his rapid success that thwarted and upset everything."
> Pasquier: "But what was your object?"
> Lavalette: "We intended going to Paris, where reliable friends were awaiting us; we should have carried off the king, together with all the members of his family near him at the time, and we should have once more politely transported them across the frontier."
> Pasquier: "And then?"
> Lavalette: "We should have given France a sovereign who would have held his crown from the nation, and not from the foreigner."
> Pasquier: "Where, then, would you have found this sovereign?"

> Lavalette: "Who can tell? Perhaps the Duc d'Orléans, if he had only showed proper understanding and reason. Such a sovereign would of necessity have had to be sincerely constitutional, and I do not think that he would have aroused any alarm in Europe which would certainly not have rushed to arms for the mere sake of Louis XVIII."[300]

As Lavalette observed, the rapidity of Napoleon's progress towards Paris and the unavailability of the Duke of Orléans doomed the Conspiracy of the North. The immediate contributing causes to its failure were the last-minute abandonment of the plot by Napoleon's former "Iron Marshal," Louis-Nicolas Davout (who would shortly become the returned Emperor's Minister of War), and the fact that royalist Marshal Mortier, sent by the alarmed Bourbons to confront the advancing column from Lille, was able to face down the insurrectionists and prevail upon their troops to return to their barracks.[301] But as will be seen, this strange and fleeting episode would nevertheless be adeptly used by Fouché to regain for himself the portfolio of the Ministry of Police.

Mortier had succeeded in reassuming control over the sixteenth division, but it was the lone example of success for the Bourbons in confronting the rapidly expanding existential danger to their rule. On March 18, Marshal Ney and his troops defected to Napoleon at Auxerre. A number of other marshals who had been welcomed in 1814 by King Louis into his defense establishment now followed the lead of the "Bravest of the Brave" or at least declared their neutrality.[302] Garrison after garrison across France tore down the *fleur-de-lys* and raised the tricolor. And Joseph Fouché finally began to receive serious overtures from the Bourbons, who were becoming ever more desperate.

Commencing on March 12, a stream of mendicant notables from the Tuileries approached the Duke of Otranto, asking for his help in rescuing royalist fortunes. The level of authority of these emissaries escalated over several days (they included counselor Blacas and Chancellor Dambray), until a meeting was hastily arranged for very late in the evening of March 15 in the home of the Princess de Vaudemont. The last supplicant to the regicide Fouché was none other than Louis' ultra-conservative brother, the haughty Comte d'Artois. On offer was the Ministry of Police, which Fouché, recognizing that the situation was irretrievable for the time being, declined. (Savary wryly commented that "It will readily be believed that he cautiously remained silent respecting the part he had taken in the movement of troops in Flanders.")[303] However, the Duke of Otranto did not burn his newly established bridge, either. He is said to have coolly advised d'Artois: *"Monsieur, sauvez le roi: je me charge de sauver la monarchie."*[304] ("Monsieur, save the King; I will take care of saving the monarchy.") If this was so, it confirms that Fouché's advance planning was already flexible enough for him to facilitate a Second Restoration of the Bourbons — if the price was right.

On March 16, the very next day after the private interview between the Duke of Otranto and Louis' brother, a detail of royalist police was dispatched to the Rue Cerutti to arrest Fouché. The reasons for this action are unclear. Perhaps the Comte d'Artois was angered by the refusal of the proffered portfolio, and believed that a non-co-opted Fouché was simply too dangerous. Perhaps word of Fouché's role in masterminding the Conspiracy of the North had coincidentally been leaked. Perhaps the arrest warrant was issued by some other authority acting independently of d'Artois; it may have emanated from the converted royalist Bourrienne, who was no friend of Fouché's, and it had allegedly been approved by Louis himself.[305] Or, in light of the bizarre attempt at arrest that followed, perhaps the whole thing was a set-up intended to position Fouché as a royalist mole within Napoleon's government, for that is at least the end result of what transpired.

On the policemen's arrival at his Rue Cerutti residence, Fouché delayed agent Foudras of the Paris prefect in the entryway with some complaints about the formalities of the arrest warrant. (Fouché would later put Foudras on his own payroll.)[306] Suddenly, Fouché bolted through a secret door and down a hallway, ran out into his garden, and scrambled up a ladder which he had left leaning against the wall. He thereupon dropped down into the adjacent garden, behind the mansion belonging to Napoleon's stepdaughter and Louis Bonaparte's estranged wife, Queen Hortense (whom Louis XVIII had benevolently recognized as the Duchess of Saint-Leu), and fled out into the street. From there the Duke of Otranto, apparently quite spry for someone almost 56, threw off his pursuers by hopping into a carriage, and made his way to the safe-house of a retired secretary-general of the Paris police (a former Oratorian), to await the imminent collapse of the Bourbons.[307]

⚜

On the same day as his attempted arrest of Fouché, Louis XVIII gave a magnificently defiant speech before the Chamber of Deputies, exclaiming "[C]ould I, at sixty years of age, better end my career than by dying in its [France's] defense?"[308] His emotional audience vociferously pledged to defend him. But three days later, in the dead of night, Louis and his entourage fled the Tuileries Palace and headed for the border, to take up residence in comfortable lodgings in Ghent and placidly await events. With his typical self-centeredness, Chateaubriand bitterly commented: "It was evident that a scamper was being contemplated: for fear of being detained, they did not even warn those who, like myself, would have been shot within an hour of Napoleon's entry into Paris."[309]

On the 20th of March, the Emperor returned to the hastily vacated palace, hoisted on the shoulders of his adoring troops. It had taken less than three weeks from his landing at the Golfe-Juan for the House of Bourbon to collapse totally and vanish from French soil. Shock on the part of the Allies turned to anger, they shelved their internecine arguments which had intensified at the Congress of Vienna, and they formed a Seventh Coalition against Napoleon. Armies which had been marching back home to Austria, Russia, and Prussia were turned around in their tracks; British forces re-boarded transports to cross the Channel. The Coalition solemnly declared Napoleon Bonaparte to be an outlaw who had "placed himself beyond the pale of civil and social relations and delivered himself to public judgment as the enemy and destroyer of world peace."[310] There was to be no such peace, no negotiations whatsoever, until Napoleon was permanently removed from power. But at the same time the Allies were at pains to emphasize that their war was with him and his devoted supporters, and not with France. What a wonderful opportunity all this presented for Fouché, who had now come out of hiding, and was about to receive from Napoleon the portfolio of the Ministry of Police for the third time!

The Emperor's grotesquely bad decision to resurrect and re-empower Fouché was taken without due heed to the Duke of Otranto's 1808-09 plotting with Talleyrand regarding Napoleon's successor, nor to his actions in flagrant excess of his authority regarding the defense of Antwerp in 1809, nor to his wholly unauthorized attempts to negotiate with Britain in 1810, nor to his prima facie counterproductive activities in Naples and Lyon in 1814 (granted that their true nature and extent may still not have been fully comprehended), nor even to his 1814 letter urging Napoleon to remove himself to the United States from Elba for the sake of France. How could such an acknowledged genius commit such a grotesque error?

First of all, Napoleon had concluded, just as his enemies were again about to do, that Fouché was indispensable. The policeman had something on everyone (including quite a lot on the Bonapartes), he knew how each and every political faction was constituted and operated, he could anticipate events and outcomes with uncanny accuracy, and it seemed better to have him on his advisory team rather than off it, as the Bourbons had just found out. Second, Napoleon repeated his error of believing that because Fouché was a regicide he would be a perpetual outcast from the Bourbon and Allied camps. In addition, the news of Fouché's "escape" from arrest had swept through Paris and Napoleon was quite amused by the Duke of Otranto's apparent cleverness and the embarrassment he had inflicted on the opposition; he certainly placed undue weight on Fouché's brief fugitive status, even if one assumes that the entire affair had not been a pretext or a sham from the start.[311] Finally, Fouché convincingly re-packaged the Conspiracy of the North as an abortive attempt to *assist* Napoleon's return, rather than to pre-empt it.[312] In his memoirs, Savary states that he could not help smiling at the "impudent falsehood" Fouché had conveyed that "he had labored in his [the Emperor's] cause by setting in motion the troops stationed in Flanders."[313] As a precaution, Napoleon placed Savary in charge of the imperial gendarmerie, since according to the Duke of Rovigo, "I had always proved his best safeguard" against Fouché,[314] but that gambit would not provide nearly enough insurance for the Emperor. Napoleon and his loyalist faction were about to be completely and fatally out-maneuvered by the Duke of Otranto.

Shortly after receiving his portfolio once again, Fouché was called upon by his old acquaintance, former police prefect Étienne-Denis Pasquier, who had served the Bourbons as commissioner of bridges and roadways and who did not subsequently rally to Napoleon. Pasquier was therefore in need of a police passport in order to be able to remain in Paris for a few days before he retreated to his estate at Le Mans, in the Auvergne. (In the coming weeks, Fouché would selectively and adeptly use his recovered police powers to bend the rules in order to ingratiate himself with his employer's enemies and his own potential allies.) Pasquier recounts that Fouché asked him to accompany him into his private garden so that they could talk freely, and that there the new Minister of Police accurately predicted that Napoleon's return would be very brief: "I declare to you that, in spite of his assertion to the contrary, the whole of Europe is going to fall on him; it is impossible for him to resist the onslaught, and within four months his fate will have been decided." Fouché then allegedly confided to Pasquier, "I ask for nothing better than the return of the Bourbons, only matters must be managed a little less clumsily than they were managed by Talleyrand; it will never do for everybody to be at their mercy. There must be conditions plainly laid down, and good and lasting pledges."[315] The individual who would be the true beneficiary of these requisite royalist pledges would soon become apparent, by the end of the four-month period clairvoyantly projected by Fouché.

CHAPTER XV

Supremo

In the early morning hours of March 21, Joseph Fouché returned to the Ministry of Police offices on the Quai Malaquais to commence exploiting the precious portfolio so foolishly entrusted to him yet again. He sat at his desk in the Hôtel de Juigne for the first time since 1810 and there, reunited with his familiar view of the Tuileries Palace across the Seine, he began implementing his master plan to permanently remove its occupant.

Two aspects of his plan were novel additions to his established repertoire. First of all, he promulgated a public policy of "enlightened policing." On April 4, after only two weeks back on the job, the Duke of Otranto published an admonition to his prefects under his name in the *Moniteur Universel* (which he had swiftly brought under his close control), advising that the police "must not be governed by any other rule than that of justice," and that they "should not restrict the free exercise of human and civil rights. . . ." He continued: "It is necessary to abandon the attributes of the *police d'attaque*, which ceaselessly agitated by suspicion, ceaselessly restless and turbulent, menaces without guaranteeing and torments without protecting. It [i.e., the Ministry of Police] must contain itself within the limits of a liberal and a positive police."[316] Chateaubriand sardonically observed: "The police, directed by Fouché, informed the world, by means of solemn proclamations, that it would henceforward serve only to spread philosophy, that it would act only in accordance with virtuous principles."[317] While the new and improved image of a kinder, more sensitive Ministry of Police appeared to dovetail nicely with the returned Emperor's pressing need to reposition himself as a liberal constitutional monarch, especially given the legacy of real reforms which the Bourbons had however reluctantly implemented, it also signaled a break with Fouché's predecessor, General Savary, and his heavy-handed, unsubtle approach to internal security. More important, this progressive-sounding ethos gave Fouché the necessary cover to confer protection and favors upon royalists and other anti-Bonapartists who were suddenly in serious jeopardy due to the political upheaval. Safe-conduct passes could be issued; warnings could be whispered; orders for arrest could be lost or ignored; unavoidable incarcerations could be ameliorated; above all, new dependencies could be created. False threats or predicaments could even be conjured up by Fouché and then obligingly neutralized or "solved" to the victims' lasting gratitude.

The second of Fouché's novel police approaches was election rigging. Napoleon, in keeping with his newly assumed liberal façade and pursuant to a proposed replacement Constitution known as the *Acte additionnel* (which awaited a June plebiscite on ratification), had grudgingly permitted French propertied voters to select a new Chamber of Representatives that would replace the members of the lower house who had been elected in 1814 under the Bourbons' *Charte*. (The upper house, the hereditary Chamber of Peers, was also reconstituted.) But Napoleon's heart was never in dealing with the vicissitudes of popular legislatures, and his attention was almost wholly fixed upon swiftly getting the nation back onto a war footing. This left Fouché, who had been provided with more than ample funding for his ministry, with carte blanche to buy candidates and votes and to pack the Chamber of Representatives with his protégés and other individuals beholden to him; he similarly spread his influence within the Chamber of Peers and diligently maneuvered himself into a position to be able to bend the legislature to his will should the Emperor's fortunes take the predicted turn for the worse.

Other aspects of the Minister of Police's preparations to unseat the Emperor at the time and place of his choosing were vintage Fouché: he took control of the media, he re-enlisted legions of his veteran agents and informers and attracted new ones, and his special couriers generally came and went as they pleased, including crossing France's borders to transmit messages to and from the Allies' camps.

However, one near-fatal exception to this unimpeded flow of police couriers occurred when an aide reporting directly to Napoleon happened to intercept a clandestine message from Prince Metternich to the Duke of Otranto. Metternich's probe (or provocation) hinted at a renewed Austrian interest in the possibility of a regency for the King of Rome, and Fouché had not disclosed it to the Emperor. Anger welled up in Napoleon; he had of course not forgotten Fouché's unauthorized communications with Britain that had led to his abrupt dismissal and flight in 1810. This chance discovery probably constituted Napoleon's last and best opportunity to arrest and summarily execute or at least imprison his Minister of Police. Yet, amazingly, Fouché managed to sidestep the consequences of his intrigues once again. Napoleon was fatally reluctant to remove such an important and high-profile member of his administration only weeks after he had appointed him and while Allied armies were massing on the borders; he may well have also rationalized the episode by convincing himself that it was a necessary part of espionage for his spy chief to be involved in duplicitous contacts with the enemy.[318] He seems either not to have fully comprehended that it was *he* who was Fouché's despised enemy, or to have been somehow mesmerized into holding back the decree which would have branded his Minister of Police as an exposed traitor. Napoleon's fate was thus sealed.

⚜

On May 2, Étienne Pasquier once again sought out Fouché at the Quai Malaquais. This time he was seeking an extension of Fouché's previously granted special permission to reside in Paris temporarily. According to Pasquier's account of this second interview, Fouché said to him: "Remain in the city as long as you like. What is there to cause you any alarm nowadays? Who is going to object? Have you not read his [Napoleon's] *Acte additionnel*, which guarantees individual liberty, and which protects persons from arbitrary exile? As you can well see, we have already drawn our nets about him much more than he expected." Pasquier was not at all convinced that he should adopt this complacent attitude, and he insisted that he only required a two-week prolongation of his permit before he finally left for his country home in the Auvergne. He records that Fouché, who was almost certainly attempting to recruit Pasquier as an accomplice in his machinations, confidently rejoined that the short time limitation was needless, as Napoleon would be absent from Paris and at the head of his army by the end of the month. The Minister of Police then continued: "As soon as he has gone, we remain masters of the field. Even admitting that he wins one or two battles, he will lose the third, and then will be the time for us to enter upon the stage. Believe me, all will have a happy termination."[319]

If this exchange was accurately reported by Pasquier, the Duke of Otranto's clairvoyance was indeed startling and impressive. For, in June 1815 Napoleon for the last time commanded the French army, leading it north, where he intended to burst across the border into what was then the Kingdom of the Netherlands (which included Belgium). There he aimed to defeat *seriatim* the Prussians under Field Marshal Blücher and then the Duke of Wellington's polyglot and improvised force of British, Dutch, Belgians, Nassavians, Brunswickers, and Hanoverians, perhaps driving it right to the Channel. The Emperor's immediate objective after achieving victory over these opponents was to occupy Brussels, and thereupon to determine whether the Russians and the perhaps wavering Austrians would consequently be inclined to halt their armies' respective marches towards the boundaries of France.

⚜

In the early morning hours of June 14, with the French army poised to launch itself across the frontier and achieve total surprise over its adversaries, Lieutenant-General Louis-Auguste-Victor de Bourmont and a group of five or six of his staff officers, reporting to General Gérard, commander of IV Corps, rode out ostensibly to inspect the perimeter of vedettes. Reaching their picket line, Bourmont and his officers trotted ahead as though reconnoitering the terrain immediately beyond the forward observers. Suddenly, they all at once spurred their mounts to the gallop, pulling white cockades from inside their tunics and making a bee-line for the Prussian cantonment roughly six miles away, where they would announce their defection to their stunned former enemies, and warn them of the unsuspected looming threat.[320]

While General Bourmont's betrayal of his command was perhaps not as pivotally decisive in the ultimate outcome of the campaign as Napoleon would subsequently make it out to be,[321] it did deprive Gérard's IV Corps of the advantages of surprise it would have otherwise almost certainly enjoyed. More importantly, it unleashed a debilitating, paranoid fear throughout the French rank-and-file, a pervasive suspicion that their own most senior leadership could not be relied upon to stay as true to the Emperor as they were, that the integrity of their orders might be suspect. In the words of one French colonel: "*partout ils voyaient des traitres*" ["everywhere they saw traitors"].[322]

Twenty years later, in 1835, the Comte de Falloux, a French monarchist politician who was a copious chronicler of his times, paid a visit to Bourmont (who had been made a Marshal of France by the Bourbons for his actions of June 14, but was subsequently exiled after the rise of the Orleanists) at his residence near Geneva. They went on hikes together in the mountains. On one such Alpine excursion, Bourmont on his own initiative raised with his companion the topic of his conduct before Waterloo, conduct that had earned Bourmont widespread and lasting opprobrium not for just abandoning his comrades in the face of the enemy, but for selling them out as well. Here is Bourmont's explaination to de Falloux as to why he was serving as a general officer in Napoleon's army in the first place, instead of leaving France with the Bourbons in March of 1815 or exercising his option of remaining on the sidelines:

> "I never for one instant," he said, "thought of re-entering the service for the 'Hundred Days.' I had proved this by ostensibly voting in the negative on the additional articles. But through accident I met Fouché, the Minister of Police, and he took the initiative in an interview which decided me. "The Emperor is mad," he said, "and we cannot allow him to plunge France once more into the abyss. The army yielded to its first excitement, but it now understands that

> patriotism should be stronger than an ill-timed enthusiasm. The Marshals themselves daily repeat this language to me, and they will find a way of ending this terrible adventure before Europe has rendered it irreparable." Fouché confirmed his statement with names and facts which convinced M. de Bourmont that by resuming his post as Lieutenant-General he would contribute to a peaceful and rapid settlement.[323]

Without questioning the fundamental veracity of Bourmont's account, one can speculate whether his encounter with Fouché was truly accidental, or whether the Minister of Police had orchestrated the seemingly chance encounter so as to enlist his services as a debilitating and demoralizing mole.

⚜

Napoleon did indeed win the first battle of the campaign, just as Fouché had predicted to Pasquier, defeating but not destroying (in part due to Bourmont's treason) the Prussians at Ligny on June 16. The second engagement simultaneously took place between Marshal Ney and Wellington at Quatre Bras, and it resulted in a draw. Then, two days later, also as forecast, Napoleon did indeed lose the third battle, spectacularly, as his superb but unsupported cavalry formations rode uphill to their deaths against stubborn Allied squares on the slopes of Mont St. Jean, as Blücher's reinvigorated Prussian force avoided pursuit by the befuddled Marshal Grouchy and slammed into Napoleon's right flank at Plancenoit, and as the vaunted Old Guard recoiled from the blazing fire of Maitland's Brigade and faded into legend. The proud French army was transformed by the cataclysm into a mass of fugitives, streaming southwards towards the border and away from the forlorn fields of Waterloo.

Napoleon raced back to Paris ahead of his shattered regiments, abandoning his imperial carriage to a squadron of Prussian uhlans and outrunning Marshal Blücher's vengeful pursuit. In so doing, he abandoned his army in order to reassure and stabilize his supporters in the capital, as he had done when he left Egypt in 1799 and as he had again in 1812, after the debacle in Russia. The Emperor failed to remain with and attempt to rally his routed but not obliterated forces, and this failure was symptomatic of his increasing lapses in judgment during the last few years of his decline and fall. Fouché awaited Napoleon's arrival in Paris, poised to exploit the gap that the Emperor had recklessly opened between himself and his only truly reliable power base, the officers and men of the regular army.

It has been claimed that Fouché was advised of the catastrophe suffered by French arms at Waterloo well before the politicians and people of Paris learned the awful news, and that would not be in the least surprising.[324] Whatever the case, by the time a weary and discouraged Emperor and his fugitive entourage had passed through the perimeter defenses of the great city and arrived at the Élysée Palace on the Rue St. Honoré approximately forty hours after the battle had ended, the Minister of Police had thoroughly assessed the situation and activated his plan for this anticipated contingency. Joseph Fouché was ready to seize control of France's destiny.

The problems confronting Fouché were interlocking, complex, and dangerous. With the triumphant Prussian and British forces now marching menacingly towards Paris, he simultaneously had to dispense with Napoleon; take control of the legislature and marginalize his potential rivals; keep restive royalists both in check and at the same time favorably disposed to himself; neutralize those bloodied but unbowed elements of what remained of the French army as well as Napoleon's veteran and highly able commander, Minister of War Marshal Davout; conduct his own secretive diplomacy with the Allies; and hand back Paris and the throne to his former enemy, the House of Bourbon, in exchange for the best terms he could possibly obtain for himself, all the while convincing everyone that he was the indispensable man, rather than the foremost candidate in the land for the firing squad. He would have to bring successfully to bear every shady skill and cunning trait he had accumulated over the long course of his manipulative career upon this host of obstacles confronting him. Here is how he managed it.

Fouché inexorably maneuvered Napoleon first into irrelevancy and subsequently into exile and imprisonment, as though he were a chess piece being forced off the board. The Emperor, not yet 46 years old, suddenly became passive and morose in his outlook and conduct in the wake of the Waterloo disaster, making this part of Fouché's agenda far easier to accomplish than it might otherwise have been. (One eyewitness describes Napoleon's facial expression as "sad and without hope" in response to being cheered on his return by a crowd of loyal Parisians — a crowd which was quickly dispersed by Fouché's police.)[325] At first, when he returned to the Élysée Palace on the morning of June 21, Napoleon was urged by his brother Lucien, who had played such a pivotal role in the coup of 18-19 Brumaire, and by Marshal Davout, to prorogue the Chambers and to take charge of the defense of Paris, where Bonaparte still retained considerable popularity among the middle and lower classes. Instead, influenced by his Minister of Police's intentionally misleading assessment that the legislature would likely respond favorably to a request for emergency powers, Napoleon approached the Chambers as a supplicant for support rather than as a confident, self-anointed dictator.[326] Fouché, via his election rigging and his ability to spread pervasive rumors on a moment's notice, had carefully prepared the battlefield. According to one of his agents, a former Oratorian named Gaillard: "To the old Jacobins and to the liberals, [Fouché] said that Napoleon in proclaiming himself dictator would dissolve the Chambers: 'Will you let him get away with it?'"[327] The result was that the Chambers preemptively conducted a coup d'état itself.

The agent of this role reversal was a ghost from the Revolution. Standing up against Napoleon in the Chamber of Deputies was the Marquis (and now Representative) de Lafayette, the darling of the United States. Lafayette's popularity was very much limited to America; on his home side of the Atlantic, he was despised by the Bourbons as a radical revolutionary who had betrayed his class, he had been excoriated as a traitor by the Jacobins because of his ineffective attempts as head of the National Guard in 1791-92 to restore order on Paris and preserve constitutional monarchy, and he had been incarcerated by the Prussians and Austrians until none other than General Napoleon Bonaparte had obtained his release pursuant to a specific clause in a 1797 peace treaty which his battlefield successes had enabled him to impose upon the Habsburgs. Napoleon's seizure of power in 1799 meant that Lafayette was eventually able to return to France. After keeping a very low profile for the fifteen years of Napoleonic supremacy, Lafayette, who remained a republican idealist, now intended to use his elected position to denounce his former liberator. In so doing, he was cynically encouraged by Fouché.

A member of the Chamber of Peers and a fellow regicide, Antoine Thibaudeau, states in his *Mémoires* that he happened to encounter the minister and the marquis engaged in deep conversation on the morning of June 21 at the Quai Malaquais. Fouché introduced Lafayette to Thibaudeau, who asserts that he initially failed to recognize the formerly *"svelte et élégant marquis"*; Lafayette had by then become rather stout and was dressed as a gentleman farmer rather than in the uniform of the dashing young general he had been twenty-three years earlier. Thibaudeau records that the following exchange took place:

> *"Eh bien*, general," Fouché said to him, "it is understood. There is not a moment to lose." "Yes, yes" responded Lafayette, "rest easy. I am heading for the Chamber." Then, turning to Thibaudeau, Fouché reportedly said of the Bonapartists: "[T]hey will be exposed to us as being divided and decimated like sheep."[328]

The ostensible prompt for Lafayette to take action against Napoleon was a speech delivered by Lucien Bonaparte to the Chamber of Representatives, in session at the Palais Bourbon, on the evening of the very same day, June 21; in representing his older brother, Lucien appeared to be attempting to re-enact his role of 19 Brumaire in the Palais Saint-Cloud. Lucien argued that this was the moment for the French people to stand by their sovereign, and unwisely observed that if they did not subjugate themselves to authority as did the subservient populaces of Russia and Germany, they would then be subdued by those countries. Lafayette thereupon heatedly declared this argument to be "a slanderous assertion," and he turned the tide against Lucien and his sibling by demanding of him what right he had to accuse the French nation "of lacking perseverance with respect to the Emperor Napoleon."

Then Lafayette added the devastating indictment that France had trustingly followed Bonaparte "in the sands of Egypt and in the wastelands of Russia, on five hundred battlefields, in defeats as well as in successes, and it is on account of having followed him that we mourn the blood of three million Frenchmen."[329] He called for the Chambers to remain in permanent session. Any attempt to suspend or dissolve the legislature would constitute an act of high treason. Lafayette's motion carried, bolstered by the arguments of Fouché's agents and allies. Napoleon could no longer persuade, and he no longer possessed the will to send the constitutionally elected representatives scrambling out the windows at bayonet point as he had done with the help of his brother Lucien and his future brother-in-law Joachim Murat sixteen years beforehand at the Palace of Saint-Cloud.

Furthermore, sixteen years earlier, Bonaparte had not been confronted by a hostile Minister of Police. This time he was.

On the next day, June 22, Napoleon responded to the Chambers' startling defiance with an offer to abdicate in favor of his son. Less than two days after returning to the Élysée, he had allowed his crown to tumble to the ground. The Chambers accepted Napoleon's resignation, and its apparent contingency upon his proposed succession by the absent and puerile King of Rome was promptly and completely ignored. In the bitter words of the Emperor's private secretary, Baron Méneval, "never was the nation represented by a political assembly more ignorant of its true interests, more below its mission, in [the] presence of circumstances of such extraordinary gravity."[330]

On June 24, the Chambers, anxious not to exercise the authority it had suddenly assumed, elected a five-man provisional government to conduct war against the Allies to the extent necessary and to negotiate with them to the extent possible, now that Napoleon himself was out of the picture and the Allies' proclaimed *casus belli* consequently no longer existed. The president of this new provisional government was none other than the calculating Duke of Otranto, whose agents, allies, and hirelings in the legislature — "a thousand hidden springs" in the words of one observer[331] — had served him exceptionally well in his bid to attain ultimate political power. The wheel of the careening ship of state had unexpectedly now passed into the death-grip of the Minister of Police.

But before we turn to how the waging of war and the concomitant search for peace were in fact conducted by acting president Joseph Fouché, it is instructive to recount the way in which he drove Bonaparte from France and ultimately to that remote rock in the middle of the Atlantic, the British-held island of Saint Helena. First, as both president and minister, and with the backing of the Chambers which, Nero-like, distracted itself from the looming crisis by immersing itself in arid theoretical debates about constitutional reform, Fouché prevailed upon Napoleon to leave Paris, where the populace and the National Guard might yet rally to him; he succeeded in getting him to decamp on June 25 to the deceased Empress Josephine's beloved chateau of Malmaison, seven miles outside the city. President Fouché accomplished this exorcism by convincing Napoleon that he was in mortal danger at the Élysée, using the ploy of mounting guards around the residence in response to the supposed emergency of manufactured death threats.[332]

Once Napoleon had arrived at Malmaison, Fouché detailed an anti-Bonapartist general by the name of Nicolas Becker, who was "personally obnoxious to the Emperor,"[333] along with a picked contingent of several hundred gendarmes to keep Bonaparte under close surveillance, for his own purported protection. Then, since for Fouché's liking Napoleon was still uncomfortably close at hand to the capital, and since the ex-ruler had, too late, commenced plaintively making renewed offers to the provisional government and to the Chambers that he was ready to take command of French forces as a field officer rather than as head of state, Fouché ruthlessly removed him much further. The Duke of Otranto accomplished this by applying pressure through Marshal Davout (who in the wake of Waterloo seemed to have abruptly lost his former confidence in and loyalty to the Emperor) and with the promise of passports to the United States, passports purportedly to be somehow obtained by Fouché's provisional government from the British. This beguiling lure brought a credulous Napoleon, under close "protective" escort by General Becker, out of Malmaison and enticed him inexorably in the direction of the port of Rochefort on the Atlantic coast. Fouché gave the following order to the surprisingly pliable Davout on June 27:

> Circumstances are such that it is absolutely necessary that Napoleon decide to leave for the Island of Aix [adjacent to Rochefort] . . . [Y]ou must put Malmaison under surveillance, in a manner that he cannot escape it. . . . These measures are to remain secret to the degree possible. General Becker, who will be charged with handing over Napoleon for arrest, will receive specific instructions from Your Excellency, and he will make him understand that he is being held in the interest of the State and for the safety of his person.[334]

And of course, the request for passports, directly made by Fouché's provisional government to the Duke of Wellington, served to alert the grateful British to Napoleon's escape plan and to his intended place of embarkation.[335]

On the Atlantic coast, Napoleon's will and fortune failed him yet again, and instead of moving with alacrity, instead of heeding the advice of the loyalists in his entourage and attempting to run the Royal Navy's blockade, as he had successfully done just months earlier, he allowed himself to be hemmed in. He surrendered to the captain of H.M.S. *Bellerophon* on July 15. The day before, Bastille Day, he had written the Prince Regent of England, despondently begging for "a seat by the hearth of the British people," and attributing his demise to "the factions which divide my country."[336] However, his hearth for his remaining six years would be located in the grim and vaporific estate of Longwood on the extinct volcanic island of St. Helena, and the "factions" directly responsible for his final downfall essentially consisted of just one man, his own Minister of Police.

Fouché had finally and completely triumphed over his master, and he had managed to do it without having to hand him over directly to the Allies by obvious force. Rather, he had skillfully herded and driven Napoleon into the arms of his ancient enemy, like a sheep to slaughter indeed. In so doing, Fouché kept a promise he had secretly transmitted to Wellington via a British agent on June 28. The English go-between had reported: "Every possible concession that a free nation will make can be granted; and the Duke d'Otrante, in the name of the French government, pledges himself to deliver up Buonaparte in any way that may be most suitable to the views of the British government."[337]

While executing his plan to eliminate the Emperor, Fouché also moved quickly to marginalize the Marquis de Lafayette, before that liberal idealist's rhetoric could revive his popularity and transform him into a significant counterforce. His method was convenient and beautifully simple: President Fouché's provisional government named Lafayette to a peace commission to seek armistice terms. The commissioners, whose number included other potential troublemakers, were sent under a white flag well away from Paris and first presented themselves to the Prussian and British headquarters, where they were sequentially rebuffed out of hand. They then journeyed further away from the capital and from their own countrymen, desperately seeking audiences with the Allied sovereigns who had based themselves on the east bank of the Rhine. These conservative rulers deeply detested Lafayette, and they remained convinced that he had richly merited his years in their dungeons. Of course, Fouché was well aware of their opinions and of the remoteness of the chance that the provisional government's amateurish peace delegation would be able achieve any diplomatic breakthroughs. In the words of Pasquier, the Duke of Otranto

> . . . was too well acquainted with the frame of mind of the foreign cabinets not to be convinced that M. de Lafayette was the last person to have any influence with them. His mere presence among the delegates, even supposing the foreigner was favorably inclined towards entering into negotiations, was capable of spoiling everything . . . no member of this deputation was in a position to hold his own in a discussion of questions of such magnitude. This was just what M. Fouché desired, as his intention was that nothing should be concluded except through himself. [338]

While the new government's official peace negotiators ineffectually meandered behind enemy lines, the victors of Waterloo were headed for the gates of Paris. Blücher's 60,000 Prussians, driven forward by their vengeful leader, were in the vanguard, and they burned and pillaged their way through France as they advanced southwards along the banks of the Oise River and toward the Seine. *"Marschall Vorwärts"* ("Marshal Forward") may not have been a brilliant strategist, but he certainly knew how to inspire and push his men. He fervently wanted Napoleon dead and his capital laid waste, to even the score for the Emperor's earlier subjugation of Prussia. Wellington's army of approximately 52,000, itself severely battered by the battles near Brussels, also made its way down the Oise, and it brought in its wake Louis XVIII and his retinue, who had finally found it safe and convenient to leave their comfortable refuge in Ghent.[339] But Wellington's columns did not move with anything like the alacrity of those of Blücher's, and a march-gap of two days soon opened up between the two Allied forces. They also found themselves moving down opposite banks of the Oise.

⚜

On June 26 a furious Marshal Ney, back from the blood-soaked road to Brussels, sent a message to Fouché in his new capacity as head of the provisional government. Ney had learned to his ire that Napoleon had made him the scapegoat for the stalemate at Quatre Bras and for the defeat at Waterloo, where the fiery marshal had had multiple mounts shot out from under him, and where by the onset of evening he was dazedly seeking death, bare-headed and brandishing his broken sword. In 1812, Ney had fought valiantly shoulder-to-shoulder as part of the rearguard, retreating meter-by-meter back from Moscow across the frozen steppes, and he reputedly fired the last shot of that campaign while the Emperor was hurrying back to Paris; now, history had repeated itself, a repetition too many. In his complaint to Fouché, Ney angrily denounced the rumors "regarding my conduct during this short and unhappy campaign; the papers repeat and seem to give credit to the most odious calumnies. After having fought for twenty-five years, and spilled my blood for the glory and independence of my country, it is me who stands accused of treason, it is me that the people and even the army are informed is the author of the disaster."[340] On June 29, Ney was given permission to address the Chambers. Ruing his decision to back Napoleon rather than to adhere to the Bourbons, he warned that the enemy would be at the capital in less than a week, that there was no possibility of further resistance, and that the only solution left was to recall King Louis. This assessment by the "Bravest of the Brave" of the hopelessness of the military situation delivered to the gullible and fearful legislators dovetailed nicely with Fouché's strategy of systematically degrading all sources of power that might rival his own.

But the problem was that Ney's report was not true. The French army in fact lived.

⚜

After Waterloo, the remnants of the last army commanded by Napoleon had begun to regroup at Laon, east of the Oise River, assembling there under Marshal Soult. This amalgam of broken French formations in and of itself would have been no match for the Allies, and its mere existence certainly did not disprove Ney's bleak assessment to the Chambers. But soon it was joined by a wholly intact and considerable force which doubled its numbers to over 50,000: Marshal Grouchy's command, given up for lost, had extracted itself from the grasping clutches of the merciless Prussians by conducting one of the more impressive fighting retreats in military history. As the reconstituted and recombined *Armée du Nord* fell back on Paris, where it would come under the authority of the eminently capable "Iron Marshal," the Prince of Eckmühl Louis-Nicolas Davout, it doubled in size yet again, being supplemented by reserves, by garrison troops brought into the capital, and by units of the highly motivated National Guard. Despite the disaster in which he had played no part, Marshal Davout now had well over 100,000 men under arms and under his command, many of them excellent veteran troops and all burning with hatred for the Prussians and with a deep desire to even the score for the disaster at Waterloo. His rapidly rebuilt force was of equal strength to that of the Allies, it enjoyed interior defensive lines and access to ample supplies on its home ground, and it threatened to defeat the strung-out Prussian and British armies sequentially.[341] On July 2, Wellington would consequently send Blücher this alarming note: "It appears to me that, with the force you and I have under our command at present, the attack of Paris is a matter of great risk. I am convinced it cannot be made on this side with any hope of success."[342]

However, the suddenly resurrected French force put into jeopardy not just the Allies' military fortunes, but also President Fouché's plans to surrender Paris to the Bourbons for the right set of *quid pro quos*. So, he methodically proceeded to remove the entire French army from the chessboard as well.

⚜

Post-Waterloo, there was undoubtedly no one in the French military command by whom the Allied leaders would less rather be confronted than Marshal Davout. The bald and bespectacled Iron Marshal possessed outstanding organizational skills – as Minister of War, he had already assembled the formidable French army which had gone on the offensive in just three months after Napoleon's return from Elba. He was brilliant on the battlefield: for instance, at Auerstadt in 1806, he had defeated two-thirds of the Prussian army with one-third of that of the French, while at the same time Napoleon fought the twin battle at nearby Jena enjoying a reciprocal two-thirds versus one-third advantage and subsequently took expansive and unjustified credit for the success of the entire campaign. Under Davout's famously strict discipline, his vaunted Third Corps had been one of the most feared fighting formations of its day, often compared to the Roman Empire's fabled Tenth Legion.[343] And Davout was undeniably tenacious; he had led the grinding defense of isolated Hamburg in 1813-14, only yielding up the besieged city to the Russians and Bernadotte's Swedes when he was expressly and emphatically ordered to do so by King Louis following Napoleon's first abdication.

But by June of 1815, Davout's outlook and fighting spirit seemed to have changed. Twenty-three years of grueling warfare weighed even more heavily on him after the army he had created was beaten at Waterloo (where he was not present, another profound error on the Emperor's part). As we have seen, his advice to Napoleon that he should seize dictatorial powers on his return to Paris had been rejected, and thereafter Davout willingly aided and abetted Fouché in removing the diminished Emperor from the picture. As soon as he had finished exploiting Davout's utility in this regard, Fouché came up with a masterstroke in order to neutralize Davout as a potential disrupter of his plans: as head of the provisional government charged with protecting the safety of the capital, the Duke of Otranto demanded that Marshal Davout and his senior officers guarantee in writing their ability to defend Paris successfully.

On July 1, President Fouché required answers to the following interrogatories from Davout and his lieutenants: (1) "Are you able to defend all of the approaches to Paris, those on the left bank of the Seine as well as those on the right?" (2) "Are you able to fight at all points at the same time without compromising the fate of a million persons?" (3) "In a word, for how much longer can you answer for the fate of the capital?"[344] These were obviously loaded questions. What level-headed and sober commander can possibly give absolute guarantees to his political overlords of complete future success against a considerable foe, given the vagaries of combat? After conferring with his fellow marshals and generals, Davout honestly but not very cannily responded on July 2 that all of the defenses encircling Paris were not completed, and that guarding every point simultaneously was simply not feasible. (Whether he would have been *required* by his enemies to do so is an entirely different matter, given Blücher's impetuousness, Wellington's caution, and the geographical distance and natural obstacles separating the two Allied forces.) In conclusion, Davout concisely allowed that "No such guarantee can be given."[345]

Thus hemmed in by the interrogatories, Davout was also to some extent seriously compromised by a meeting (orchestrated by Fouché) in full view of his own staff which the Marshal had held with a well-known royalist agent, the Comte de Vitrolles (conveniently sprung from prison by the Minister of Police). The Iron Marshal wearily conceded that he had "overcome my prejudices," that Louis XVIII should be invited back as the nation's only hope, and that he would indeed be obliged to seek a military armistice from the Allies, an armistice which would remove the *Armée du*

Nord well to the south to positions on the Loire River, and a considerable distance away from the perimeter of Paris.[346] Fouché as president gladly authorized this action. He wrote to Davout: "I am persuaded, as you are, *Monsieur le Maréchal*, that there is no better course for us than to treat for an armistice," and stated that Davout should make "all sacrifices compatible with our duties and our dignity." [347] But he also assured Davout that before the Bourbons could hope to be restored, as Wellington was demanding, the provisional government would be sure to extract political guarantees of French freedoms in exchange for the return of Louis XVIII. He finally warned Davout to limit himself to negotiating a military withdrawal from the capital and to stay out of the realm of politics.

President Fouché of course meant to claim for himself all of the Bourbons' gratitude for the turnover of Paris and their Second Restoration. He would indeed extract guarantees, but they would inure to his own benefit alone. Marshal Davout, for his part, would reportedly later tell his friends that he would never forgive himself "for having been put to sleep by Fouché." [348]

⚜

That other man of iron, the Duke of Wellington, had already made it known to the Chambers via the provisional government's and Marshal Davout's emissaries that they had better accept the return of the King quickly and unconditionally to avoid the violent subjugation of Paris by Allied forces. As we have already noted, however, Wellington did not in fact believe that those forces were actually capable of enforcing his ultimatum against the legions of determined French defenders of the capital. But the British — Foreign Secretary Castlereagh as well as the Iron Duke — very much wanted to engineer a Second Restoration, as they had in their hip pocket the highly dependent Anglophile King Louis and his feeble entourage, who had found a welcoming asylum in England prior to his first accession to power in 1814. France under the House of Bourbon was slotted to become part of Great Britain's sphere of influence and control.

⚜

On June 28, an English agent stationed in Paris sent a note to Wellington through the defensive perimeter lines by means of a French cavalry courier, named Captain Maceroni, who had formerly served as the aide-de-camp to Joachim Murat. Maceroni was now in the employ of Fouché, although he insists in his memoirs that he was an unwitting pawn. The note which Maceroni carried under a white flag to the British supreme commander advised that President of France and Minister of Police Joseph Fouché was fully aligned with the pro-Louis faction.[349] The communication assured the Duke of Wellington that he could "most fully depend upon" the Duke of Otranto, "and that there is nothing he can do which your Grace may point out which he is not willing to undertake."[350]

Captain Maceroni, after delivering the English agent's message and subsequently attempting to return to Paris through one of the barrier gates, had to display his award of the Legion of Honor to avoid being shot by French pickets who were "furious at the appearance of anything like negotiation with the enemy."[351]

⚜

Louis XVIII, uncertain that this time around he was still the "Desired One," cautiously followed in the wake of the British army as it methodically worked its way down the Oise and towards Paris. He had finally been joined by his foreign minister, Prince Talleyrand, who even more cautiously, had taken his time traveling from Vienna to join his threatened sovereign until he was completely assured of Napoleon's decisive defeat at Waterloo. When Louis crossed the border back into France and reached the town of Le Cateau on June 23, he rashly issued a proclamation which had been drawn up for him. It stated that he would still govern according to the *Charte* but it also warned that he would use existing laws to punish the guilty. The last thing Wellington wanted in the midst of hostilities was to repeat the Duke of Brunswick's mistake in 1792 of threatening the population of Paris, thus prompting inspired resistance similar to that which had led to the defeat at Valmy. He therefore had the proclamation of Le Cateau immediately suppressed.[352] (This was in itself a telling indication of the shortness of the leash on which the British leaders held the French monarch.) On June 27, Louis and his royalist entourage had moved ever so tentatively south to Cambrai, and it was there that a second, substitute proclamation was issued which, under the editorial control of Talleyrand, allowed that mistakes had been made by the Bourbons — much to the ire of the Comte d'Artois — and which emphasized pardon over punition for those who had served the usurper Bonaparte during Louis XVIII's recent interregnum as a fugitive. The right to pursue those who had supposedly engineered Napoleon's return and thereby engaged in "treason unmatched in world annals" was, however, expressly reserved.[353]

One week later, on July 3, the question of amnesty and forgiveness was addressed in the armistice convention agreed to by Marshal Davout. As we have noted, Davout's negotiations had been authorized by President Fouché, but the document carried the signatures of neither of them; instead it was executed for the French by the provisional government's minister with the ostensible foreign affairs portfolio and by Davout's chief of staff, while senior Prussian and Britsh officers signed it for the Allies. The instrument provided that Davout would yield up Paris and remove his army south to the Loire, and it contained an Article 12, which stated that the French would "continue to enjoy their rights and liberties, without being pursued, be it by reason of the positions they have occupied or their conduct or their political opinions."[354] Thus, as Davout's sullen, nearly mutinous forces withdrew from the capital in the face of the enemy, their commander believed that he had obtained an ironclad guarantee against reprisals. But as Wellington was later quick to point out in a letter dated July 13 to Britain's Secretary for War, the Earl of Bathurst, "the convention binds nobody excepting the parties to it; viz., the French army on the one side, and the allied armies under Marshal Prince Blücher and myself on the other; and the 12th article cannot be considered, and never was intended, to bind any other persons or authorities whatever, unless they should become parties to the convention."[355] In other words, the returning Bourbons were not obliged to honor it.

So the task fell to Fouché, who had consciously and intentionally rid himself of the trump card of a powerful army, to try to negotiate additional guarantees on behalf of republican liberties and against revenge and reprisals. He adroitly presented himself to his increasingly fearful and suspicious fellow members of the provisional government as being fully committed to extracting every possible guarantee and concession from the Allies' Bourbon clients to protect the gains of the Revolution and to avoid vengeance being taken against those who had not stood with (or more accurately, had fled to Ghent with) the *fleur-de-lys*. Of course, the Duke of Otranto's agenda as he proceeded to British headquarters located on an estate at Neuilly, just to the west of Paris, to engage in personal talks with Wellington, was first and foremost to look out for himself.

⚜

The Duke of Wellington was already favorably disposed towards the Duke of Otranto. This was not because of Fouché's flattering notes to him ("My Lord Duke, there is no man at this moment with greater power than you to put all of humanity . . . in a better condition"); the acerbic British commander was notoriously scornful of sycophants, commenting about a crowd of Belgians cheering him after Waterloo, "If I had failed they would have shot me."[356] Rather, Wellington was impressed by results: Fouché had driven Bonaparte onto a British warship, and he had prepared Paris for an Allied victory parade down the Champs Elysées rather than for a costly siege with a highly problematic outcome. Maceroni claims that the Iron Duke informed King Louis that he owed his throne to Fouché: "Neither Blücher nor myself would have been able to restore to you your crown. We had to do with an army of eighty thousand furies [a numerical understatement] who would have repulsed us."[357]

Wellington, who was no doubt well aware that Fouché had already once been offered the ministry by the Comte d'Artois in their late-night meeting right before the Bourbon collapse, was also convinced that the veteran Minister of Police was essential to maintaining order in the capital once the Allies had entered it, as well as in future years after the foreign military occupation of France inevitably wound down. For his viewpoint, the British commander surprisingly found a supportive chorus of echoes amongst the French aristocracy. The Minister of Police had exploited his stratagem of a liberalized police force like a virtuoso, and scores of royalists believed they owed their lives to his enlightened approach, many of them not realizing that he had saved them from manufactured and illusory threats. According to Chateaubriand, "on every hand the cry was heard 'No safety for the King without Fouché, no salvation for France without Fouché.'"[358] The highly influential Comte de Vitrolles became a ceaseless advocate of Fouché with the Bourbons. The archconservative monarchist the Bailly de Crussol also aggressively lobbied the King on the Duke of Otranto's behalf, stating to a confidant of Louis, the more skeptical former royalist Minister of Police the Comte de Beugnot, "Fouché has preserved all of us since the King left; it was due to him alone that M. de Vitrolles was not shot . . . he holds them [the Jacobins] in his hand . . . My dear Monsieur Beugnot, we are old in the faubourg Saint-Germain; we have suffered too much, it is necessary for us to rest."[359]

Against this background of pressure from Wellington and the swelling paeans of praise and pleas for Fouché by French aristocrats, Louis reluctantly dispatched Foreign Minister Prince Talleyrand to Wellington's headquarters at Neuilly for the unavoidable parley with the Duke of Otranto. Fouché's long-time rival and occasional ally out of mutual self-interest had once again come into brief planetary alignment with him. Talleyrand must have been grudgingly impressed by the Duke of Otranto's successful destabilization of their mutual enemy, Napoleon. He was doubtless also convinced of the short-term utility of having a cunning and resourceful policeman to help keep the peace. Talleyrand, who had lost some standing at court because of his foot-dragging reluctance to leave Vienna and join the King in Ghent while the issue of Napoleon's Flanders campaign was still in doubt, may also have felt that there were self-preservational advantages to having someone in the new Bourbon regime with considerably more radical revolutionary baggage than his own.

⚜

Just before the meeting took place between the three men who were shaping France's destiny, the following conversation took place between Louis XVIII and the Comte de Vitrolles, as reported by the latter in his *Mémoires*:

> Louis: "Do you know that the prince de Talleyrand and the Duke of Wellington are leaving for Neuilly, where they have a meeting with the Duke of Otranto?"
> Vitrolles: "Yes, Sire, Madame de Talleyrand came to tell me that."
> Louis: "But you do not know the instructions which I have given them."
> Vitrolles: "I do not know them, Sire."
> Louis: "I have said to them: you go to Neuilly, you see the Duke of Otranto there, do anything you believe to be in my service, only be gentle and think of my virginity."[360]

⚜

As it transpired, the Duke of Wellington and Prince Talleyrand defended Louis' virtue, but only up to a point. The Duke of Otranto apparently requested that as part of the final settlement making way for his return, the King should retain the revolutionary symbols of the tricolor and the cockade. This gambit went nowhere, with Louis once again being completely unyielding on the issue of state symbolism. Fouché also allegedly requested a more sweeping amnesty than was provided for by the modified royal proclamation of Cambrai; this too was rejected, but Wellington cannily advised him that the best assurance against royalist retribution was for Fouché to possess the Ministry of Police portfolio under the Bourbons' Second Restoration.[361]

So it was only with the firm promise of that precious portfolio that acting president Fouché returned to Paris on July 6 and issued a proclamation declaring the provisional government to be immediately dissolved, stating that "we must stop the useless shedding of blood" and that "we have finally received guarantees."[362] The next day, Prussian troops moved in behind him and surrounded the Chambers, unceremoniously terminating its theoretical debates about a new constitution. Blücher's guns were now trained on the Tuileries from close range. And on July 8, Fouché wrote to the Duke of Wellington: "I have the honor to inform your lordship that the [provisional] commission of government has ceased to exist; that the government is in the hands of the King."[363]

The word "treason" (*"trahison"* in French) comes from the Latin *traduire*, meaning to hand over. The hand-over of Paris to the Allies and their client, Louis XVIII, by Joseph Fouché was now complete.

Before Fouché could receive his portfolio as a devoted servant of His Majesty, there was some paperwork that needed to be executed. Talleyrand asked the Comte Beugnot if he had a number of official decrees for the King to sign, and when Beugnot replied that he did, Talleyrand gave him an additional one naming Fouché to the Royal Ministry of Police. Beugnot put it at the bottom of the stack of documents to be signed by Louis. In his *Mémoires*, he describes what transpired:

> His Majesty's countenance had lost none of its accustomed calm and he appeared rather disposed to express contentment . . . .He gave me without difficulty and according to his habit, the first signatures which I had asked of him, and then took the occasion to make fun of my impatience to get back to Paris, as if, he said, I could not separate myself from the Opera for two or three days . . . I presented at the same time the ordinance for the nomination of Monsieur the Duke of Otranto. The King stared at it and let it drop to his desk; the quill fell from his hand; the blood rose in his face, his eyes became somber and he completely withdrew into himself as though overwhelmed by the thought of death. A mournful silence had suddenly interrupted a conversation heretofore light-hearted and pleasing. This silence lasted several minutes, after which the King said to me, after sighing deeply:
> "It must be done! We are going to do it! . . ."
> He picked up his quill, stopped himself again before writing some characters and pronounced these words:
> "Ah! My unhappy brother, if you could see me you would forgive me!"
> He finally signed, but, at the same time that he did it, laboriously and with trembling, great tears fell from his eyes and blotted the paper. I took back the ordinance, I bowed and left.[364]

Chapter XVI

Anathema

On July 7, 1815, Louis XVIII returned once again to the ancient Abbey of Saint-Denis, on the northern outskirts of Paris, where his older brother and his queen constituted the sole royal occupants among the vacant, violated crypts and cadaver tombs. In addition to communing with his guillotined predecessors and making preparations for his re-entry into his capital the following day, the King had another important duty to perform: personally to receive the regicide Joseph Fouché into his new cabinet of ministers. In one of the cloistral halls of the hallowed Abbey, the Comte Beugnot, spotting Chateaubriand (who had perhaps too forcefully for his own good argued to Louis that he should refuse to employ the Duke of Otranto), knowingly commented to him: "That which we are about to see is worthy of the pen of Tacitus, and happily you are there."[365]

Chateaubriand proved himself to be a worthy witness indeed; Tacitus would have relished the account that resulted. In a famously riveting passage in his *Memoirs from beyond the grave*, the legitimist writer captured or created the spectral and surreal moment of the first meeting between corpulent royalty and gaunt regicide, brokered by the club-footed, heavily powdered, perpetually insouciant Prince Talleyrand:

> I first entered the church: a piece of wall adjoining the cloister had fallen; the old abbey church was lit only by a lamp. I said

> my prayer at the entrance to the vault where I had seen Louis XVI lowered: full of dread as to the future, I do not know that I ever felt my heart drowned in a more profound and religious melancholy. Next I went to His Majesty's: shown into one of the rooms which preceded the King's, I found no-one there; I sat down in a corner and waited. Suddenly, a door opened: silently vice entered leaning on the arm of crime, M. de Talleyrand walking supported by M. Fouché; the infernal vision passed slowly before me, penetrated into the King's closet, and vanished. Fouché was coming to swear fealty and homage to his lord; the trusty regicide on his knees laid the hands which caused the head to fall of Louis XVI between the hands of the brother of the royal martyr; the apostate bishop [i.e., Talleyrand] was surety for the oath.[366]

The next day, Louis XVIII received his quid pro quo. Too obese to mount a horse and ride into Paris as did his brother the Comte d'Artois and his nephew the Duc de Berry, he entered the city via the Barrière de Saint-Denis in his closed coach. The weathervane *Moniteur Universel* dutifully reported that the air resonated with cries of *"Vive le Roi!"*,[367] but the truth appears to have been that the King's reception was decidedly more mixed. Marshal MacDonald, a veteran of Napoleon's wars who had nevertheless honored his oath of loyalty to Louis during the "Hundred Days" just ended, observed the scene as he cantered into the heart of the capital with the procession, alongside d'Artois:

> The reception by the Parisians was less demonstrative than at the first entry [i.e., in 1814]. On the boulevards they were even colder than in the suburbs and the Rue St. Denis. At that point Marshal Moncey joined the procession. The King turned his head away from his salute, and Monsieur [i.e., d'Artois] withdrew his hand indignantly when the Marshal advanced respectfully to take it. He was in disgrace for having continued in office during the Hundred Days.[368]

Thanks to the royalists' vengeful mood, and thanks to their newly annointed Minister of Police, Joseph Fouché, Marshal Moncey would soon be sharing that disgrace with many others who had sided with the Emperor.

As the royal procession made its way towards the Tuileries Palace, already ringed by Blücher's fiercely posturing Prussians, shouts of *"Vive l'Empereur!"* could also be heard. But not all of these retrograde outcries nececessarily emanated from diehard Bonapartists. According to former police prefect Bourrienne, Fouché had infiltrated the crowd with *agent provocateurs* paid to create the impression that the Bourbons were entering an acutely hostile environment, as to which only their new Minister of Police was equipped to protect them. These sham Bonapartists were quickly and ostentatiously rounded up by other elements of Fouché's men.[369] In this one episode, we can readily see Fouché's strategy for continued survival: to keep the Bourbons feeling threatened by the revolutionaries, and vice versa, with the indispensable man ostensibly preserving both sides against calamity. It was a balancing act that even Fouché could not maintain indefinitely, especially because one side of the scale was now being pressed down upon: the Allies had no intention of leaving France quickly and without inflicting pain, unlike the last time they had held the upper hand. The royalists' fears of a repeat of 1789 were tempered by their realization that there would be no concerted revolutionary uprising against them for as long as France remained occupied by Allied forces.

⚜

The day after Louis had re-entered the Tuileries, where he was "protectively" encircled by legions of foreign occupiers, British Prime Minister Lord Liverpool anxiously minuted to Viscount Castlereagh, his emissary to the interrupted Congress of Vienna (which was about to reconvene in the conquered capital of France):

> It will be a Herculean task, I think, to give any real strength to his [Louis'] government. For what is a King unsupported by opinion, by an army, or by a strong national party? I am glad, upon the whole, that he has determined to employ Fouché. He may betray him, but he may likewise feel it is in

> his best interest to save him. In a desperate state of affairs we must try desperate remedies.[370]

But part of the reason that Louis was so weak and the situation was so desperate was that Britain, to some extent, and the other members of the Seventh Coalition, especially Prussia, to a much greater extent, were intent on making it so, even though their common enemy, Napoleon Bonaparte, had been permanently removed from the Continent and was now a prisoner en route to Saint Helena. In his note to Foreign Secretary Castlereagh, Lord Liverpool had already conceded his lack of confidence in Louis' ability to govern, and five days later, in a second letter to his foreign minister, he underscored the Allies' determination to make things extremely difficult for the country which the House of Bourbon was attempting to rule: "It might have been not unwise [a carefully turned phrase here!] last year to try the effect of a more magnanimous policy [towards France]; but in the result of that we have been completely disappointed, and we owe it to ourselves now to provide in the best manner we can for own security."[371] And the Duke of Wellington, who counted himself a friend of the House of Bourbon for as long as it could be manipulated by Great Britain, would later bluntly opine as he prepared to have his troops empty the Louvre of treasures which had been plundered from all over Europe by Bonaparte: "It is . . . desirable, as well as for their own happiness as for that of the world, that the people of France, if they do not already feel that Europe is too strong for them, should be made sensible of it; and that whatever may be the extent at any time, of their momentary and partial success against any one, or any number of individual powers in Europe, the day of retribution must come."[372]

The retribution Wellington, Castlereagh, and Lord Liverpool had in mind entailed, in addition to the forced repatriation of stolen works of art, vast indemnities, significant territorial concessions, the total disbandment of Marshal Davout's hastily renamed "Army of the Loire," and the demolition or occupation of French border fortresses. What none of the British leaders had envisioned as part of the Allied Judgment Day, however, was the terrorization of France's cities, towns, and countryside by the vengeance-minded Prussians and come-lately occupation forces from other German states and principalities (Prussia was now the dominant part of the German Confederation created by the Congress of Vienna), in a grim foreshadowing of the horrors, crimes, and indignities which would again be visited upon France during its tortured history by the Second and the Third Reichs. Under Field Marshal Blücher, who loathed the French for their subjugation of his country in 1807, and for the defeat inflicted on him at Ligny in Napoleon's final campaign, where he was thrown from his horse and nearly killed, the Prussians engaged in widespread and systematic looting, arson, vandalism, peremptory executions of civilians who got in their way, vicious and random rape, and the demeaning arrests of Bourbon-appointed prefects who attempted to mitigate the mayhem.[373] Wellington, who apparently intervened to stop Blücher from blowing up the Pont de Iéna in Paris (named for Napoleon's crushing 1806 victory over the Prussians for which, as noted earlier, Marshal Davout had been largely responsible), was deeply shocked. He wrote to his brother regarding his comrades-in-arms: "I am a little afraid of them. They are all behaving exceedingly ill."[374]

The Prussians' widespread depredations were threatening to break down the social order in France, rapidly diminishing Louis' stature as the guardian of his people. They also brought into sharper focus the stark consequences of the devil's bargain to which Fouché had subscribed, removing the French army as both the nation's shield and as a major bargaining chip for which concessions of a far greater general benefit than his own selfish retention of the Ministry of Police could likely have been gained.

⚜

While they may have regretted the violent excesses being perpetrated against the French population, the Allied sovereigns and their foreign ministers had pointedly insisted upon diplomatic, economic, and political vengeance; they also demanded retribution against the Bonapartist leaders who had "so treasonably disturbed the peace of Europe," costing the Seventh Coaliton much blood and treasure.[375] In this one particular punitive demand, the Allies had the concurrence, even the enthusiastic concurrence of many of the members of the House of Bourbon, who simmered under the humiliation of being ousted from Paris and forced into exile at Ghent less than four months earlier at the hands of the escapee from Elba and his backers. The Bourbons insisted that the sudden and complete collapse of their halcyon First Restoration could only have been accomplished by treacherous plotting in order to set the stage for the tumultuous welcome which Bonaparte had received on his triumphant northward march from the Golfe-Juan, when a bullet from just one loyally commanded infantryman could have cut short the outlaw's return to the Tuileries. To fulfill the Allies' demands, and to eliminate or at least punish the leaders of the Bonapartist army and political clique, the Bourbons turned to the individual who actually *had* been involved in high-level treasonous plotting against them in the early part of 1815, that of the "Conspiracy of the North." In one of his first acts upon returning to the throne, Louis XVIII ordered his new Minister of Police to draw up a list of proscribed traitors. The operative benchmark given to Fouché was whether each individual in question had gone over to Napoleon before the King fled Paris on March 23. In the cynical but perceptive words of Talleyrand: "Treason, it is a question of the date."[376]

Fouché's response to the task assigned him was quite confounding. He diligently compiled an immense list of everyone who was anyone during the Hundred Days, including but not limited to his close associates and subordinates, inserting the names of minor actors as well as ministers, of ostensible allies as well as his enemies. Estimates and accounts vary, but Fouché's first draft may have called for the proscription of upwards of 300 individuals as alleged traitors.[377] Talleyrand is said to have commented sarcastically, "We must give the Duke of Otranto credit for one thing, he did not forget any of his friends in drawing up the list."[378] Fouché's fellow minister Pasquier records "our surprise on seeing him unroll before our eyes two enormous lists, which included three or four times as many names as was necessary, and in which he had, without any scruple, included both his most intimate political friends and a few very obscure enemies . . . The entire council [of ministers] revolted against such unheard-of numbers, and the spirit which had presided over the designations."[379]

What was Fouché up to? Pasquier concedes that his motives were "a difficult matter to discover," but that he was inclined to believe that

Fouché "wished to render the measure nugatory, nay ridiculous, by extending it beyond all limits." [380] Perhaps, but the more names Fouché listed for prosecution, the more pleased the vindictive Allied powers would be with him and, in keeping with his usual *modus operandi*, the more people there would be for the Minister of Police to "save," either by subsequently deleting them from the list or by leaving them on it while assisting in their escapes and evasions and thereby rendering them beholden to him.[381] If the list shrank, as it inevitably did with interested and powerful parties striking off names left and right — Louis himself removed that of the liberal political philosopher Benjamin Constant, and Czar Alexander personally intervened to save the French diplomat the Marquis de Caulaincourt, who had been a prominent member of Fouché's provisional government[382] — Fouché could use that winnowing process as an opportunity to distribute broadly the responsibility for oversights, inclusions, and exclusions.

After a frenzy of excisions emanating from a variety of supplicants, sponsors and saviors, Fouché's blacklist contracted to fifty-seven individuals. These names were divided into two categories, as spelled out in a royal ordinance published on July 24 1815 and known as the "Act of Proscription." The notorious Act bore the respective signatures of Louis XVIII and of the Duke of Otranto, as "The Minister Secretary of State for the police department." The first category consisted of "generals and officers who have betrayed the King before the 23rd of March, or who have attacked France and the government by force of arms." Nineteen high-ranking military men who had served Napoleon were to be "seized and brought before the competent courts-martial in their respective divisions." The list was headed up by Marshal Ney; Savary, the Duke of Rovigo, the longtime archenemy of Fouché and overseer of the execution of the Duc d'Enghien, was unsurprisingly named on it as well.[383]

The second category, while it also included a few high-ranking military officers, was primarily aimed at ministers and politicians; it comprised thirty-eight individuals. (See Appendix I for the full text of the Act of July 24.) The accused were ordered to leave Paris in three days and to report to locations within France assigned them by the Minister of Police, where they were to remain under surveillance until the new

Chamber of Deputies (then in the process of being elected) "shall declare which of them are to quit the kingdom, or to be sent for trial before the tribunals."[384]

Those of the fifty-seven proscribed "traitors" who possessed a modicum of good sense instead immediately scattered for the borders, in many cases carrying false passports issued by the Ministry of Police. Some received secret relocation funds. Not all of these sudden fugitives were grateful to Fouché. One of the men appearing on the second list was Lazare Carnot, an accomplished military planner and a fellow regicide, who had served Napoleon as Minister of War during the Consulate and as Minister of the Interior during the Hundred Days. Carnot was a fervid anti-royalist, and as a member of the provisional government he had been pathetically out-maneuvered by Fouché. He was appalled by what Fouché had wrought post-Waterloo. According to numerous contemporary sources, the outlawed Carnot angrily demanded of the Bourbon's Minister of Police: "Where should I go now, traitor?" Fouché's acid response: "Wherever you want, imbecile!"[385]

Carnot may have been Fouché's dupe, but he was not in fact an imbecile; he promptly left France for Poland. Marshal Ney, however, was another story. Despite being provided with passports (one false, one not) and possibly even a disguise by the Minister of Police, he inexplicably wandered about France for almost a month instead of heading straight for the Swiss border.[386] He may have been compromised by leaving his ornate dress sword in plain view at a chateau where he was staying in central France; in any event, the "Bravest of the brave" was apprehended soon thereafter, on August 3. Louis XVIII, recognizing that the trial of such a man would lead to a groundswell of sympathy for him, is said to have commented that "this arrest is more disastrous than his defection."[387] And the momentum was irreversible, as Ney was certainly the most prominent of the men proscribed, having personally represented to Louis just five months earlier that he would make Bonaparte his prisoner. By the end of the year, after a trial before the already purged Chamber of Peers (which he foolishly demanded, instead of appearing before what might well have been a much more lenient and sympathetic military tribunal), and in a climate of rising ultra-royalist fervor for revenge, he would lie dead in his civilian clothes on a Paris street, executed by a hastily assembled French firing squad, after having survived the retreat from Russia, the carnage of Waterloo, and a hundred other battles and engagements under the tricolor, for his country and his Emperor.

⚜

Unlike Marshal Ney, Marshal Davout's name did not appear on the July 24 proscription list (although it would be interesting to know whether the "Iron Marshal," Minister of War during the Hundred Days and Fouché's collaborator in removing the Emperor, in fact appeared on Fouché's initial draft). The reason for the omission apparently was that Davout had never sworn his allegiance to the King under the First Restoration, remaining sequestered on his estate; he therefore had broken no oath of loyalty. However, Davout, who had agreed to order the restless and fuming officers and men of his Army of the Loire to submit to the Bourbons on the immensely symbolic date of July 14 (just as Bonaparte was about to board H.M.S. *Bellerophon*) and to switch to the white cockade, was stunned when he saw a copy of the Act of Proscription. He had assumed that his general officers were protected by Article 12 of the capitulation of Paris; as we have seen, however, that document was not considered binding on or by the Bourbons, who had not been a party to it. The scales suddenly fell from Davout's eyes; he agonizingly realized he had been made to play the fool by Fouché. He wrote from Bourges on July 27 with great angst and passion to his replacement as Minister of War, Gouvion Saint-Cyr (an outspoken member of the marshalate who himself had had a trying relationship with Napoleon and who, consequently, had opted to honor his 1814 oath to Louis):

> I see in article I the names of generals, Gilly, Grouchy, Clausel, and Delaborde . . . they have done nothing but obey orders which I have given them in my role as minister of war. It is therefore necessary to substitute my name for theirs . . . Do not think, *Monsieur le maréchal*, these reflections are dictated by a fit of bad temper; they are the result of the profound sorrow with which I am distressed on account of the evils afflicting our unhappy country . . . You know the French

> army well enough, *Monsieur le maréchal*, to know that most of the generals named in the royal ordinance of 24 July are distinguished by their enormous talent and service . . . May I take upon myself alone the consequences of this proscription! It is a favor I request in the interests of the King and the country . . . Put this letter before the King's eyes.[388]

Davout's self-sacrificial gesture was heroic and no doubt heartfelt, but it was far too late. Marshal MacDonald came down from Paris personally to oversee the disbandment of the Army of the Loire, which had been shrinking in strength daily from desertions after it had abandoned the capital of France to the enemy, and which was waning even more rapidly after its debasing and demoralizing submission to the King. The *Grande Armée* was no more.

Marshal Davout thereupon relinquished his command to Marshal MacDonald. Several months later, in December, he would appear as a witness for the defense at the trial of the doomed Marshal Ney in the Chamber of Peers. Davout insisted that he had believed that Article 12 of the convention conferred a blanket amnesty on the French army's high command, and averred that if he had thought otherwise, "I would have given battle."[389] Three weeks after Ney's execution, before the end of the cataclysmic year 1815, a disgraced Davout was placed under surveillance and restricted to "internal exile" in Louviers in Haute Normandie, sixty miles from Paris, yet another prominent victim of the ceaseless and poisonous intrigues of Fouché.[390]

⚜

At the same time the purges were being promulgated from the top down, grassroots, vigilante revenge against the Bonapartists and the Jacobins was percolating up throughout the royalist-leaning regions of the South. The so-called "White Terror" typically involved mob action precipitated by gangs of rightist thugs. Some of them were called *les verdets* because they wore green livery, the color of the Angoulême nobility, while others were known as *"Les Chevaliers de la Foi"* (Knights of the Faith); despite their aristocratic-sounding names, they quickly became feared for their brutality. Marshal Guillaume Brune, who had not made it onto the final proscription list, was nevertheless attacked by a bloodthirsty crowd in Avignon who dragged him through the streets, hacked him to pieces, and threw his mutilated remains into the Rhône. An estimated two hundred Bonapartists were hunted down and killed in Marseilles, including members of the Emperor's Mameluke bodyguard, who had accompanied Napoleon on his return from Egypt. In Bordeaux, two brothers, both of whom had served as generals, and who were also not included on the July 24 list, were summarily executed for defiantly wearing the tricolor cockade. The disorders took on a particularly nasty religious aspect in Nîmes, where Protestants were assaulted and a general dispatched by the King's government to try to restore calm and open up their house of worship was murdered.[391] The center was not holding, violent counterrevolution was in full cry. Pasquier, now serving as Minister of the Interior and of Justice, darkly observed that "assassinations were following close upon one another in rapid succession, evidently deriving encouragement from a powerful source," pointing in the direction of the ultra-monarchist Comte d'Artois and his sons.[392] The King promised "solemn, national, and regular punishment" of the traitors of 1815 but worriedly warned against "the effects of private revenge . . . which would constitute an outrage on justice, perpetuate discord, and open the door to numberless disturbances . . . to an upheaval of the social order."[393]

As the nation writhed under a brutal Teutonic occupation, as the Allied sovereigns were preparing an ultimatum that would reduce France to impotent penury, as Bonapartists, republicans and revolutionaries were fleeing to escape retribution visited upon them from both above and below, as it was "time to hunt down the marshals" in the words of the avenging Comte d'Artois,[394] the widower Joseph Fouché, the architect of capitulation, decided that this was an excellent occasion for him to marry into the aristocracy.

The object of Fouché's desire was almost thirty years younger than he, and she was by all accounts very attractive. Her name was Ernestine de Castellane, and she was a member of the prominent ancient nobility of Provence, with a family line traceable back to at least the ninth century.[395]

Fouché had met her in Aix during his wilderness time in 1814, and he calculated that the moment had come for a Bourbon minister risen from a bourgeois merchant family from Nantes to make both an advantageous marital alliance and a noticeable splash in royal Paris.

Why did not Ernestine de Castellane's noble family summarily spurn the regicide's request for their daughter's hand in marriage, a proposal coming from a 56-year-old whom a contemporary depicts as then possessing "bloodshot and piercing eyes, white hair like an albino's, a ferocity, elegant and agile that made him resemble a panther"?[396] Part of the answer may be found in the last part of the foregoing description: the aura of fear and intimidation that surrounded the suitor. Another factor was likely money: over the lucrative years of the Empire, Fouché had amassed a huge personal fortune and it is entirely possible, even likely, that the House of Castellane had been stretched very thin in order to survive the Revolution.[397] Finally, there was the aphrodisiac of power: in July of 1815, the Duke of Otranto could understandably be seen by those not within the very inside circle to be riding quite high as the indispensable man who had outmaneuvered Bonaparte and who had enabled the King to regain his throne. Perhaps the old news of the accolades the Duke of Otranto had received from anxious aristocrats in late June and early July had traveled slowly to Aix, accolades which were quickly diminishing after the throne had been regained and the royalists' collective safety was, for the most part, being secured by Allied bayonets.

In any event, the parents of the bride would have been reassured that this was a fortunate and promising match by the fact that Louis XVIII actually witnessed the notarization of the marriage certificate. This royal sign of approval occurred several days before the former de-Christianizer's second wedding took place on August 1, 1815 at the Abbaye-aux-Bois, a Bernardine convent that had been restored to its holy functions after serving as a prison during the Terror.[398] It seems certain that the members of the House of Castellane who attended the subsequent lavish reception hosted by the Fouchés at the headquarters of the Ministry of Police at the Hôtel de Juigne on the Quai Malaquais did not sense the fault lines which were beginning to appear beneath the feet of the newlywed Minister of Police. Neither could they predict that the bride, now become the *Duchesse d'Otrante*, would very soon share in the groom's complete disgrace.

The brand-new prefect of police for Paris would likely have attended the nuptial celebrations on that summer evening by the Seine. His name was Élie Decazes and he was a handsome and very ambitious young man, an appellate-practice attorney and a widower, a royalist but not an aristocrat, who had helped to shut down and secure the Chamber of Deputies as the capital capitulated, but whose political views were relatively moderate. He also possessed an ample amount of cunning. Fouché, perhaps noting Decazes' obliging role in the recent legislative lockdown, had offhandedly consented to appoint him to this important open position within his organization when his name was suggested; neither Fouché nor Talleyrand apparently knew him particularly well, a surprising lapse for the all-seeing eye of the Duke of Otranto. Decazes had also almost immediately come to the attention of Louis himself, and the monarch was very favorably impressed by his loyalty and intelligence, by his engaging sycophancy and charm. When the King encouraged Decazes to advise him directly, regularly, and in one-on-one sessions, rather than indirectly through his superior, the Minister of Police, the newly minted prefect enthusiastically obeyed.

Pasquier commented that the King never once saw Fouché "come into his presence but with disgust," and the perceptive Prefect Decazes, with his invaluable direct line of communication to the throne — which disconcerted other cabinet ministers and royal advisors as well as the Minister of Police — lost no time in setting to work to marginalize and further discredit a man whom Louis already reviled.[399] Decazes had taken the lead in personally interrogating Ney before his trial, pre-empting Fouché from involvement in an exercise in which he probably would not have wanted to be visibly engaged anyway.[400] More threateningly, Fouché's new subordinate surreptitiously created a clandestine organization called *"Francs régénérés,"* to assemble and chronicle the past crimes and misdeeds of his boss, and he became adept at spreading rumors that played to the King's fear and distrust, including rumors about a supposed assassination plot that, if it had actually existed and come to fruition, would have made the Duke of Otranto a repeat regicide.[401] And Decazes, enterprisingly taking another leaf from Fouché's own manual, further ingratiated himself with both Louis and the increasingly influential Czar Alexander by flaunting his men's adept "solution" of a bogus plot to poison the Allied sovereign while he was residing in Paris.[402]

⚜

Alexander I, the alleged target of that discredited attempt, himself increasingly constituted another threat, and not only to Fouché, but to Prime Minister Talleyrand as well, and therefore to Louis' entire cabinet. Talleyrand had once served as the Czar's highly valuable informant against Napoleon (see Chapter X), and he later had graciously turned over several floors of his chateau to the Russian ruler during the first occupation of Paris by the Allies in 1814. But Alexander now found him to be exceptionally distasteful. During the Congress of Vienna, before Napoleon's return from Elba, Talleyrand had engineered a secret alliance of convenience between France, Britain, and Austria to oppose territorial claims of Russia and Prussia, and the Czar had discovered it and was deeply resentful.[403] Also, Czar Alexander had his own favorite whom he very much wished to see in Talleyrand's place as the head of the King's council of ministers: Armand-Emmanuel de Vignerout du Plessis, the Duc de Richelieu. A close friend of the Czar, Richelieu was an intelligent, upright, and accomplished royalist émigré who had actually served Alexander and the Russian Empire as the governor of Odessa during several of his many years of exile from Napoleon's France. Adding to the potential domino effect were two additional dynamics. First of all, the royalist Richelieu abhorred Fouché, and he had adamantly refused to serve in Louis' council of ministers for as long as the regicide was Minister of Police. Second, Louis himself had soured on his prime minister as well. Talleyrand, although an aristocrat, had also been a man of the Revolution, the Directory, the Consulate, and the Empire; like Fouché, he plotted incessantly, and certainly not always in the Bourbons' best interests; he was exceptionally venal, even for his time; he had clashed publicly and in front of the King with the Comte d'Artois (although this did not in and of itself weigh too heavily against him, as Louis was also suspicious of his extremely illiberal younger brother, next in line to the throne); his sporadic and diffident attempts at diplomacy with the Allies in 1815 had proved fruitless; and, perhaps worst of all in Louis' eyes, Talleyrand had appeared at his side in Ghent only after it was clear that the Seventh Coalition had in fact triumphed at Waterloo. [404] Richelieu in place of Talleyrand — which would also of necessity mean an ascendancy of Russian over British interests — was a substitution that Louis XVIII would be delighted to effect. Joseph Fouché was very much in the way, impeding not only the Richelieu-for-Talleyrand swap, but also the appointment of Louis' new favorite, Élie Decazes, as Minister of Police.

Yet another potent force to be reckoned with was inexorably bearing down upon the uneasy ministerial partnership of Fouché and Talleyrand: the election of the new Chamber of Deputies was not unfolding in the way that the two inveterate schemers had hoped and planned. Instead of a relatively liberal legislature which would help shape the government of France into a constitutional monarchy and complement the King's more moderate instincts, the elections of the summer of 1815, in spite of the ministers' attempts to manipulate them, resulted in an ultra-right wing, revenge-minded Chamber which was seen as more monarchist than the monarch himself and which was a natural ally of the Comte d'Artois and his sons. With voting rights in the hands of a small electorate qualified by using very restrictive tax and property-holding criteria, and with rightist intimidation taking place in some districts, of 402 available seats in the Chamber, 370 were won by fervent royalist "Ultras."[405] This newly elected body soon came to be called *"La Chambre introuvable."* This appellation has been variously translated, but it connotes a Chamber which was incredibly reactionary, one which couldn't have been more so if that had actually been the end desired by the King and his ministers, which it decidedly was not. Louis was suddenly concerned about being outflanked to his right, and by his own family members. And both Fouché — unable to duplicate the results of his election-rigging just four months earlier — and Talleyrand correctly saw that they were both imperiled by the unanticipated influx of angry legislators who detested them.

⚜

Fouché concluded that it was high time for him to tip the scales and slide the situation back into that state of tense equilibrium in which he had always thrived. He decided to raise the spectre of revolution from the left in order to convince the forces of the right that they were the ones who were actually in jeopardy, at least without his suppressive services. The tactic that Fouché chose to spring, without any forewarning, was to submit a scarifying and sobering report which he had commissioned about the current situation in France. He oddly chose to read it aloud at a meeting of the King and his ministers in cabinet at the Tuileries on August 15. His report focused on the excesses of the Allied troops, and it concluded that the nation was at the breaking point, ready to rise against the occupiers and perhaps itself to be destroyed. In his presentation, Fouché melodramatically intoned:

> A nation of thirty millions of inhabitants may disappear from the earth, but in this war of man to man, more than one tomb will enclose, by the side of each other the oppressors and the oppressed! The calamities of France [are] complete: ruin, devastation, and destruction are taking place, as if for us there was neither peace nor compromise to be hoped for . . . Despair will soon listen to no voice of authority.[406]

The King immediately cut off any discussion of the Minister of Police's grim and highly sensitive report. He thanked Fouché for frankly describing the situation as he saw it, and strongly cautioned all his ministers that the report itself must remain strictly top secret and that "the walls of this closet have no ears."[407] But Fouché's alarming assessment, as well as a second report prepared for the King by the Ministry of Police and predicting a popular uprising against the royalists by a predominantly liberal and republican populace ("the destinies of France are not in your hands alone, fatal circumstances exist which excite fears in the minds of the people"[408]) were promptly leaked and were very soon in widespread circulation. Almost all fingers pointed to Fouché as the culprit. Louis was understandably furious, and he resolved to be done with him, once and for all.

Setting aside the irony of Fouché's warnings of "calamities" which he had played a central role in creating, it appears that he was at the same time trying to re-establish his leadership credentials with downtrodden forces of the left and center, who now viewed him as a traitor. But his efforts floundered, and Fouché was immediately consumed by tendering excuses and denials, and by being humiliatingly called onto the carpet by the Prussians' own *Polizeidirektor* for Paris, Karl Justus von Gruner.[409] To von Gruner, and to anyone else who would listen to him, including Wellington himself, Fouché claimed that his reports had been altered. The British diplomat Charles Arbuthnot was not buying it, referring in a message to Lord Liverpool to Fouché's "report to the King of the interior (so shamefully made public by him)," while nevertheless conceding that he thought it was "the truest representation of the country that could be given."[410] But Fouché was apparently more convincing in his explanations to the British commander-in-chief, whom he assured that "all measures are being taken to seize the work and the author"; Wellington would later write "I know there are courtesans who published his last report to the King."[411] And the truth of the matter may very well have been nuanced and complicated: while Fouché had desperately attempted to influence public spirit against the royalist Ultras and force the King towards the center, it is also very possible that Prefect Decazes and his undercover agents of *Francs régénérés* had made sure that altered and even more inflammatory versions of the reports by the Minister of Police were widely circulated.

The King, at once outraged by the leaks and relieved that he had a gold-plated excuse to fire Fouché, set in motion the paperwork to remove him. According to Minister Pasquier, Louis was especially delighted that with the return of the Duchess of Angoulême to Paris, the surviving child of Louis XVI "will no longer be exposed to see that odious face."[412] But on the very day on which Pasquier had been instructed to bring the ordinance to the King for signature, it turned out that Fouché — who had gotten wind of his imminent dismissal, perhaps via Vitrolles — had one last potent ace to play.[413] The Duke of Wellington appeared in person at the Tuileries, sought and of course received an audience with His Majesty, and either demanded or respectfully requested that the Duke of Otranto be retained. In this mission, Wellington was temporarily successful, and British influence over the course of French politics seemed to have been maintained. Louis, no doubt grievously embarrassed by his obvious impotency, admitted to Pasquier that the dismissal was countermanded because "he could not resist the entreaties of a personage who played so important a part in the coalition, and to whom he believed he was under special obligations."[414] Subsequent cabinet meetings at which Fouché was present were now rendered "as painful as possible" with the "position so false that it could not last for any length of time"; Pasquier notes that while it did, "it cast the greatest discredit on the council."[415]

The stay of execution would in fact prove quite fleeting. The overwhelming hatred for the Minister of Police could no longer be contained within intra-cabinet maneuverings or dealt with in private conversations between the British Field Marshal and the King of France. The 370 *revanchist* members of the *Chambre introuvable* were headed for Paris in mid-September for the opening legislative session, and they and their allies among the princes at court threatened to submerge the ministerial cabinet and to marginalize the King himself unless Fouché was removed. Also, Russian influence was now revealed as in the ascendancy at the Tuileries over that of Wellington and the British. The Czar, acting in the interests of his protégé, the Duc de Richelieu, and of course in his own country's best interests as well, suggested that should Louis rid himself of both Fouché and Talleyrand, "your Majesty will win doubly."[416] It would actually be a triple victory, because Alexander, if he obtained what he wanted, was willing to use his great leverage to ameliorate the harsh peace terms which would otherwise be imposed by the Allies, and in so doing help place the Duc de Richelieu on much more solid footing than his predecessor.

⚜

In a ministerial meeting in September, Prime Minister Talleyrand prepared to open the trap door underneath the Minister of Police and thereby save himself and the rest of the King's cabinet. He took an oblique approach, praising the virtues of America and directing his words to Vitrolles and Pasquier, but with his intended audience being Fouché, who was also present and becoming increasingly uncomfortable. "It is such a beautiful country!" Talleyrand intoned. "Do you know it, Monsieur de Vitrolles? I do, I have travelled it, I have lived there, it is superb." As

Talleyrand continued to extoll the splendors of North America's primal forests in general and those of the Potomac River in particular, Fouché began to glare.[417] He realized full well that the ambassadorship to the United States was vacant and available, and that it was being dangled before him as the consolation prize for his exit from the first ministerial cabinet of the Second Restoration. The King was against him, and the King feared the Duchess of Angoulême and the rest of his own family more than he feared Wellington; the King's ministers, hoping to save their own skins, were against him; the new legislature abhorred him; the Czar's increasing influence was obvious; Fouché's one-time natural constituencies, the leftists and centrists, the revolutionaries and the Bonapartists, reviled him as a traitor; his new constituency, once-fearful and clinging royalists, were fearful and clinging no longer.[418] Fouché also likely sensed that he was being rapidly destabilized from below as well, from within his own organization. The game was finally at an end. It was time for him to try to obtain the best severance arrangement possible from a relentlessly hostile regime.

On September 19, 1815, after less than three months in Louis' cabinet, Fouché resigned as Minister of Police. Instead of opting for Washington on the Potomac, however, he decided upon accepting an ambassadorial assignment to the court of Dresden on the Elbe, in the Kingdom of Saxony, as recompense for his departure. It was probably only a short-term mistake on his part, as it appeared he had no long-term future representing his homeland given the rise of the *Chambre introuvable*, but he may have been better off taking what was on offer from Talleyrand, as his American reception would likely have been more welcoming, at least initially, in the land of revolutionaries, rather than within the confines of another royal court permeated with marital alliances with the House of Bourbon and aristocratic victims of the French Revolution.

⚜

With his fellow scorpion now removed from the cabinet bottle, Prince Talleyrand returned his attention to the oppressive terms of the draconian peace treaty upon which the Allies were insisting. He also had to cope with the looming threat posed by the incoming *Chambre introuvable*.

The Comte de Vitrolles records that two of Talleyrand's agents overheard a conversation involving several of the new deputies, in which one said "Fouché has been sent from the ministry and it is M. de Talleyrand who has done it." His fellow deputies responded "[T]he King has done well to get rid of Fouché; but when will he send away the other?"[419] The answer came just days after Fouché was expunged. In the words of Vitrolles, in orchestrating his rival's exit, Talleyrand had "nimbly jumped across the stream before him, without seeing on the other side he would fall into a swamp."[420]

On September 24 Talleyrand had a meeting with the King. He sought assurances from Louis that he would be backed unreservedly in his negotiations with the Allies, regardless of the results, and in the face of a chorus of criticism from the new Ultra deputies. In the absence of such assurances, Talleyrand stated that he would offer to resign, along with the entire rest of the cabinet. Perhaps to his astonishment, as he certainly had always thought of himself as the indispensable man, especially now with Fouché out of the picture, the King blithely accepted his hypothetical proffered resignation on the spot. (It is also possible that Talleyrand welcomed and perhaps even engineered this outcome, in order to avoid the blame for what he expected would be a harsh and humiliating peace treaty.) In any event, Talleyrand notes in his *Mémoires* that the King reacted to his proposed departure with the air of a man who was *"fort soulagé"* ("greatly relieved"), and that Louis' reaction was doubtless shared by the Czar, "who did me the honor of personally hating me."[421]

A new cabinet was quickly formed, with the Duc de Richelieu taking over Talleyrand's roles as presiding minister and foreign secretary. Bolstered by the intervention of his close friend, the Czar, Richelieu was eventually able to arrive at peace terms for France much less onerous than would have been possible for the reviled Talleyrand to obtain. Russia became ascendant over Britain in influence exerted upon the weak executive government of Louis XVIII. And Élie Decazes became the new Minister of Police.

⚜

Joseph Fouché, perhaps somewhat consoled by the fact that his own demise had been followed immediately by that of his long-time rival, quickly headed for the border with his young bride. He is said to have affected a disguise, anticipating that he would be targeted by any of the universe of factions who viscerally hated him and who also despised him now that he had been relieved of his pervasive police powers. He may have had particular reason to fear falling into the hands of Decazes' agents, who were now working for a proper Bourbon Ministry of Police, inheriting the organization which Fouché had so painstakingly built, polished, and perfected since the last year of the Directory.[422]

The sacked minister turned ambassador is said to have regretfully admitted to an English visitor to Dresden in late 1815, Philip Henry, the Fourth Earl of Stanhope, that the Duke of Wellington had counselled him against accepting the Saxony posting, bluntly warning that "You will get into a hole which you will never be able to leave."[423] While the available options may have in fact been somewhat limited, the Duke's advice to Fouché would nevertheless prove prescient.

Chapter XVII

Exile

Joseph Fouché's ambassadorial appointment to the Saxon court in Dresden proved to be a most ephemeral one. At the beginning of 1816, the Ultra royalists of the *Chambre introuvable* forced additional acts of vengeance upon the King's new presiding minister, the comparatively moderate Duc de Richelieu. They embodied these retaliatory acts in an ordinance which, in addition to banning permanently all members of the Bonaparte family from France, contained the following provision:

> Those of the regicides who, scorning a clemency nearly without precedent [a reference to the amnesty provision of Louis' *Charte* of 1814], voted for the *acte additionnel* [Napoleon's proposed constitution] or accepted positions in the employ of the usurper, and who therefore declared themselves the irreconcilable enemies of France and its legitimate government, are hereby excluded from the Kingdom in perpetuity, and are required to leave in one month, under the penalty carried by article 33 of the penal code [i.e., public execution]; they will no longer enjoy any civil rights.[424]

The evening after the ordinance was signed by Louis XVIII, *Par La Grace de Dieu, Roi de France et de Navarre,* Fouché was summarily stripped of his ambassadorship. He would not be viewed or treated as a member of those legions of dispossessed noblemen or outspoken philosophers who rode out the vicissitudes of politics for a finite period in a sympathetic safe haven, only to be permitted to return when passions in their homeland eventually calmed, as had been the case with the émigrés. On the contrary, Fouché had suddenly become a perpetual outcast, an ostracized and reviled regicide, a branded pariah.

Thus began Fouché's four-year odyssey through *Mitteleuropa* on his way to a foreign grave. On this journey he was accompanied by his young wife, who was stunned and shaken by her husband's precipitous fall from prominence, and by his four surviving children (who were almost his wife's age) from his first marriage (three sons, Joseph-Liberté, Armand, and Athanase, and a daughter, Josephine).[425] The family's wanderings took place within the bounds of the Habsburg Empire, for that is where the exiled Fouché applied to reside, in the hope that Prince Metternich would be mindful and duly appreciative of all of his former back-channel intelligence and advice. The wily Metternich did indeed desire that Fouché be situated within the Austrian Empire, but at a place very much of Metternich's choosing, a place where police surveillance of the master policeman would be at maximum effectiveness and where any intrigues could be discovered and thwarted instantaneously. Therefore, Fouché's entreaties for permission to locate himself in the political epicenter of Vienna were repeatedly denied and, after due consideration and the approval of the Emperor Francis, he was ordered by Metternich to proceed directly from Dresden to Prague.

When Fouché arrived in the baroque capital of Bohemia in August of 1816, he had one not inconsiderable consolation in addition to the company of his wife and children: he was still an extraordinarily wealthy man. While he had forfeited his landholdings in France, he had been permitted to take with him that portion of his immense fortune that was liquid or transportable; the King's repugnance for the regicide was perhaps tempered somewhat by the fact that he owed his easy return to the throne to him.[426] Wealth did not equate to happiness in Prague, however, as the local aristocracy shunned the Fouchés, the police marked his every move and intercepted and vetted all his correspondence, and his attractive young wife began to draw the persistent and seemingly unsolicited and unwanted attentions of Adolphe Thibaudeau, the son of a fellow exiled regicide, whose family was also domiciled in Prague courtesy of the watchful Hapbsurg administrators. Rumors of the young Thibaudeau's attempts at alienating the affections of Ernestine de Castellane from her 57-year-old husband soon became conflated into false reports of a lurid extramarital affair. These reports were gleefully spread throughout Europe by the prurient legions of Fouché-haters eager to conclude that the once-feared Minister of Police, the man with something on everyone, the man who so shortly before had held the life-and-death power to proscribe (Thibaudeau *père* had himself been included on the July 24 proscription list), had now been publicly and ridiculously cuckolded.[427]

This embarrassment was simply too much for the secretive and opaque Fouché, certainly not a man very used to being on the defensive, let alone being in the public eye in a matter of private scandal. He pleaded with Metternich for permission to relocate, and the Prince relented. Fouché – no longer officially referred to by the Austrians as the Duke of Otranto - was allowed to troop his beleaguered and mortified wife and children, along with his servants and horses and furniture, to the much smaller, relatively isolated, and very provincial town of Linz, on the upper Danube, where the third stayover in his wanderings commenced in August of 1818. There, the scrutiny of the imperial Habsburg police was every bit as intense as it had been in Prague, and the ostracism of the Fouchés by the locals was just as marked, although in Linz it was further tinged with a rural superstitious dread of the "Butcher of Lyon." Fouché had, ominously, arrived in Linz during a particularly violent thunderstorm, and he proceeded to rent the menacingly named Weissenwolf ("White Wolf") Palace. One local chronicler referred to it as "the lair of this emaciated man with his pale face who was the incarnation of the bloody troubles of the Revolution."[428]

Fouché's domestic household was infiltrated by informants, his rare visitors were interrogated and harassed, a code he attempted to use was compromised and cracked, his correspondence (nearly all outgoing) continued to be opened and read by Metternich's efficient *Polizei*.[429] It was an ironic reversal of fortune indeed: the all-seeing eye was itself under relentless observation. Attempts by Fouché to correspond with various men of note – Wellington, Richelieu, Decazes, Metternich, the Czar even, typically yielded no response. At one point in Fouché's exile, Wellington quizzically wrote to Richelieu: "Monsieur Le Duc: I send you two letters which I have received from Monsieur the Duke of Otranto. I do not know exactly why he wrote me, nor that which he wishes to explain to me by all this; but it is good for you to see it."[430] The indispensable man, the master intriguer who had pulled the strands of his overlapping webs for decades, was scorned, neutralized, and rapidly fading into oblivion.

Then, into the unhappy Fouché domicile at Linz, on her way back from the mineral spas of Franzensbad in Bohemia, came an unexpected, albeit evanescent, reprieve in the person of fellow exile Élisa Bonaparte. That she was no longer the Grand Duchess of Tuscany thanks in considerable measure to the destabilizing machinations of Fouché in 1813-14 with her sister and her sister's husband, the grasping Murats, seems never to have occurred to Élisa. Rather, she was filled with solicitude for the Fouchés, and she lent a sympathetic ear to the complaints of the aristocratic Ernestine, now age thirty-two, about her new family's reduced station in life ("What good is it to come into this world if it is only to live the way we are living?").[431] Élisa thought it would be something of a coup to recruit an ex-Minister of the Empire into the small community of prominent and not-so-prominent Bonapartists she headed. Her exiles' enclave was located in the Italianate city which was the Habsburg Empire's chief outlet into the Mediterranean, the exotic polyglot port of Trieste on the Adriatic.[432] Élisa implored Joseph Fouché and his family to join her there. Her audience was most receptive to packing up their belongings and leaving behind the Weissenwolf and the cold, unwelcoming Austrian hinterlands for the sunny and cultivated south, which Fouché remembered well and favorably from his earlier sojourn in the now-extinct Province of Illyria.

On October 20, 1819, at Élisa's entreaty, Prince Metternich (who had once had a useful affair with her sister Caroline, before she became the Queen of Naples)[433] granted permission for the Fouchés to decamp within the Austrian Empire for a final time. Joseph Fouché's request for an en route stopover in Vienna was immediately and firmly denied, however.[434] He and his entourage of family members and servants were ordered to proceed directly from Linz to Trieste.

Trieste had long been under Austrian rule — with a brief Napoleonic intermission which had included Fouché's 1813 Illyrian governancy — but in 1820 its diverse population of approximately 35,000 was comprised of Italians, Slovenes, Croats, Jews, Germans, French, and Greeks, as well as Austrian officialdom. The city occupied a crescent-shaped sliver along the Adriatic coast; behind it towered the Kras plateau, a limestone escarpment which psychologically as well as physically separated the port from Continental Europe, and which increased the isolated feelings of its resident exiles. Trieste was known for a sudden and extremely powerful katabatic winter wind called the *bora,* which without warning would sweep down over the Kras and blast through the streets of the city, attaining speeds of over one hundred miles an hour; later in the century, cables were installed along the city's walkways to keep pedestrians from being propelled by the *bora* out into traffic.

The Kras was also noted for being permeated with expansive caves and deep natural tunnels. The Timavo River plunges from its sources above ground to the northeast and follows a subterranean route through the massive Kras itself before again finding sunlight and the Adriatic. The Romans, whose north-south route, the *Via Germania*, traversed the plateau, believed, as did Dante later, that a gate to Hades could be found in the depths of the Kras.[435]

The Fouchés reached Trieste in January of 1820. They resided in a rented *palazzo* which had been constructed in the late 1790s and where Joseph Fouché had stayed briefly during the course of his forced exit from Illyria seven years earlier. But the social center of the exiles' activities was Élisa's magnificent home in the city, the villa de Campo Marzio, which overlooked the Adriatic and was surrounded by exotic flowers and vine-covered *allées*. The Austrian authorities had required Élisa to forfeit her title of *Duchesse*, and they only permitted her to be formally referred to as the *Comtesse de Compigniano*. She seems to have prudently barred any political discussion from her soirées, and the policemen at this Adriatic outpost detailed with conducting surveillance of the Bonapartes and Fouché relaxed the level of their vigilance somewhat, and proved to be not as intrusive in their oversight as had been their counterparts to the north.

In addition to the Fouchés, Élisa's other most-noteworthy, frequent visitor was her brother Jérôme Bonaparte, whom we have not encountered earlier in this work. Jérôme was the youngest of the eight Bonaparte siblings, and he had led a rakish existence, having had his non-advantageous marriage to an American annulled upon the order of his angry imperial brother, and subsequently ruling the Kingdom of Westphalia, which he had been awarded in 1807, in such a sybaritic manner that he was referred to by the locals as the *König Lustig* – "the lusty king." He had rejoined Napoleon for the final act, fighting quite bravely if ineffectively as the commander of a division at Waterloo, where he had been wounded as he stubbornly ordered repeated and fruitless French assaults on the Château Hougomont. While Jérôme had witnessed some of Fouché's duplicitous political machinations in the aftermath of the great battle, he nevertheless was apparently grateful to the erstwhile Minister of Police and head of the provisional government for having provided the precious passports he needed to escape quickly from France just ahead of the advancing Prussians.[436] After being held for an unpleasant period of time as the virtual prisoner of his father-in-law, the King of Württemberg, Jérôme and his second (or, technically, his first) wife Catharina, the former Queen of Westphalia, were permitted by Prince Metternich to reside in Trieste as well. There, Jérôme was just as friendly and cordial to Fouché as was his sister Élisa.

It appears that Fouché may have tried to reposition himself as an ardent advocate of Napoleon's return from Elba — although, he asserted, just not at the precise time at which it had been attempted — but it is likely that such transparent attempts by the former Minister of Police to rationalize and reshape his conduct and thus ingratiate himself with the two Bonaparte siblings were unnecessary.[437] Jérôme and Élisa, and Élisa's husband, Prince Félix Baiocchi who, like Jérôme, had a keen eye for pulchritude, were quite gratified simply to have his company and that of the lovely Ernestine at their parties, concerts, card games, and expeditions to the countryside where Élisa had a second home, the Villa Vicentina, close by the Roman ruins at Aquileia. Fouché's children became fast friends of Élisa's son and daughter. It was quite sufficient for Jérôme, now re-titled by Metternich as the Comte de Montfort, that Fouché had helped to save his skin in 1815, and both Bonaparte siblings had experienced enough of their own unnerving run-ins with their domineering older brother to be forgiving if others harbored reservations about the conduct, personality, and career of Napoleon as well.

⚜

So it was that, during the first half of the year 1820, Élisa and Jérôme and their families happily consorted with Joseph Fouché and his wife and children in picturesque, seaside Trieste, under the looming shadow of the Kras. Meanwhile, Napoleon was enduring the fifth year of his heavily guarded existence on an unforgiving volcanic rock almost four thousand miles away in the middle of the South Atlantic, and over twelve hundred miles distant from the nearest landmass. There, in dank Longwood House, "General Bonaparte" or *"Monsieur N"* (he too had been stripped of his imperial title by his jailer, Sir Hudson Lowe), in a comment made to a member of his own small and closely monitored entourage, ruefully and bitterly condemned the Duke of Otranto: "I ought to have had Fouché hanged. That was indeed my intention. If I had been conqueror at Waterloo, I would have had him shot immediately."[438]

The imprisoned Emperor would nevertheless soon have the faint and dubious pleasure of narrowly outlasting his exiled Minister of Police.

Chapter XVIII

Death in Trieste

The next summer, in August of 1820, Élisa Bonaparte died suddenly at the age of 43. She had contracted malaria while exploring the ruins of another empire, those from the second century adjacent to her Villa Vicentina country retreat. Thus the center and mainstay of the little Bonapartist enclave at Trieste was removed from the stage.

Élisa was buried with much ceremony on September 6 at the great Cathedral of Trieste, San Giusto, on the heights overlooking the Adriatic. The building was completely swathed in black-and-white fabric decorated with the letter "E." One hundred and sixty torchbearers preceded her coffin, and a forty-piece orchestra accompanied William Byrd's *Mass for three voices*. Joseph Fouché served as a pallbearer. The Austrian *Polizei* were there to observe. They likely noted in their reports that the image of a vacant throne was provocatively displayed in the procession, in accordance with the ancient usages of French royalty.[439] But back in Paris, *Le Moniteur Universel* dismissively referred to the deceased as "Mme Élisa Bacciochi, sister of Bonaparte," although it duly noted that she had left "considerable properties."[440]

Soon it was Fouché's turn. He had been in the habit of taking long, solitary walks along the promenades overlooking the Adriatic. During one of them, in early December, he contracted pneumonia. He lingered several weeks, his condition steadily worsening. A member of the Napoleonic entourage in Trieste, one Louis Planat de la Faye, a former aide-de-camp who had actually accompanied the Emperor onto H.M.S. *Bellerophon* and who was persistently but unsuccessfully seeking permission to join his idol on St. Helena, paid the failing Duke of Otranto a courtesy visit, even though the young officer was understandably quite ill-disposed towards him. Planat de la Faye recorded his brief bedside encounter with the dying man in his *Mémoires*, noting, "After a life so tumultuous, after navigating so happily our devouring revolutions, he came to die in Trieste, in exile and with the sorrow of not seeing his enemies confounded."[441]

Shortly before he died, Fouché is said to have instructed one of his sons to burn his papers, in his own eyesight and in that of other witnesses.[442] Assuming that this indeed occurred, the smoke and embers billowing out into the December air from one of the *palazzo's* chimneys may have contained the last trace particles of the Minister of Police's personal files on the Bonapartes, as well as on many of the other illustrious personages whose paths Fouché had crossed and stalked.

He lingered through Christmas Day, and expired in the early morning hours of December 26. The sacrament of extreme unction was administered to him on Christmas Eve, perhaps at the behest of his wife.[443] The serpentine, secretive trail Joseph Fouché had traversed over his sixty-two years had led him to forsake successively the Church, the Crown, the Revolution, the Directory, the Empire, the Restoration (if he was indeed, as likely, the leaker of his own confidential report to the King), and virtually anyone and everyone who had assisted him along the way. It had now led him, finally and ironically, in a complete circle all the way back to his starting point: the Church.

⚜

Fouché was to be interred, like his protector Élisa, at the Cathedral of San Giusto. The legend arose, perhaps true, perhaps not, but impossible to prove or disprove conclusively, that on the way to the funeral service, the wintry *bora* suddenly rocketed down from over the the summit of the

Kras escarpment and violently propelled his coffin from the top of the hearse and sent it tumbling into the roadside.[444]

Be that as it may, Fouché's mortal remains finally reached the great Cathedral. There, they were lowered into a small, subterranean crypt. By an odd coincidence, that crypt had also been the last resting place of two aunts of Louis XVI, the princesses Victoire and Adélaide, who had themselves once found refuge from the furies of the Revolution in the city of forlorn exiles on the shores of the Adriatic.[445]

Epilogue: The Sinister Basket

On January 16, 1821, a terse death notice in *Le Moniteur Universel,* after erroneously stating that Joseph Fouché had resided in Trieste for several years, reported that his last words to his wife were, *"Maintenant, vous pourrez rentrer en France."*[446] ("Now, you can go back to France.") Ernestine de Castellane, Duchess of Otranto, did indeed soon depart the Hapsburg outpost for her native land, but on her return she was scorned and shunned as the wife of a regicide who had supposedly carried on an adulterous affair with the son of yet another regicide. She therefore decamped once again, this time taking her very considerable inheritance to Switzerland, where she immersed herself in charitable works until her death in 1850.[447] However, two of Fouché's sons, Armand and Athanase, were received much more warmly, and by royalty, albeit quite *nouveau* royalty: they were welcomed into the court of King Charles XIV at Stockholm. In his prior existence, this newly crowned monarch had been none other than the Jacobin general and Napoleon's Marshal of France Jean-Baptiste Bernadotte, he who had played the part of Fouché's cat's-paw during the siege of Antwerp, who had incongruously been invited to serve Sweden first as its regent and its crown prince, and who had then ascended to the throne when the incumbent, the childless Charles XIII, died in 1818.

Thus it was in his role of grand chamberlain to the founder of the line of the House of Bernadotte (which constitutes the royal family of Sweden to this day), that Athanase Fouché, the third and only surviving son and the fourth Duke of Otranto, accompanied his father's exhumed coffin back to France in 1875, where it was reburied at the cemetery of Ferrières-en-Brie, close by the family's former estate, and next to the remains of Fouché's first wife, Bonne-Jeanne. The monument incorporated no religious symbolism whatsoever; neither did it make reference to Death as an "eternal sleep."

⚜

Auguste Regnaud de Saint-Jean d'Angély, an officer who served on Napoleon's personal staff at Waterloo, who was censured in the Act of Proscription, and who would survive to later become a marshal under the Second Empire, has been quoted as saying of Joseph Fouché: "I shall distrust him even after his death."[448] In September 1824, nearly four years after Fouché had been buried for the first time, d'Angély's words proved prescient, as a sepulchral literary fog emanated in the name of the deceased Duke of Otranto, in the form of "his" *Mémoires.* Fouché had threatened to do just this periodically during his exile, and he had even at one point contracted with a publisher in Leipzig.[449] As noted, however, it had been thought that any such work (or its underpinnings) had vanished up the chimney in his Trieste *palazzo* just before he died. The publisher in this event was a French house called Le Rouge, and the touted autobiography came on the scene at a pivotal time for France: Louis XVIII had just died and his ultra-royalist brother the Comte d'Artois was ascending to the throne as Charles X, the last member of the senior line of the House of Bourbon to do so, to the rejoicing of monarchists and the despair of republicans.

Le Rouge's *Mémoires de Joseph Fouché* opens with a statement in the preface by the purported author that "I shall find means to disappoint the expectations of those who are already anticipating the spoils of my reminiscences and revelations, of those who are preparing to lay snares for my children."[450] Fouché's well-provided-for offspring, however, were intent upon laying their own snare for the publisher: they immediately brought a lawsuit styled *Famille d'Otrante contre Le Rouge* in the Chambre du Tribunal de la Seine. The children denied that their father had left any memoirs whatsoever and their lawyer called the work in question a "lying fabrication produced by a literary rag-merchant."[451]

The attorney defending the interests of Le Rouge was Antoine Berryer, a prominent royalist who had nonetheless assisted his father in unsuccessfully representing Marshal Ney at his trial before the Chamber of Peers in 1815. Interestingly, Berryer's defense in this instance consisted of asserting that because Fouché was a notorious historic figure, his name had posthumously come into the public domain and that it really did not matter whether it was being used in connection with a third-person history or a first-person memoir. (This defense in and of itself obviously raises red flags as to the *Mémoires*' authenticity.) For good measure, Berryer asserted that Fouché's heirs deserved to lose control of their father's "voice" because of his "persecutions, incarcerations, [and] confiscations of works published in honor of the Bourbons."[452] Le Rouge's chances of prevailing on this unorthodox legal basis were not helped at all when it aggressively published the second (and final) volume of the *Mémoires* right in the middle of the proceedings, an act that apparently angered the court and which resulted in the printer being joined as a defendant as well. It also provoked an open letter in the newspapers from an aggrieved bookseller named Delaunay, who asserted that "numerous passages" in the new volume have been "taken literally from the *Manuscript of 1813* of which I was the editor."[453]

As the trial continued and drew increasing public attention, it developed that the "editors" of Fouché's *Mémoires* were two individuals who both had strong royalist leanings and connections to Fouché as former police agents. The first member of the notorious duo was Alphonse de Beauchamp, who had been a security officer for the Committee of Public Safety and for the Directory, and who had served as a Ministry of Police watchdog over the press while writing numerous planted articles in *Le Moniteur* and other journals. In 1807, Beauchamp had also written a history of the wars against the *Chouans* and in the Vendée, and this work had gotten him into serious trouble with Fouché because he had apparently failed to obtain advance authorization for it and because it was too slanted towards the insurgents' cause for the official line at that time.[454] After enduring years of internal exile and pervasive surveillance, Beauchamp harbored a significant grudge against his former boss. In 1822, two years before the publication of the *Mémoires*, Beauchamp wrote the then director general of the Bourbons' Ministry of Police seeking employment and stating that "I am the victim, as you know, of an arbitrary act of the regicide Fouché who, depriving me of employment, made me forfeit fourteen years of work and public service."[455]

The second Le Rouge "editor" to come into the public eye as a result of the litigation was one Pierre-Louis-Pascal Jullian. In his case, Bourbon sympathies went farther back than Beauchamp's: Jullian had attempted to rescue Louis XVI when the King was arrested at Varennes in 1791 and had languished in revolutionary prison as a result. After he was liberated thanks to the post-Robespierre Thermidorian reaction, he had denounced Fouché's accomplice at Lyon, Collot d'Herbois, and headed up an anti-Jacobin vigilante group. The ever-pragmatic Fouché had made use of his services during the siege of Antwerp in 1809, and thereafter in Italy as a special agent at the court of Murat.[456]

The royalist credentials of its two editors were not sufficient to save the publisher Le Rouge and its co-defendant printer from courtroom defeat, and the involvement of Beauchamp in the creation of other apocryphal memoirs as well as with prior libel and plagiarism charges probably helped to seal it.[457] At the end of a two-month trial, the presiding judge ruled that the work was fraudulent, that the plates used to print the Le Rouge *Mémoires* were to be broken, that copies of the two books were to be retrieved and destroyed, and that the children of the Duke of Otranto were entitled to receive damages as well, based on those volumes which could not be retrieved. The surviving first editions became, of course, extremely rare collector's items, and a number of subsequent editions would be printed in the future. [458]

⚜

But what of the style and content of the disputed work? Both volumes, particularly the second, contain many extremely long and tedious passages of narrative filler (e.g., the war in Spain and Portugal, the invasion of Russia, the numbing details of territorial adjustments and naval deployments), which imperial episodes were common knowledge and, for the most part, tangential to Fouché's experience and career; awkwardly inserted first-person explicatory references to third-party informants (e.g., "I learned from my correspondents"); huge narrative gaps (e.g., no mentions of de-Christianization, the massacre in Lyon, the entente with Talleyrand, the subornation of Augereau); occasional lame explanations of these gaps ("I must limit the range of my excursion and condense my narrative"; "This framework is immense; and that is an additional reason to set aside all that is unworthy of the graving tool"[459]); easily manufactured ex-post-facto opinions ("Spain, the gulf in which Napoleon was about to plunge, raised in me many gloomy forebodings"[460]); some ridiculously stilted and histrionic dialogue (e.g., "'Unfortunate man!' said I unto him, 'you have introduced yourself into my cabinet by means of a subterfuge.' 'Yes,' cried he, 'my life is in your hands, and if it be necessary, I shall willingly sacrifice it for my God and my king.' 'No,' rejoined I, 'you are seated on my hearth, and I will not violate the hospitality due to misfortune . . .'"[461]); and glaring inconsistencies (e.g., the author asserts that during his 1810 disgrace he had no fear of Napoleon's vengeance and then four pages later he refers to his "sleepless nights"[462]). There are numerous errors, including with regard to the street address of the "author's" Paris residence; a particularly egregious one has Fouché stating that he received his dukedom after Napoleon's victory of Austerlitz in 1806 when, as we have seen, he in fact received it after the victory at Wagram and on the Emperor's birthday in August of 1809.[463] The account of Fouché's unauthorized peace initiative of 1809-10 omits pivotal figures Louis Bonaparte and Pierre-Cèsar Labouchère, and makes no mention of Napoleon's forceful but unsuccessful demand that Fouché hand over his dossiers.[464] And there is blatant politicization of the work: in the rushed-out second volume, in remarking upon the Bourbons' First Restoration in 1814, "Fouché" asserts that he was "[m]oved, I confess, by the affecting picture of royal affability, intermingling with royalist intoxication, I was subjugated by the feeling." The French editor (probably Beauchamp, sounding suspiciously like the florid and melodramatic "voice" of Fouché which is elsewhere on display), thereupon decides to ladle it on very thickly by adding his own sycophantic footnote, stating:

> What a sublime and affecting spectacle was that return of a son of France on the immortal day of the 12th of April, 1814. That spectacle affected the soul of a regicide; the feeling of remorse overcomes him; he recognizes in the great catastrophe

> the hand of Divine Providence, which prepared, ten years before, the way for the mild and paternal rule of Charles X. [Again, this is a reference to the new monarch. Six years later the former Comte d'Artois would provoke his own ouster and exile by suspending the Constitution he so despised and in so doing, trigger the July 1830 revolution and the permanent loss of the French throne by the senior branch of the House of Bourbon.][465]

And yet. There are several quotations in the first volume which, while impossible to verify, do ring rather true, perhaps because they may actually have been directly or indirectly captured by the editors from Fouché himself in some way and at some point: "I thought and I still think, that it is better to prevent criminal attempts than subsequently to exert the power of punishing them"; "Bonaparte was then the only man in a position to maintain us in the possession of our property, our distinctions, our employments"; "I have avoided more evil than was permitted me to do"; "In my own secret mind I saw nothing in this result but an ill-formed and dangerous piece of work." [466] Perhaps these excerpts are nothing more than examples of the more elegant turns of phrase created by the experienced fabricator Beauchamp and by his collaborator Jullian, or perhaps, as the great French historian Louis Madelin has argued, the two "editors" actually had somehow obtained access to portions of Fouché's writings pertaining to events which are covered in somewhat more convincing fashion in the first volume, writings that were not included among the papers putatively burned at his death-bed instructions.[467] Madelin, who seemingly conceded the fabricated nature of much of the second volume, also argued that Fouché's survivors, settling comfortably into aristocratic ways, did not want the *Mémoires* to see the light of day.[468] But this ignores the fact that Le Rouge's concoction, replete with examples of the regicide's remorse, his strident anti-Bonapartism, and the gaping omission of his revolutionary excesses, may have been as flattering a portrait of the plaintiffs' father as they were ever likely to get during the retributive Second Restoration. In any event, it is entirely appropriate that this literary legacy of Fouché is one that is highly assailable, at least quasi-spurious, and shrouded in controversy and deceit. It is also perhaps fitting that the fraudulent aspects of the work were contributed by the "editorial" hands of two individuals who had honed their duplicitous skills during the heyday of the Third Division of the Ministry of Police, and who then revealed themselves as vengeful former pawns.

⚜

Let us now return to the opening epigraph taken from the epic poem by Victor Hugo, and observe as Death opens "the fatal ledger." What can possibly be said in defense of the real Joseph Fouché before this grim and final arbiter? That he was a devoted family man who had consistently led a sober, settled, and mundane domestic existence, in spite of his tremendous wealth, is undisputed. But that immediately brings to mind Hannah Arendt's famous reflection on "the banality of evil."[469] That Fouché's actions in late June and early July of 1815 may have saved the city of Paris from being razed had the Allies ultimately been victorious following a protracted French resistance can certainly be argued. But that outcome was very much in doubt, and here one notes the rebuke of British Foreign Secretary Sir Anthony Eden that "there are worse things than the destruction of cities."[470] Eden was commenting upon the devil's bargain made in June of 1940 by the aged Marshal Henri Pétain in capitulating to and soon collaborating with the enemy: the vacant City of Light was thereby kept intact for a triumphal personal inspection visit by the Führer, at the expense of the honor and dignity of France. And that Fouché in his three successive tours as Minister of Police did not perpetrate wanton mass executions, nor engineer waves of deportations, nor establish concentration camps (although his ministry's prison-system population was certainly robust) may also be factored favorably into this final accounting. However, as we have seen, he had demonstrated himself quite capable of the most depraved cruelty in 1793 Lyon. Thereafter, he simply found that committing such revolting atrocities was unnecessary and counterproductive. The more mature and seasoned Fouché would have adroitly coerced, cajoled, and converted his Lyonnais captives into becoming heavily surveilled agents and informants, instead of exterminating them.

Turning to his amazing virtuousity in intrigue, betrayal, and sheer survival, one is tempted to conclude that this is the essence of Fouché's life and legacy. Louis XVI, Robespierre, Barras, Napoleon, Lafayette, and Davout comprised his most imposing personal trophies. As we have seen, the supporting cast of his duped victims was legion. Napoleon in exile observed that Fouché's very lifeblood was intrigue, that "he intrigued all the time, everywhere, in every manner, and with everyone."[471] Surely, the most direct road to ruin for anyone was to act in furtherance of Fouché's career: witness the manipulated Gracchus Babeuf, the disgraced Joachim Murat, the toppled Élisa Bonaparte, the compromised Louis XVIII. Certainly, Fouché's protean yet consistent facilities for promoting himself as indispensable, for seemingly being worth far more positioned on the inside than on the outside, for sensing and predicting not only the course of events but also how to exploit them to his own insidious advantage, are simply breathtaking.

However, one can point to an even more sweeping and profound legacy of this chameleonic antihero, a legacy with more chilling ramifications than the transfixing litany of course reversals, shattered allegiances, and opportunites cleverly snatched from disastrous events. Joseph Fouché transformed the mission of the police from that of arresting criminals and breaking up riots into that of a preventive political role, of anticipating and suppressing dissent before it boiled out into the streets. But he accomplished far more than launching surgical preemptive strikes at nascent or hypothetical enemies of the state. He carefully constructed his own bureaucracy which, fueled by legions of police spies and paid police informants, collected intelligence on anything and anyone, not necessarily because it had immediate use or apparent value, but because knowledge itself was seen to be power, potential power to be exercised, perhaps sooner or perhaps later, but always held in reserve. He shaped public opinion via his control of the media and via his infiltration of the full spectrum of political, cultural, and social organizations. And as his own bureaucracy grew, it relentlessly impinged upon the purviews of other state bureaucracies and power centers – that of the interior ministry, which he actually subsumed for a time; that of foreign policy and diplomacy, with his agents avidly collecting and transmitting data from around the world and not just domestically, and with the Minister of Police himself engaging in unauthorized negotiations of the highest order with Great Britain in 1810; and that of the army: witness his mobilization of the National Guard in 1809 on a scale which the Emperor never would have countenanced, his activation of the Conspiracy of the North in 1815, and his clever elimination of Marshal Davout's formidable force of defenders from the gates of Paris several months later. Moreover, "popular" electoral processes and the mechanisms of royal succession - be they Bonapartist or Bourbon - were fair game for his clandestine interference.

⚜

In 1805, the Ministry of Police distributed a curious circular which Fouché may well have authored or at least edited and which he undoubtedly approved. It contained the following stunning mission statement for the police, expressed as a strange amalgam of physics and theology. It has a distinctly Oratorian ring to it:

> The regulating [police] power which can be felt everywhere without being in any way visible, holds in the center of the State the same place which is held in the Universe by the power which maintains the harmony of celestial bodies, a power which impresses us with its regularity without our being able to understand its cause . . . Each of the branches of the administration has a part which is subordinated to that of the police.[472]

The police were no longer to be a mere servant of government or the tool of a regime: they were to act as the centripetal force, the very essence of power and legitimacy.

⚜

Inexorably, this systemic regulating power of Fouché's Ministry of Police developed the requisite resources and weapons — not just and not even principally brutish repression, but propaganda, censorship, intelligence, surveillance, provocations, the ability to penetrate and corrupt the electoral system — the whole arsenal of devices that were available in the early nineteenth century. It vastly perfected these tools beyond anything that had preceded them. All the while, Fouché carefully positioned his monstrous creation to take over control of the State itself. We have witnessed how he relentlessly undermined and brought down the Emperor Napoleon and briefly became the acting president of France. In the next century, SS Reichsführer and Minister of the Interior (with control over the Gestapo) Heinrich Himmler would attempt to supplant Adolf Hitler during the final death throes of Nazism, while frantically and delusionally seeking a deal with the Allies which would allow him to continue as the head of the German police. Several years later, the malevolent NKVD overlord Lavrenti Beria would effect the demise of his own formidable boss, Joseph Stalin, who had once patronizingly and at his own peril, although likely also admiringly, referred to him as "our Himmler."[473] Begining with Fouché, the security state within the State, no longer a mere defensive shield or handy implement, would voraciously seek to overwhelm and eclipse the State. That most police state malignancies have not yet been successful in terms of longevity, gives us no assurance that, as their arsenals continue to evolve towards technological perfection, pernicious outcomes can ultimately be averted.

Thus, to answer squarely Death's pointed question, posed in the opening epigraph (and adroitly ducked by Victor Hugo's respondent in a most Fouché-esque manner), the historic forces that were molded and unleashed by Minister of Police Joseph Fouché ever threaten to place *both* the severed head of the people *and* that of the king into the "sinister basket."

Appendix: The Act of Proscription of July 24, 1815

"Desirous, by the punishment of an attempt without example, but graduating the penalty, and limiting the number of the guilty — of conciliating the interest of our subjects, the dignity of our crown, and the tranquility of Europe, with what we owe to justice and to the full security of all other citizens, without distinction, we have declared and do declare, have ordered, and do order as follows:

"Art. I. The generals and officers who have betrayed the King before the 23rd of March, or who have attacked France and the government by force of arms, and those who by violence have possessed themselves of power, shall be seized and brought before the competent courts-martial in their respective divisions; viz. Ney, Labédoyère, Lallemand senior, Lallemand junior, Drouet d'Erlon, Lefebvre, Desnouettes, Ameil, Brayer, Gilly, Mouton-Duvernet, Grouchy, Clausel, Laborde, Debelle, Bertrand, Drouot, Cambronne, Lavalette, and Rovigo [i.e., Savary].

"Art. II. The individuals whose names here follow: viz. Soult, Alix, Excelmans, Bassano, Marbot, Felix Lepelletier, Boulay de la Meurthe, Méhée, Freissinet, Thibeaudeau, Carnot, Vandamme, General Lamarque, Lobau, Harel, Piré, Barrère, Arnault, Pommereul, Regnault de St. Jean d'Angely, Arrighi de Padoue, Dejean jun., Garrau, Réal, Bouvier, Dumolard, Merlin (de Douai), Durback, Dirat, Defermon, Bory de St-Vincent, Félix Desportes, Garnier (de Saintes), Hullin, Mellinet, Cluys, Courtin, Forbin-Janson jun., Lelorgne d'Ideville, - shall quit Paris in three days, and shall retire to the interior of France, to the places which will be indicated by our minister of general police, and where they shall remain under his superintendence, until the Chambers shall declare which of them are to quit the kingdom, or to be sent for trial before the tribunals.

"Art. III. Those individuals who shall be condemned to quit the kingdom shall have the power of selling their estates and property, within the term of one year; to dispose of and transport the produce out of France, and to receive during this period the revenue thereof in foreign countries on condition, however, of furnishing the proof of their obedience to the present ordinance.

"Art IV. The lists of all the individuals to whom Articles I and II may be applicable, are and shall remain closed by the names designated in these articles, and can never be extended to others for any cause or pretext whatsoever, other wise than in the forms and according to the constitutional laws; from which deviation is only made for this special case.

(Signed) Louis

"By the King.
The Minister Secretary of State for the police department.
(Signed) Duke of Otranto"

Index

G

H

J

K

L

M

N

O

P

R

S

T

V

W

Bibliography

Adams, Michael, *Napoleon and Russia*. New York: Hambledon, 2006.

Alary, Eric, *L'Histoire de la Gendarmerie: de la Renaissance au IIIe millénaire*. Paris: Calmann-Lévy, 2000.

Andress, David, *The French Revolution and the People*. London: Hambledon, 2003.

Andress, David, *The Terror: Civil War in the French Revolution*. London: Little, Brown, 2005.

Andrew, Christopher and Vasili Mitrokhin, *The Sword and the Shield: the Mitrokhin Archive and the secret history of the KGB*. New York: Basic Books, 2001.

Arendt, Hannah, *Eichmann in Jerusalem: a report on the banality of evil*. New York: Penguin, 2006.

Armstrong, Eva, and Hiram Lukens, "Jean-Antoine Chaptal, Comte de Chanteloupe," *Journal of Chemical Education*. 1936 13 (6).

Arnold, James R, *Crisis on the Danube: Napoleon's Austrian campaign of 1809*. New York, Paragon House, 1990.

Auger, Antoine, J. Garnier, et al., *Napoléon Bonaparte*. Paris: Larousse, 2004.

Baczko, Bronislaw, *Ending the Terror: the French Revolution after Robespierre*. New York: Cambridge University Press, 1994.

Barante, Amable-Guillaume-Prosper, *Souvenirs du baron de Barante . . . 1782-1866*. Paris: Calmann Lévy, 1890-1901.

Bardoux, A., *Madame de Custine, d'après des documents inédits*. Paris: Calmann Lévy, 1891.

Barras, Paul, *Mémoires de Barras, membre du Directoire*. Paris: Hachette, 1895.

Barton, D. Plunket, *Bernadotte and Napoleon, 1763-1810*. London: J. Murray, 1921.

Beach, Vincent W., *Charles X of France: His Life and Times*. Boulder, Colo.: Pruett Pub. Co., 1971.

Belloc, Hillaire, *Robespierre, a study*. New York: Charles Scribner's Sons, 1901.

Benoit, Bruno, and Roland Saussac, *Guide Historique de la Révolution à Lyon: 1789-1799*. Lyon: Editions de Trévoux, 1988.

Bertaud, Jean Paul, *Bonaparte et le duc d'Enghien; le duel des deux France*. Paris: R. Laffont, 1972.

Bertaud, Jean Paul, *Le duc d'Enghien*. Paris: Fayard, 2001.

Bertier de Sauvigny, Guillaume de, *The Bourbon Restoration*. Philadelphia: University of Pennsylvania Press, 1967.

Bertier de Sauvigny, Guillaume de, *Metternich*. Paris: Fayard, 1998.

Beugnot, Jacques-Claude, comte, *Mémoires du comte Beugnot: ancien ministre (1783-1815)*. Paris: E. Dentu, 1889.

Biard, Michel, *Collot d'Herbois: légendes noires et Révolution*. Lyon: Presses universitaires de Lyon, 1995.

Boudon, Jacques-Olivier, *Le roi Jérôme: frère prodigue de Napoléon, 1784-1860*. Paris: Fayard, 2008.

Bourrienne, Louis Antoine Fauvelet de, and R.W. Phipps (ed.), *Memoirs of Napoleon Bonaparte*. New York: Merrill and Baker, 1885.

Bourrienne, Louis Antoine Fauvelet de, *Mémoires de M. de Bourrienne, ministre d'état; sur Napoléon, le directoire, le consulat, l'empire et la restauration*. Paris: Lavocat, 1829.

Brougham and Vaux, Henry Brougham, Baron, *Historical Sketches of Statesmen Who Flourished in the Time of George III*. Philadelphia: Lea and Blanchard, 1844.

Buisson, Henry, *La Police: son histoire*. Paris: Nouvelles Éditions Latines, 1958.

Cambacérès, Jean Jacques Regis de, *Mémoires inédits: éclaircissements publiés par Cambacérès sur les principaux événements de sa vie politique*. Paris: Perrin, 1999.

Campbell, Peter R., T. E. Kaiser, et al., *Conspiracy in the French Revolution*. New York: Manchester University Press, 2007.

Caratini, Roger, *Dictionnaire des Personnages de la Révolution*. Paris: Le Pré aux clercs, 1988.

Carrot, Georges, *Histoire de la Police Francaise: tableaux, chronologie, iconographie*. Paris: J. Tallandier, 1992.

Castelot, André, *Napoléon Bonaparte*. Paris: Libr. académique Perrin, 1984.
Castelot, André, *Fouché: le double jeu*. Paris: Perrin, 1989.
Caulaincourt, Armand Augustin Louis, marquis de, *Mémoires du Général de Caulaincourt*. Paris: Plon, 1933.
Caulincourt [sic], Armand Augustin Louis, marquis de, *Napoleon and His Times*. Philadelphia: E. L. Carey & A. Hart, 1838.
Chaix d'Est-Ange, G., *Dictionnaire des Familles Francaises Anciennes ou Notables à la Fin du XIXe Siècle*. Évreux: C. Hérissey, 1903.
Chandler, David G., *Napoleon's Marshals*. London: Weidenfeld and Nicolson, 1987.
Chaptal, Jean-Antoine-Claude, comte de Chanteloup, *Mes souvenirs sur Napoléon*. Paris: E. Plon, 1893.
Charrier, Pierre, *Le Maréchal Davout*. Paris: Nouveau monde, 2005.
Chaboulon, Fleury de, *Mémoires de Fleury de Chaboulon*. Paris: L. Cornet, 1901.
Chastenay, Madame de, *Deux Révolutions pour une Seule Vie: mémoires, 1771-1855*. Paris: Tallandier, 2009.
Chateaubriand, Francois-René, *The Memoirs of Francois René, Vicomte de Chateaubriand, sometime ambassador to England: being a translation by Alexander Teixeira de Mattos of the Mémoires d'outre-tombe*. London: Freemantle and Co., 1902.
Cole, Hubert, *The Betrayers — Joachim and Caroline Murat*. London: Eyre Methuen Ltd., 1972.
Conrad, Joseph, *The Duel: a military tale*. Garden City, N.Y.: Garden City Publishing Co., 1924.
Conte, Arthur, *"Sire, ils ont voté la mort."* Évreux: le Cercle du bibliophile, 1971.
Couturaud, Laurence, *Augereau: l'enfant maudit de la gloire*. Paris: H. Veyrier, 1990.
Crook, Malcolm, *Napoleon Comes to Power: democracy and dictatorship in revolutionary France, 1795-1804*. Cardiff: University of Wales Press, 1998.
Cubberly, Ray E., *The Role of Fouché During the Hundred Days*. Madison: State Historical Society of Wisconsin for the Dept. of History, University of Wisconsin, 1969.
Dallas, Gregor, *The Final Act: the roads to Waterloo*. New York: Henry Holt, 1996.

Davout, Louis Nicolas, duc d'Auerstadt, *Correspondance du Maréchal Davout, prince d'Eckmühl*. Paris: E. Plon, Nourrit et cie., 1885.

De Polnay, Peter, *Napoleon's Police*. London: W. H. Allen, 1970.

Débordes, Jean, *Les Mystères de l'Allier: histoires insolites, étranges, criminelles et extraordinaires*. Clermont-Ferrand: De Borée, 2001.

Desmarest, Pierre-Marie, *Quinze Ans de Haute Police sous le Consulat et l'Empire*. Paris: Garnier frères, 1900.

Despatys, Omer, *Un Ami de Fouché d'apres les Mémoires de Gaillard*. Paris: Plon-Nourrit, 1911.

DuPâquier, Jacques (ed.), *Carrier: procès d'un missionaire de la Terreur*. [Paris?]: Editions des Etannets, 1994.

Dwyer, Philip G., *Talleyrand*. New York: Longman, 2002.

Edmonds, W. D., *Jacobinism and the Revolt of Lyon, 1789-1793*. New York: Oxford University Press, 1990.

Epstein, Robert W., review of *Napoleon's Finest: Davout and His 3rd Corps* by Matthew Delameter et al., in *Journal of Military History*. Vol. 71., no. 2 (April 2007).

Espitalier, Albert, *Napoleon and King Murat*. Felling, Tyne & Wear [England]: Worley Publications with Brigade Library, 1998.

Esposito, Vincent J. and J. R. Elting, *A Military History and Atlas of the Napoleonic Wars*. New York: Praeger, 1964.

Etèvenaux, Jean, *Fouché: Nantes, Nevers, Moulins, Lyon, Paris, itinéraires d'un révolutionnaire*. Bourg-en-Bresse [France]: La Taillanderie, 1990.

Falloux du Coudray, Alfred-Frédéric-Pierre, comte de, and C. B. Pitman (ed.), *Memoirs of the Count de Falloux*. London: Chapman and Hall, 1888.

Fay, Sidney B., "The Execution of the Duc d'Enghien II," *The American Historical Review*, vol. 4 no. 1 (Oct. 1898).

Forssell, Nils, and Anna Barwell (trans.), *Fouché, the Man Napoleon Feared*. London: Allen & Unwin, 1928.

Fouché, Joseph, duc d'Otrante, *Letter [January 1, 1816] of M. Fouché, Duke of Otranto, to the Duke of Wellington*. London: H. Colburn, 1818.

Fouché, Joseph, duc d'Otrante [purported author], *The Memoirs of Joseph Fouché, Duke of Otranto, Minister of the General Police of France*. London, Charles Knight, 1825.

Fouché, Joseph, duc d'Otrante [purported author] and Louis Madelin (ed.), *Les Mémoires de Fouché*. Paris: Flammarion, 1947.

Fouché, Joseph, duc d'Otrante [purported author] and Michel Vovelle (ed.), *Mémoires de Joseph Fouché, duc d'Otrante*. Paris: Imprimerie nationale, 1992.

Fouché, Joseph, duc d'Otrante, *Réflexions de J. Fouché, (de Nantes) sur le jugement de Louis Capet*. Paris: Imprimerie nationale, 1793.

Fouché, Joseph, *Réflexions de Fouché (de Nantes), sur les calomnies répandues contre lui*. Paris: Imprimerie nationale, 1795.

Fouché, Joseph, duc d'Otrante, *Second report made to Louis XVIII being an inquiry into the present state of France by the Duke of Otranto, then Minister of the General Police, a few days previous to his departure from the ministry*. New York: A.T. Goodrich, 1815.

Gallaher, J. G., *The Iron Marshal: a biography of Louis N. Davout*. Carbondale: Southern Illinois University Press, 1976.

Gamichon, Louis, *Napoléon et les Lyonnais 1779-1815*. Lyon: Editions Bellier, 2001.

Garnier, Jean Paul, *Barras, le Roi du Directoire*. Paris: Perrin, 1970.

Goethe, Johann Wolfgang von, and R. Farie (trans.), *Campaign in France in the Year 1792*. London: Chapman and Hall, 1849.

Gourgaud, Gaspard, Baron, and Sydney Gillard (trans.), *The St. Helena Journal of General Baron Gourgaud, 1815-1818; being a diary written at St. Helena during a part of Napoleon's captivity*. London: John Lane, 1932.

Gueniffey, Patrice, "Robespierre," *A Critical Dictionary of the French Revolution*, Francis Furet and Mona Ozouf, ed., Cambridge, MA: Belknap, 1989.

Hall, John R., *General Pichegru's Treason*. London: Smith, Elder, 1915.

Hardman, John, *Robespierre*. New York: Addison Wesley Longman, 1999.

Hauterive, Ernest d', *Napoléon et Sa Police*. Paris: Flammarion, 1944.

Hauterive, Ernest d' (ed.), *La Police Secrète du Premier Empire: bulletins quotidiens addressés par Fouché à l'empereur*. Paris: Perrin, 1908-64.

Hearsey, John E. N., *Marie Antoinette*. London: Constable, 1972.

Herriot, Edouard, *Lyon n'est plus . . .* Paris: Hachette, 1937.

Horricks, Raymond, *Military Politics from Bonaparte to the Bourbons: the life and death of Michel Ney, 1769-1815*. New Brunswick: Transaction Publishers, 1995.

Hortense, Queen, consort of Louis Bonaparte, and Arthur Griggs (trans.), et al., *The Memoirs of Queen Hortense*. New York: Cosmopolitan Book Corp., 1927.

Houssaye, Henry, *1815: la première restauration, le retour de l'ile d'Elbe, les cent jours*. Paris: Perrin, 1894.

Houssaye, Henry, *1815: la seconde abdication, la terreur blanche*. Paris: Perrin, 1918.

Hulot, Frédéric, *Le Maréchal Ney*. Paris: Pygmalion, 2000.

Hyde de Neuville, Jean Guillaume, Baron, *Mémoires et Souvenirs du Baron Hyde de Neuville*. Paris: E. Plon, 1888.

Jordan, David P., *The Revolutionary Career of Maximilien Robespierre*. New York: Free Press, 1985.

Kieswetter, James, "Étienne-Denis Pasquier: The Last Chancellor of France," *Transactions of the American Philosophical Society*. Vol. 67, no. 1 (1977).

Kirchberger, Joe H., *The French Revolution and Napoleon: an eyewitness history*. New York: Facts on File, 1989.

La Revellière-Lépeaux, Louis-Marie de, *Mémoires*. Paris: E. Plon, 1895.

Lacour-Gayet, Georges, *Talleyrand, 1754-1838*. Paris: Payot, 1928.

Lacour-Gayet, Michel, *Joachim et Caroline Murat*. Paris: Perrin, 1996.

Lafayette, Marquis de, and H. Fournier (ed.), *Mémoires, Correspondance et Manuscrits du General Lafayette*. Paris: H. Fournier, 1838.

Lamartine, Alphonse de, *The History of the Restoration of Monarchy in France*. New York: Harper & Brothers, 1851.

Lavisse, E. and Philippe. *Histoire de France Contemporaine depuis la Révolution jusqu'à la Paix de 1919*. Paris: Hachette, 1920.

Lawday, David, *Napoleon's Master: a life of Prince Talleyrand*. London: Jonathan Cape, 2006.

Le Blond, Yves, *Gouvion Saint-Cyr, Maréchal de l'Empire: pour que vive la République*. Nantes: Normant, 2008.

Le Clère, Marcel, *Histoire de la Police*. Paris: Presses universitaires de France, 1964.

Le Nabour, Eric, *Barras: le vicomte rouge*. Paris: J.C. Lattes, 1982.

Lebrique, Arlette, "Les Régicides," *Le Bicentaire du Procès du Roi*, ed. Charles Goyard, et al. Paris: F.-X. de Guibert, 1993.

Lefebvre, Georges, and Henry F. Stockhold (trans.), *Napoleon, from 18 Brumaire to Tilsit, 1799-1807.* New York: Columbia University Press, 1969.

Legrand, Robert, *Babeuf et Ses Compagnons de Route.* Paris: Société des études Robespierristes, 1981.

Lenôtre, G. [pseudo.], and M. K .Stawell (trans.), *The Last Days of Marie Antoinete* [sic]. Philadelphia: J.B. Lippincott 1907.

Lentz, Thierry, *Le 18-Brumaire: les coups d'état de Napoléon Bonaparte (novembre-décembre 1799).* Paris: Jean Picollec, 1997.

Lentz, Thierry, *Savary: le séide de Napoléon.* Paris: Fayard, 2001.

Linton, Marisa, "'Do You Believe That We're Conspirators?': conspiracies real and imagined in Jacobin politics, 1793-94," in *Conspiracy in the French Revolution*, P. Campbell (ed.) et al. New York: Manchester Univ. Press, 2007.

Liris, E., *L'Allier en Révolution: sur les pas de Joseph Fouché, représentant en mission, en 1793.* Saint-Julien-Chapteuil: Roure, 2000.

Longford, Elizabeth, *Wellington.* New York: Harper & Row, 1969.

Louis Bonaparte, ex-Roi de Hollande, *Documens* [sic] *Historiques et Réflexions sur le Gouvernement de la Hollande.* London: Lackington, Hughes, 1820.

Macdonald, Etienne-Jacques, duc de Tarente, and Camille Rousset (ed.) et al., *Recollections of Marshal MacDonald, Duke of Tarentum.* New York: Charles Scribner's, 1893.

Maceroni, Francis, *Memoirs of the Life and Adventures of Colonel Maceroni.* London: J. Macrone, 1838.

Madelin, Louis, and E. F. Buckley (trans.), *The Consulate and the Empire.* London: W. Heinemann, 1934.

Madelin, Louis, *Fouché.* Paris: Plon, 1901.

Mansel, Philip, *Louis XVIII.* London: Blond & Briggs, 1981.

Mansfield, Paul, "The Repression of Lyon, 1793-94: Origins, Responsibility, and Significance," *French History.* 1988 2 (1).

Marmottan, Paul, "La Grande-Duchesse Élisa et Fouché," *Revue d'Histoire Diplomatique.* Oct.-Dec. 1926.

Martel, Arnaud Louis Raoul, Comte de, *Types Révolutionnaires: étude sur Fouché et sur le communisme dans la pratique en 1793.* Paris: E. Lachaud, 1873.

Masson, Frédéric, and J. E. Matthew (trans.), *Napoleon at Home; the daily life of the Emperor at the Tuileries.* Philadelphia: J.B. Lippincott, 1894.

Matrat, Jean, and Alan Kendall (trans.) et al., *Robespierre: or, the tyranny of the majority.* New York: Scribner, 1975.

Melchior-Bonnet, Bernadine, "Élisa Bonaparte," in *Dictionnaire Napoléon*, Jean Tulard ed. Paris: Fayard, 1989.

Melchior-Bonnet, Bernardine, *Le Procès de Louis XVI.* Paris: Perrin, 1992.

Méneval, Claude-Francois, Baron de, and Proctor Jones (ed.), et al., *Napoleon, an Intimate Account of the Years of Supremacy, 1800-1814.* New York: Random House, 1992.

Méneval, Claude-Francois, Baron de, and N. J. E. Méneval (ed.), et al., *Memoirs Illustrating the History of Napoleon I from 1802 to 1815.* New York: D. Appleton, 1894.

Metternich, Clemens Wenzel Lothar, Fürst von, and R. C. L. Metternich-Winneburg (ed.), et al., *Memoirs of Prince Metternich, 1773-1815.* New York: H. Fertig, 1970.

Michaud, L. G. (ed.), *Biographie Universelle, Ancienne et Moderne.* Paris: Michaud, 1811.

Molé, Louis-Mathieu, comte, *Le Comte Molé, 1781-1855: sa vie, ses mémoires.* Paris: E. Champion, 1922.

Mollien, Francois Nicolas, comte, *Mémoires d'un Ministre du Trésor Public 1780-1815.* Paris: Guillaumin, 1898.

Le Moniteur (Paris), No. 50, Decadi 20 Brumaire (Nov. 10, 1799), from *Réimpression de l'ancien Moniteur, seule histoire authentique et inalterée de la Révolution francaise depuis la réunion des États-Généraux*, vol. 29, Paris.

Le Moniteur Universel (Paris): 4 Avril, 1815; 6 Juillet, 1815 (no. 187); 9 Juillet (no. 190); 28 Août, 1820 (no. 241); 1 Septembre 1820 (no. 245); 16 Janvier, 1821 (no. 16); 4 Février, 1821 (no. 35); 6 Janvier 1825 (no. 6).

Le Monument Religieux des Brotteaux. Lyon: Éditions Lyonnaise d'arts et d'histoire, 1989.

Morris, Jan, *Trieste and the Meaning of Nowhere.* New York: Simon & Schuster, 2001.

Moulin, Michel, *Mémoires de Michelot Moulin sur la Chouannerie Normande.* Paris: A. Picard, 1893.

Mounier, Claude Philibert Edouard, and Comte d'Herisson (ed.), *Souvenirs Intimes et Notes du Baron Mounier, secrétaire de Napoléon ler, pair de France, directeur général de la police.* Paris: P. Ollendorff, 1896.

Nafziger, George F. and Marco Gioannini, *The Defense of the Napoleonic Kingdom of Northern Italy, 1813-1814.* Westport, Conn.: Praeger, 2002.

Napoleon I, Emperor of the French, and Henri Plon (ed.) et al., *Correspondance de Napoléon Ier.* Paris: Plon, 1858.

Napoleon I, Emperor of the French, and Michael Kerautret (ed.) et al., *Napoléon Bonaparte: correspondance générale.* Paris: Fayard, 2008.

Napoleon I, Emperor of the French, and J. J. S. A. Damas-Hinard (ed.), *Napoléon. Ses opinions et jugements sur les hommes et sur les choses.* Paris: Duféy, 1838.

Napoleon I, Emperor of the French, and J. M. Thompson (ed.), *Napoleon self-revealed, in three hundred selected letters.* New York: Houghton Miffin, 1934.

Napoleon I, Emperor of the French, and Jean Massin (ed.), *L'Oeuvre et l'Histoire.* Paris: Le Club francais du livre, 1969.

Ney, Michel, duc d'Elchingen, *Lettre de M. le maréchal prince de la Moskowa, a S. Exc. M. le duc d'Otrante, June 26, 1815.* Houghton Harvard Depository.

Nodier, Charles, *Souvenirs de la Révolution et de l'Empire.* Paris: Charpentier, 1850.

Oliver, A. Richard, *Charles Nodier, Pilot of Romanticism.* Syracuse, N.Y.: Syracuse University Press, 1964.

Ophuls, Marcel, *The Sorrow and the Pity; a film.* New York: Outerbridge & Lazard, 1972.

Orieux, Jean, and Patricia Wolf (trans.), *Talleyrand; the art of survival.* New York: Knopf, 1974.

Ouvrard, Gabriel-Julien, *Mémoires de G.-J. Ouvrard, sur sa vie et ses diverses opérations financières.* Paris: Moutardier, 1826.

Palmer, R. R., *Twelve Who Ruled: the year of the Terror in the French Revolution.* Princeton: Princeton University Press, 2005.

Pasquier, Étienne-Denis, and E. A. G. Audiffret-Pasquier (ed.), et al., *A History of My Time: memoirs of Chancellor Pasquier.* New York: C. Scribner's Sons, 1893.

Patrick, Alison, *The Men of the First French Republic; political alignments in the National Convention of 1792*. Baltimore: Johns Hopkins University Press, 1972.

Patrick, Alison, "Regicides and Anti-Regicides in January 1793: the significance of Joseph Fouché's vote," *Historical Studies*. Vol. 14, no. 55 (1970).

Pelletier, André, *Histoire de Lyon: de la capital des Gaules à la métropole européenne*. Lyon: Editions lyonnaises d'art et d'histoire, 2004.

Picaut, Jean-Étienne, *Madame Napoléon, Princesse Baciocchi*. Colpo: Liv'éditions, 2007.

Pierre, Michel Désiré, *Ney: du procès politique à la réhabilitation du "brave des braves," 1815-1991*. Paris: S.P.M., 2003.

Planat de La Faye, Nicolas Louis, *Vie de Planat de la Faye, Aide de camp des Généraux Laribosière et Drouot*. Paris: Paul Ollendorff, 1895.

Postic, Marcel, *Carrier et la Terreur à Nantes*. Paris: L'Harmattan, 2001.

Price, Munro, *The Perilous Crown: France between revolutions*. London: Macmillan, 2007.

Proudhon, Pierre-Joseph, and C. Rochel (ed.), *Commentaires sur les Mémoires de Fouché: suivis du parallèle entre Napoléon & Wellington*. Paris: Société d'Éditions Littéraires et Artistiques, 1900.

Quynn, Dorothy Mackay, "Destination: America, Marshal Ney's attempt to escape," *French Historical Studies*, Duke University Press, vol. 2, no. 2 (Autumn 1961).

Rain, Pierre, *L'Europe et la Restauration des Bourbons, 1814-1818*. Paris: Perrin, 1908.

Recoules, André, *Moulins, Yzeure, Avermes, Toulon-sur-Allier*. Thionne: Editions du Signe, 1995.

Révérend, Albert, *Armorial du Premier Empire: titres, majorats et armoiries concédés par Napoléon Ier*. Paris: H. Champion, 1974.

Rigotard, Jean, *La Police Parisienne de Napoléon: la préfecture de police*. Paris: Tallandier, 1990.

Roberts, Andrew, *Napoleon and Wellington*. London: Weidenfeld & Nicolson, 2001.

Roberts, J. M. (ed.), R. C. Cobb (ed.), et al., *French Revolution Documents*. Oxford: Blackwell, 1966.

Robiquet, Jean, and Violet MacDonald (trans.), *Daily Life in France under Napoleon*. New York: Macmillan, 1963.

Robiquet, Paul, "Fouché Pendant Les Cent Jours," *La Révolution Francaise.* Vol. 71, 1918.

Rose, R. B., *Gracchus Babeuf: the first revolutionary Communist.* London: Edward Arnold, 1978.

Rouchette, Thérèse, *Le dernier des régicides: Antoine-Claire Thibaudeau (1765-1854).* La Roche-sur-Yon: Centre vendéen de recherches historiques, 2000.

Rougeron, Georges, "Après les Bourbons," in *Allier Bourbonnais.* Paris: Encyclopédies Bonneton, 1979.

Sapori, Julien, *L'Exil et la Mort de Joseph Fouché: entre légende romanesque et vérité historique.* Parcay-sur-Vienne: Anovi, 2007.

Savant, Jean, *Les Ministres de Napoléon.* Paris: Hachette, 1959.

Savary, Anne-Jean-Marie-René, duc de Rovigo, *Extrait des mémoires de M. le duc de Rovigo concernant la catastrophe de M. le duc d'Enghien.* Paris: Chez Ponthieu, 1823.

Savary, Anne-Jean-Marie-René, duc de Rovigo, *Memoirs of the Duke of Rovigo,* London: H. Colburn, 1828.

Schama, Simon, *Citizens: A Chronicle of the French Revolution.* New York: Knopf, 1989.

Schama, Simon, *Patriots and Liberators: revolution in the Netherlands, 1780-1813.* New York: Knopf, 1977.

Sebag Montefiore, Simon, *Stalin: the court of the Red Tsar.* London: Weidenfeld & Nicolson, 2003.

Smith, W. H. C., *The Bonapartes: the history of a dynasty.* London: Hambledon, 2005.

Soboul, Albert, *Le Procès de Louis XVI.* Paris: Julliard, 1966.

Sournia, Jean-Charles, and Angela Dzelzainis (trans.), *A Guide to Revolutionary Paris.* Paris: Editions de Sante, 1989.

Sparrow, Elizabeth, *Secret Service: British agents in France, 1792-1815.* Rochester, NY: Boydell Press, 1999.

Staël, Madame de (Anne-Louis-Germaine), *Ten Years' Exile.* London: Treuttel and Würtz, 1821.

Stead, Philip John, *The Police of Paris.* London: Staples Press, 1957.

Stead, Philip John, *The Police of France.* New York: Macmillan, 1983 .

Stewart, John Hall, *The Restoration Era in France, 1814-1830.* Princeton: Van Nostrand, 1968.

Sutherland, Donald, *The French Revolution and Empire: the quest for a civic order.* Malden, MA: Blackwell, 2003.

Talleyrand-Périgord, Charles Maurice de, prince de Bénévent, and G. Pallain (ed.), *Correspondance Inédite du Prince de Talleyrand et du Roi Louis XVIII pendant le Congrès de Vienne*. Paris: E. Plon, 1881.

Talleyrand-Périgord, Charles Maurice de, prince de Bénévent, and duc de Broglie (ed.), et al., *Memoirs of the Prince de Talleyrand*, New York: Putnam, 1891.

Talleyrand-Périgord, Charles Maurice de, prince de Bénévent, and P. L. Couchoud (ed.), et al., *Mémoires, 1754-1815*. Paris: Plon, 1982.

Thibaudeau, Antoine-Claire, *Mémoires de A.-C. Thibaudeau*, 1799-1815. Paris: Plon, 1913.

Thiébault, Paul Charles Francois, Baron, *Mémoires du Général Bon [Baron] Thiébault*. Paris: Plon, 1895.

Thiers, Adolphe, *History of the Consulate and the Empire of France Under Napoleon*. London: Willis and Sotheran, 1861.

Thompson, J. M., "Napoleon's Journey to Elba in 1814. Part I. By Land," *The American Historical Review*. Vol. 55, no.1 (Oct. 1949).

Thompson, J. M., *Robespierre*. New York: Blackwell, 1988.

Thornton, Michael J., *Napoleon after Waterloo; England and the St. Helena decision*. Stanford: Stanford University Press, 1968.

Thorold, Algar Labouchere, *The Life of Henry Labouchere*. London: Constable, 1913.

Tondeur, Jean-Philippe, et al., *Charleroi: la journée du 15 Juin 1815*. Brussels: Editions de la Belle Alliance, 2011.

Tondeur, Jean-Philippe, *Walcheren 1809: l'expédition anglaise au jour le jour, les lettres de Napoléon à ses ministres*. Brussels: Editions de la Belle Alliance, 2009.

Tracy, Nicholas, *Who's Who in Nelson's Navy: 200 naval heroes*. London: Chatham, 2006.

Tranié, Jean and J. C. Carmigniani, *Napoléon et l'Angleterre: vingt-deux ans d'affrontements sur terre et sur mer, 1793-1815*. Paris: Pygmalion, 1994.

Tulard, Jean (ed.), *Dictionnaire Napoléon*. Paris: Fayard, 1989.

Tulard, Jean, *Le 18 Brumaire: comment terminer une révolution*. Paris: Perrin, 1999.

Tulard, Jean, *Les Thermidoriens*, Paris: Fayard, 2005.

Turquan, Joseph, and W. R. H. Trowbridge (trans.), *The Sisters of Napoleon: Elisa, Pauline, and Caroline Bonaparte after the testimony of their contemporaries.* New York: Charles Scribner's Sons, 1908.

Vartier, Jean, *Fanfan-la-conspiration, ou, La vie aventureuse de Charles Nodier.* Jarville-la-Malgrange: Est Republicain, 1986.

Vidal, Florence, *Caroline Bonaparte.* Paris: Pygmalion, 2006.

Vitrolles, Eugène Francois Auguste d'Arnaud, Baron, and Eugené Forgues et al., *Mémoires.* Paris: Gallimard, 1950.

Vyshinsky, Andrey, "The Treason Case Summed Up," *Soviet Russia Today.* Vol. 7, no. 2, April, 1938, transcribed by *Red Flag Magazine.*

Waldburg, Friedrich Ludwig Truchsess, Graf von, *Nouvelle Relation de l'Itinéraire de Napoléon, de Fontainbleau à l'Ile d'Elbe.* Paris: Panckoucke, 1815.

Walzer, Michael (ed.), *Regicide and Revolution; speeches at the trial of Louis XVI.* New York: Cambridge University Press, 1974.

Weil, M. H., *Le Prince Eugène et Murat, 1813-1814; opérations militaires, négociations diplomatiques.* Paris: A. Fontemoing, 1902.

Wellington, Arthur Wellesley, Duke of, and Lt. Col. Garwood (ed.), *The Dispatches of Field Marshal the Duke of Wellington 1799 to 1818.* London: J. Murray, 1838.

Wellington, Arthur Wellesley, Duke of, and A. R. W. Wellington (ed.), *Supplementary Despatches and Memoranda of Field Marshal Arthur, Duke of Wellington, K. G.* London: J. Murray, 1858.

Wise, Thomas A., "Life and Naval Career of Admiral Sir Richard Strachan," *Transactions of the Royal Historical Society.* Vol. ii (1883).

Wismes, Armel de, *Le Vieux Nantes.* France: Infolio, 1992.

Zins, Ronald, 1814, *L'Armée de Lyon: ultime espoir de Napoléon.* Massieux: H. Cardon, 1998.

Endnotes

1 The debate at the Palace as to the identity of the perpetrators is related in *The Memoirs of Queen Hortense*, Jean Hanoteau (ed.), vol. i, 54 (Hortense being a survivor of the Rue Nicaise blast), and in Louis-Antoine Bourriennne's *Mémoires de M. de Bourrienne*, vol. iv, 202-03; it is also treated in Hyde de Neuville's *Mémoires et Souvenirs du Baron Hyde Neuville*, 360.
2 Rigotard, Jean, *La Police Parisienne de Napoléon*, 86-67.
3 Among the deportees after the Rue Nicaise attempt were several left-wing legislative deputies who had opposed Napoleon's coup bringing him to power in 1799. Lefebvre, Georges, *Napoleon from 18 Brumaire to Tilsit*, 126.
4 Wismes, A., *Le Vieux Nantes*, 16.
5 Forssell, Nils, *Fouché: The Man Napoleon Feared*, 20.
6 Le Clère, Marcel, *Dictionnaire Napoléon*, Tulard, ed.,747.
7 Caratini, Roger, *Dictionnaire des personages de la Révolution*, 280.
8 Etèvenaux, Jean, *Fouché*, 12.
9 See Chapter VI.
10 Le Clère, 747; see also Etèvenaux, 14, who points out that Fouché apparently reversed a pro-abolition stance he had initially taken in order to bring himself into alignment with local mercantile interests.
11 Madelin, Louis, *Fouché*, vol. i, 361.
12 Andress, David, *The Terror*, 82-83.
13 Goethe, Johann Wolfgang von, *Campaign in France in the Year 1792*, 81.
14 Louis, who remained calm, almost serene, during the proceedings nevertheless bridled at being called Louis Capet: "My ancestors had that name, but I have never been called that." Schama, Simon, *Citizens*, 658.
15 Patrick, Alison, *The Men of the First Republic*, 41.
16 Melchior-Bonnet, Bernardine, *Le Procès de Louis XVI*, 59.
17 Kirchberger, J. H., *The French Revolution and Napoleon: An Eyewitness History*, 65.
18 Soboul, Albert, *Le Procès de Louis XVI*, 114.
19 Fouché, Joseph, *Réflexions de J.Fouché (de Nantes) sur le jugement de Louis Capet.*
20 Paine — perhaps too cleverly for his own safety — also pointed out that "It has already been proposed to abolish the punishment of death, and it is with infinite satisfaction that I recollect the humane and excellent oration pronounced by Robespierre on that subject in the Constituent Assembly." Paine would later be expelled from the Convention and imprisoned, and he escaped execution only

when Robespierre fell on 9 Thermidor, thanks to the plotting of Fouché. Walzer, Michael, *Regicide and Revolution: Speeches at the Trial of Louis XVI*, 210-213.

21 See, Lebrique, Arlette, "Les Regicides," *Le Bicentaire du Procès du Roi*, ed. Claude Goyard, 117; and also Patrick, Alison, "Regicides and Anti-Regicides in January 1793: The Significance of Joseph Fouché's Vote," *Historical Studies*, vol. 14, no. 55 (1970); and Conte, Arthur, *Sire Ils Ont Voté La Mort*, 72-73.

22 Conte, 73; Patrick, 321.

23 General Baron Thiebault, *Mémoires*, vol. v, 375; Conte, 342.

24 Liris, Élisabeth, *L'Allier en Révolution*, 232.

25 Liris, 115.

26 Liris, 99-100.

27 Martel, Arnaud, Étude sur Fouché, 158-59. It is interesting to note that in this proclamation, Fouché does make mention of the Church having gone astray from its ancient principles, which shows a vestigial glimmer of reformism on his part rather than abolitionism. But he may simply have felt the reference to be an expedient one.

28 Débordes, Jean, *Les Mystères de l'Allier*, 346.

29 Liris, 123-25; Débordes, 346; Martel,168-69.

30 Débordes, 347; Recoules, André, *Moulins*, 18, 58.

31 Etèvenaux, 30-31.

32 For an in-depth view of Lyon in the 1780s, see W.D. Edmonds, *Jacobinism and the Revolt of Lyon 1789-1793*.

33 Edmonds, 269. When the Convention's initial force proved inadequate, its numbers were increased by 5000 additional troops and heavy siege artillery.

34 Benoît, Bruno, and Roland Saussac, *Guide Historique de la Révolution à Lyon 1789-1799*, 86.

35 Benoît and Saussac, 87.

36 In *Twelve Who Ruled*, R.R. Palmer perceives the seeds of Collot's violence in his antipathy for his former Lyonnaise audiences: "Years before, as manager of the theater in that city, occupying a position that was then only partly respectable, he had seen the social pretensions and the snobbery of the moneyed classes. He had grudges and grievances and a sense of dramatic retribution." 160. In *Citizens*, Simon Schama notes Collot's adversarial relations with management, critics, and theater-goers, and acidly remarks: "A good portion of them were to learn the penalties of tepid applause." 781. See also, Mansfield, Paul, "The Repression of Lyon, 1793-94: Origins, Responsibility, and Significance," *French History*, 1988.

37 Edmonds, 279.

38 Mansfield, 83.

39 Edmonds, 287; Herriot, Édouard, *Lyons N'est Plus . . .*, vol. iii, 134-35.

40 Rougeron, Georges, "Après les Bourbons," in *Allier Bourbonnais*, 74.

41 *Le Monument Religieux des Brotteaux*, iii-xi.

42 At the end of the *ancien régime*, Lyon had around 150,000 inhabitants; just after the siege, the population had dropped to 102,167 and by the time of Napoleon's coup in 1799 it was under 90,000. *Histoire de Lyon*, André Pelletier (ed.), *et al.*, 673.

43 Matrat, Jean, *Robespierre*, trans. by Alan Kendall, 250.

44 Matrat, 265.
45 Jordan, David, *The Revolutionary Career of Maximilien Robespierre*, 195-96, 198.
46 Gueniffey, Patrice, "Robespierre" in *A Critical Dictionary of the French Revolution*, Francois Furet (ed.) et al., 310.
47 Hardman, John, *Robespierre*, 181-82.
48 Tulard, Jean, *Les Thermidoriens*, 49.
49 Andress, 329.
50 Sournia, J.-C., *A Guide to Revolutionary Paris*, 138.
51 Matrat, 269.
52 Matrat, 270.
53 Thompson, J.M., *Robespierre*, 558.
54 *French Revolution Documents*, J.M.Roberts (ed.), et al., vol. ii, 1792-95, doc. nos. 139 (a) and (b), 252.
55 Belloc, Hilaire, *Robespierre*, 319.
56 Tulard, 48.
57 Linton, Marisa, "'Do You Believe That We're Conspirators?': Conspiracies Real and Imagined in Jacobin Politics, 1793-94," in *Conspiracy in the French Revolution*, 145.
58 Hardman, 183.
59 Thompson, 563; Matrat, 274.
60 Belloc, 370, 377.
61 Baczko, Bronislaw, *Ending the Terror*, 139.
62 Postic, Marcel-Vincent, *Carrier et la Terreur à Nantes*, 296; Andress, David, *The French Revolution and the People*, 224; DuPaquier, Jacques (ed.), *Carrier*, 10.
63 Sutherland, D.M.G., *The French Revolution and Empire*, 245.
64 Bachelier, qtd. in Postic, 289.
65 Legrand, Robert, *Babeuf et Ses Compagnons de Route*, 178; Etèvenaux, 141.
66 Baczko, 146.
67 Postic, 291.
68 Postic, 291.
69 Biard, Michel, *Collot d'Herbois*, 199.
70 Biard, 176.
71 Fouché, Joseph, *"Réflexions de Fouché (de Nantes), sur les calomnies répandues contre lui, Prairial, l'an III,"* 4.
72 Sutherland, 250.
73 Le Clère, 748; Etèvenaux, 146.
74 Legrand, 178; Etèvenaux, 147.
75 Le Nabour, Eric, *Barras*, 148.
76 Rose, R.B., *Gracchus Babeuf, the First Revolutionary Communist*, 208.
77 Herriot, vol. v, 165; Legrand, 198.
78 Rose, 208.
79 In the Year IX, Babeuf's widow would be one of the Jacobins who were arbitrarily rounded up by Fouché's police after the Rue Nicaise bombing. Rose, 328.
80 Legrand, 198.
81 Garnier, Jean-Paul, *Barras: roi du Directoire*, 20.
82 The decision of a majority of the Directors was taken as a decision of the whole.

83 Garnier, 158.
84 Garnier, 159.
85 La Révellière-Lépeaux, *Mémoires*, vol. i, 338.
86 Barras, Paul, *Mémoires*, vol. iii, 287.
87 Barras, vol. iv, 112.
88 Barras, vol. iii, 272.
89 Barras, vol. iii, 11.
90 Barras, vol. iii, 288.
91 Barras, vol. iii, 379.
92 Sieyès' tract, *What is the Third Estate?*, published in 1789, was one of the seminal documents of the French Revolution, leading to the formation of the National Assembly.
93 Barras, vol. iii, 414; Talleyrand, *Mémoires*, 279.
94 Barras, vol. iii, 415.
95 Sutherland, 293.
96 Barras, vol. iii, 442.
97 Stead, Philip, *The Police of Paris*, 72.
98 Bourrienne, *Memoirs of Napoleon Bonaparte*, vol. i, 266.
99 According to one eyewitness, the crowd at Fréjus ignored warnings about the risks of approaching the non-quarantined landing party, and exclaimed in unison, "We prefer the plague to the Austrians." Bourrienne, *Memoirs of Napoleon Bonaparte*, vol. i, 255. Be that as it may, such public-health scruples on the part of Napoleon's entourage were not in evidence as they continued to receive acclaims during their journey through the cities of Aix and Lyon on the way to Paris.
100 Garnier, 204.
101 Lentz, *Le 18-Brumaire*, 231.
102 Madelin, *Fouché*, vol. i, 264-65.
103 Lentz, 263; Madelin, *Fouché*, vol. i, 267.
104 Bourrienne, *Memoirs of Napoleon Bonaparte*, vol. i, 279.
105 Crook, *Napoleon Comes to Power*, 39.
106 Tulard, *Le 18 Brumaire*, 122.
107 Bourrienne, *Memoirs of Napoleon Bonaparte*, vol. i, 292.
108 Napoléon, *L'Oeuvre et L'Histoire*, vol. i, 465-67.
109 Crook, 59.
110 Bourrienne, *Memoirs of Napoleon Bonaparte*, vol. i, 287.
111 *Le Moniteur*, No. 50, Decadi 20 brumaire (10 Nov. 1799), from *Réimpression de l'ancien Moniteur, seule histoire authentique et inalterée de la Révolution francaise depuis la réunion des États-Généraux*, vol. 29, Paris, 1850-54; accessed via The Making of the Modern World, Gale 2009, Princeton University Library.
112 Bourrienne states: "[W]ithout speaking as positively as if I had myself been an eye-witness of the scene [he apparently was at Saint Cloud but not in the hall of the Council of the Five Hundred], I do not hesitate to declare that all that has been said about assaults and poniards [daggers] is pure invention. I rely on what was told me, on the very night, by persons well worthy of credit, and who were witnesses of all that passed . . .Bonaparte never mentioned a word of anything of the sort to

me, either on the way home or when I was with him in his chamber." *Memoirs of Napoleon Bonaparte*, vol. i, 293.

113 Barras, vol. iv, 113.

114 Le Nabour, 285-86.

115 Garnier, 219; Le Nabour, 169.

116 Garnier, 309; Le Nabour, 289.

117 Cambacérès, *Mémoires inédits*, vol. i, 639-40.

118 Cambacérès, vol. i, 642.

119 In *General Pichegru's Treason*, Sir John Hall outlines official British complicity in the plot to overthrow Napoleon: "Hammond and Arbuthnot, the Under-Secretaries for Foreign Affairs, Flint, the Superintendent of Aliens, and Huskisson, the Under-Secretary-at-War, were unquestionably privy to the designs of the conspirators." 306.

120 In his *Memoirs*, Baron Claude-Francis Méneval, Napoleon's personal secretary, notes that "Fouché has succeeded in making himself necessary by his extreme activity. He used often to come and tell the First Consul news which he had obtained, thanks to the influence which he had retained over the police-agents, and the confidences which he had extracted from them, beating the Grand Judge in his own department." Vol. i, 251.

121 Regarding the double agent, see Bertaud, Jean-Paul, *Le Duc d'Enghien*, 316, and Hall, 320. Regarding the Fouché quotation, see Bertaud, Jean-Paul, *Bonaparte et le duc d'Enghien*, 111.

122 Lacour-Gayet, Georges, *Talleyrand*, vol. ii, 127; Lawday, David, *Napoleon's Master*, 145.

123 Méneval, Claude-Francois, *Napoleon: An Intimate Account of the Years of Supremacy*, ed. Proctor Patterson Jones, 86.

124 Pasquier, Étienne-Denis, *A History of My Time*, vol. i, 191-92.

125 Lacour-Gayet, Georges, vol. ii, 127. In his memoirs, Chancellor Pasquier, a future prefect of police, states flatly and without identifying his source that "M. de Talleyrand declared that the prince should be sent to his death." Pasquier, who later describes Fouché "as capable of sacrificing for the smallest interest the man who might consider himself the day before his best friend," notes Fouché's presence at the meeting but attributes no opinion or advice to him. Vol. i, 191, 258.

126 Fay, Sidney B., "The Execution of the Duc d'Enghien II," *The American Historical Review*, vol. 4 no. 1 (Oct. 1898), 24-5.

127 Bertaud, *Le Duc d'Enghien*, 378.

128 Pasquier, vol. i, 205, 209.

129 Castelot, Andre, *Napoléon Bonaparte*, 130. On April 5, 1804, Pichegru was found strangled in his Temple cell, probably by his own hands (using a board to twist a scarf), but possibly not. The popular Moreau was exiled to the United States in the wake of the widespread outrage over the killing of d'Enghien. (Making his way back to side with the Allies of the Sixth Coalition, Moreau would be killed by a French cannonball at the battle of Dresden in 1813.) In *Secret Service*, Elizabeth Sparrow asserts that Fouché was influential in the clemency shown Moreau, and that he was particularly keen to protect Moreau's secretary, Fresnière, "before he

could be compromised by the interrogations of others, for [he] was also Fouché's agent." 292.

130 Pasquier, vol. i, 201.

131 Méneval, *Memoirs*, vol. i, 270; Dwyer, Philip, *Talleyrand*, 94.

132 Méneval, *Napoleon: An Intimate Account*, 92.

133 Fay, 23; Méneval, *Memoirs*, vol. i, 266.

134 *Mémoires du Général de Caulaincourt*, vol. ii, 253. Caulaincourt reports that later in their conversation, Napoleon complained to him that Talleyrand, Fouché, and Murat were often telling him that the royalist faction viewed him as merely a transitional phase back to Bourbon rule. 254.

135 Savary, *Extrait des Mémoires de M. Le Duc de Rovigo Concernant la Catastrophe de M. Le Duc d'Enghien*, 66-70. See Duff Cooper, Alfred, *Talleyrand*, 140-41; Orieux, *Talleyrand*, 546-49.

136 Talleyrand, *Mémoires*, Plon, 301.

137 Lacour-Gayet, Georges, vol. ii, 125-26.

138 Pasquier, vol. i, 214; see Auger, Antoine, J. Garnier, et al., *Napoléon Bonaparte*, 121; Lentz, Thierry, *Savary*, 121; and Staël, Anne-Louis-Germaine de, *Ten Years' Exile*, 122-23. See also the quasi-fabricated *Memoirs of Joseph Fouché*, vol. i, 224 (discussed in the Epilogue of this work), and the "Biographical Sketch" introducing vol. ii, xxxix, appearing in the *Biographie Universelle*, 1856.

139 Buisson, Henry, *La Police Son Histoire*, 132.

140 Alary, Éric, *Histoire de la Gendarmerie*, 63.

141 Le Clère, 59.

142 Buisson, 148.

143 Buisson, 150.

144 Buisson, 150.

145 Buisson, 148-49.

146 Buisson, 149.

147 Stead, *The Police of Paris*, 80; Carrot, Georges, *Histoire de la Police Francaise*, 114.

148 Napoleon to Fouché, from Milan on 1 June 1805, item 10183 in *Napoléon Bonaparte: Correspondance Générale*, vol. v, p.367.

149 Napoleon to Fouché, from Milan on 30 May 1805, item 10163 in *Napoléon Bonaparte: Correspondance Générale*, vol. v, 359.

150 Stead, *The Police of France*, 47.

151 Stead, *The Police of France*, 50.

152 Andrew, Christopher and Mitrokhin, Vasili, *The Sword and the Shield*, 545.

153 Hauterive, Ernest d', *Napoléon et Sa Police*, 228 et seq., and Lefebvre, 86. With regard to passports, Cambacérès noted that "The charges for each example, covering fabrication and the stamp, were fixed at the sum of two francs. At first glance the royalty appears modest, but the consumption was so great that it resulted in a considerable benefit for the Police." Cambacérès, vol. ii, 179.

154 Robiquet, Jean, *Daily Life in France Under Napoleon*,175.

155 Buisson, 149.

156 De Polnay, Peter, *Napoleon's Police*, 47.

157 Le Clère, 58.

158 By way of example, on May 3 1805 Napoleon wrote to Fouché, "I see in the bulletin of the 5th an article on the deparment of Cher which leads me to suspect that there is an insurrectionary plot established in this department." Napoleon to Fouché, from Alexandrie, item 9967 in *Napoléon Bonaparte:_Correspondance Générale*, vol. v, 263.
159 Hauterive, *Napoléon et Sa Police*, 29.
160 Hauterive, Ernest d' (ed.), *La Police Secrete du Premier Empire*, vol. i, 1804-1805, 521-542.
161 Hauterive, *La Police Secrete du Premier Empire*, vol. i, 1804-1805, 145-146.
162 Hauterive, *La Police Secrete du Premier Empire*, vol. v, 1809-1810, 315-317.
163 Buisson, 135.
164 Cambacérès, vol. ii, 202.
165 Madelin, Louis, *The Consulate and the Empire*, 431.
166 Pasquier, vol. i, 378.
167 Pasquier, vol. i, 376-377.
168 Moore was killed defending the embarkation perimeter at Corunna on January 16, 1809.
169 Cambacérès, vol. ii, 250.
170 Madelin, 363.
171 Pasquier, vol. i, 379.
172 Dwyer, 119.
173 As recounted by Comte Francois Nicolas Mollien in his *Mémoires d'un Ministre du Trésor Public 1780-1815*; Mollien's likely source for this portrayal of the Emperor's words would have been Lebrun. Vol. ii, 339.
174 Dwyer, 171 et seq.; Orieux, 355 et seq.
175 Pasquier, vol. i, 381.
176 Dwyer, 120.
177 Arnold, James, *Crisis on the Danube*, 24.
178 Pasquier, vol. i, 381.
179 Cambacérès, vol. ii, 251.
180 Desmarest, Pierre Marie, *Quinze Ans de Haute Police*, 219.
181 After personally interrogating his assailant, Napoleon commented in a message to Fouché: "He did not seem to know much about Brutus." Madelin, 472.
182 The source for these and other statistics for the Danube campaign portion of this chapter is Vincent Esposito and John Elting's *A Military History of the Napoleonic Wars*.
183 Tranié, Jean and Carmigniani, J.-C., *Napoléon et l'Angleterre*, 192.
184 Later in the nineteenth century, the Eastern Scheldt was cut off from the Western Scheldt and the main river by a dike.
185 Tondeur, Jean-Philippe, *Walcheren 1809*, 25.
186 Hauterive (ed.), *La Police Secrète du Premier Empire*, vol. v, 1809-1810, 110, 121, 123.
187 Tondeur, 3.
188 Tondeur, 21.
189 Hauterive, *La Police Secrète du Premier Empire*, vol. v, 1809-1810, 137.

190 At the trial of Louis XVI, Cambacérès made a series of statements as to which historians have stated it is difficult to ascertain whether he was in fact for or against the death penalty. See, for example, Le Clère, 333.

191 Madelin, 371.

192 Desmarest, 219.

193 Tondeur, 46.

194 Chandler, David, (ed.), *Napoleon's Marshals*, 20-23.

195 Bernadotte had wanted to bring charges of desertion and violation of quarantine against Napoleon when he landed at Fréjus on his return from Egypt. Chandler, 26.

196 Item 15595 in *Correspondance de Napoléon I*, vol. xix, Henri Plon (ed.) et al., 288-89.

197 It appears that one other marshal, Bon-Adrien Jeannot de Moncey, was also near at hand, but at that time Moncey possessed nothing like the stature and reputation of Bernadotte; Napoleon mentioned him as a possible alternative or adjunct to Bernadotte, but did not state him to be his preference. See Item 15636 in *Correspondance de Napoléon I*, vol. xix, 330.

198 Item 15620 in *Correspondance de Napoléon I*, vol. xix, 313.

199 Item 15625 in *Correspondance de Napoléon I*, vol. xix, 316.

200 Item 15633 in *Correspondance de Napoléon I*, vol. xix, 328.

201 Item 15636 in *Correspondance de Napoléon I*, vol. xix, 330.

202 Reverend, Albert, *Armorial du Premier Empire*, vol. i, 175.

203 Item 15636 in *Correspondance de Napoléon I*, vol. xix, 330.

204 Wise, Thomas, A.,"Life and Naval Career of Admiral Sir Richard Strachan," *Transactions of the Royal Historical Society*, vol. ii (1873), 49.

205 Barton, Dunbar, *Bernadotte and Napoleon 1799-1810*, vol. ii, 241.

206 Barton, vol. ii, 240. Soon thereafter, Bernadotte became the King of Sweden through a most unusual set of circumstances. He led the Swedish Army against Napoleon as part of the victorious Allied Coalition of 1813-14; at the decisive Battle of Leipzig ("The Battle of the Nations") in 1813, Napoleon's Saxon troops defected to the side of Bernadotte and the Allies. (See the "Epilogue" herein.)

207 Tracy, Nicholas, *Who's Who in Nelson's Navy*, 336.

208 Barton, vol. ii, 234-35. The eminent duelists were Foreign Secretary George Canning and Secretary for War Lord Castlereagh; the latter shot the former in the thigh.

209 Item 15787 in *Correspondance de Napoléon I*, vol. xix, 454.

210 Cambacérès, vol. ii, 283-84.

211 Cambacérès, vol. ii, 288.

212 Madelin, *Fouché*, vol. ii, 122; Hulin seems to conveniently ignore the fact that Fouché was also wielding the Ministry of the Interior portfolio.

213 Both Fouché and Cambacérès, a clear regicide and an ambiguous one, counseled Napoleon to effect an alliance with Russia via marriage rather than with Austria. Talleyrand, at this point in the Habsburgs' pocket — or, quite as accurately, with his hands in their pockets — strongly favored the latter. Bonaparte, Louis (Comte de Saint-Leu), *Documens [sic] Historique sur La Hollande*, vol. iii, 253.

214 Pasquier, vol. i, 417.

215 Madelin, 49.

216 Bonaparte, Louis, vol. iii, 128.
217 Bonaparte, Louis, vol. iii, letter of December 21, 1809 from Napoleon, 224, 231.
218 Schama, Simon, *Patriots and Liberators*, 547-48. Schama also recounts Louis' immensely popular actions in personally helping to fight a massive fire in the city of Leiden and then immediately instituting a sweeping relief program for its displaced inhabitants. 498.
219 Thorold, A.L., *Life of Henry Labouchère*, 2, 8. (The author was the nephew of Pierre-César Labouchère.)
220 Ouvrard, G.J., *Mémoires de G.J. Ouvrard*, vol. i, 154.
221 Ouvrard, vol. i, 157.
222 Pasquier, vol. i, 417.
223 Pasquier, vol..i, 418. While Counsellor Pasquier was certainly no friend to Fouché – he concludes his passage about Fouché's dismissal with the observation that "We shall find him more than once in our pathway, and his presence will never cease being an ill omen" (431) - there is no reason to believe his report of the Emperor's insult-laden dressing down of Fouché to be inaccurate.
224 Ouvrard, vol. i, 60.
225 Pasquier, vol. i, 416, 420.
226 Savary, *Memoirs of the Duke of Rovigo*, vol. ii, 214.
227 Savary, *Memoirs of the Duke of Rovigo*, vol. ii, 215.
228 Thorold, 11.
229 Ouvrard, vol. i,162.
230 Bonaparte, Louis, vol. iii, 277, 279, 282, 286.
231 In Switzerland, Louis would ineffectually try to regain custody of his children from Hortense, and he would work on his account of his role as the attempted protector of the Dutch against his domineering older brother; this is the account cited immediately above. In his last will and testament, dictated on St. Helena, Napoleon included the following message: "I forgive Louis the libel he published in 1820, full of false assertions and forged evidence"; that was the only testamentary provision made for the former King of Holland and the father of the future Napoleon III. Smith, William H.C., *The Bonapartes*, 86.
232 Savary, *Memoirs of the Duke of Rovigo*, vol. ii, 215-16.
233 Ouvrard, 159.
234 Turquan, Joseph, *The Sisters of Napoleon*, 49; Picaut, Jean-Étienne, *Madame Napoléon*, 45.
235 Melchior-Bonnet, Bernadine, "Élisa Bonaparte," *Dictionnaire Napoléon*, Jean Tulard (ed.), 657.
236 Picaut, 132. Note Fouché's clever and careful wording here: he refers to errors for which he had been reproached, not to any errors which he may have in fact committed.
237 Picaut, 132; Marmottan, Paul, "La Grande-Duchesse Élisa et Fouché," *Revue d'Histoire Diplomatique*, Oct.-Dec. 1926, 416.
238 Marmottan, 413.
239 Picaut, 132.
240 Marmottan, 418-19.

241 Marmottan, 419.

242 Adams, Michael, *Napoleon and Russia*, 267; Madelin, *Fouché*, vol. ii, 340.

243 Vartier, Jean, *Fanfan-la-Conspiration ou la Vie Aventureuse de Charles Nodier*, 117.

244 "La Napoléone" by Charles Nodier, qtd. in A. Richard Oliver, *Charles Nodier: Pilot of Romanticism*, 35.

245 Oliver, 35-39.

246 Nodier, Charles, *Souvenirs de la Révolution et de l'Empire*, vol. ii, 307-08.

247 Lacour-Gayet, Michel, *Joachim et Caroline Murat*, 253.

248 Espitalier, Albert, *Napoleon and King Murat*, J.Lewis May (trans.), 301.

249 Lacour-Gayet, Michel, 261, and Espitalier, 303.

250 Espitalier, 305.

251 Weil, M.H., *Le Prince Eugène et Murat 1813-1814*, vol. iv, 202. The treaty with Austria provided that Murat would lead the Neapolitan Army and an Austrian corps attached to it against the French, while Austria would guarantee the territorial integrity of the Kingdom of Naples and recognize Murat as its ruler; the Emperor Francis also secretly agreed to the Kingdom's territorial expansion. See, Nafziger, George and Gioannini, Marco, *The Defense of the Napoleonic Kingdom of Northern Italy, 1813-1814*, 137.

252 Cole, Hubert, *The Betrayers*, 203.

253 Cole, 204.

254 Weil, M.H., vol. iv, 134.

255 Weil, vol. iv, 204.

256 Espitalier, 306.

257 Picaut, 187.

258 Turquan, 77.

259 Nafziger and Gionanni's work, cited above, provides a very detailed account of the military and diplomatic aspects of the Viceroy's 1813-14 campaign in Italy against Austrian, Neapolitan, and British opponents.

260 Couturaud, Laurence, *Augereau: L'Enfant Maudit de la Gloire*, 154.

261 Zins, Ronald, 1814: *L'Armée de Lyon, ultime éspoir de Napoléon*, 38.

262 Gamichon, Louis, *Napoléon et les Lyonnais*, 140-41. The author notes that Edouard Herriot, a former prime minister of France and the then Mayor of Lyon, would in parallel manner declare it to be an open city in June 1940, in order to save it from the Wehrmacht.

263 Zins, 97.

264 Zins, 102-03.

265 Armstrong, Eva, and Lukens, Hiram, "Jean-Antoine Chaptal, Comte de Chanteloupe," *Journal of Chemical Education*, 1936, 13 (6), 260.

266 Chaptal, Jean-Antoine Claude, Comte de Chanteloup, *Mes Souvenirs Sur Napoléon*, 313-14.

267 Chaptal, 314.

268 Chaptal, 315.

269 Item 189, *Memoirs of Prince Metternich*, Prince Richard Metternich (ed.), et al., vol. ii, 549.

270 They included Oudinot, Ney, Marmont, Victor, Lefebvre, Mortier, and Berthier.

271 Thompson, J.M., "Napoleon's Journey to Elba in 1814. Part I. By Land," *The American Historical Review*, vol. 55, no. 1 (Oct., 1949), 11.

272 During his second exile, Napoleon wrote of Augereau: "It is a long time since the Marshal was truly a soldier; his courage, his outstanding virtues certainly elevated him far above the crowd; but honors, titles, and money plunged him back into it. The conqueror of Castiglione could have left a cherished name to France; but she will recall the memory of the deserter of Lyon." Chandler, David, "Introduction," *Napoleon's Marshals*, lv.

273 Savary, *Memoirs of the Duke of Rovigo*, vol. iv, 168.

274 Waldburg, Friedrich Ludwig Truchess, Graf von, *Nouvelle rélation de l'intineraire de Napoléon, de Fontainebleau à l'île d'Elbe*, Paris 1815, access via galenet.galegroup.com, Princeton University Library, 21. Interestingly, von Waldburg records that Augereau's troops in Valence, already wearing royalist white cockades, nevertheless greeted the Emperor warmly and looked upon his Allied escort with sullen hostility; if so, they may well have been removed from the fray in Lyon while there was still plenty of fight remaining in them. 22.

275 Zins, 105-06, Couturaud, 176-77.

276 Lenôtre, G. [pseudo.], *The Last Days of Marie Antoinete* [sic], 274.

277 Chateaubriand, Francois-René, *The Memoirs of Francois René Vicomte de Chateaubriand*, Alexander Texeira de Mattos (trans.), 103.

278 The remains of Marie Antoinette were allegedly identifiable by some shreds of clothing; Louis' purported bones, found adjacent to hers, had very badly disintegrated. There was also the problem of a considerable time lag having occurred between the time of execution and the time of interment. See, Lenôtre, 264-283; Hearsey, John, *Marie Antoinette*, 243-44. I am, however, unaware of any calls for re-exhumation and DNA testing.

279 Lenôtre, 283.

280 Houssaye, Henry, *1815: La première restauration; le retour de l'Ile d'Elbe; les cent jours*, 95; Savary, *Memoirs of the Duke of Rovigo*, vol. iv, Part 1, 235-36.

281 For example, the pastor of Saint-Germain-l'Auxerrois fulminated to his congregation: "Swear to pursue without let-up the villains who committed this crime." Houssaye, *1815: La première restauration*, 95.

282 Chateaubriand, 104.

283 That is, dating from the alleged death in 1795 of Louis XVI's incarcerated orphan son, the Dauphin, recognized by Bourbon legitimists as Louis XVII, in the Temple prison.

284 Longford, Elizabeth, *Wellington, Pillar of State*, 14. One instance of a hundred-oyster intake occurred while Louis was in his 1815 exile at the Comte de Steenhuyse's comfortable Hôtel in Ghent. Mansel, Philip, *Louis XVIII*, 230.

285 Houssaye, *1815: La première restauration*, 77.

286 Mansel, Philip, 179.

287 Jaucourt to Talleyrand, January 21, 1815, in *Correspondance Inédite du Prince de Talleyrand et du Roi Louis XVIII*, 470.

288 Chateaubriand, 17.

289 Earl of Liverpool to Rt. Hon. G. Canning, April 19, 1815, *Supplementary Despatches, Correspondence, and Memoranda of Field Marshal Arthur Duke of Wellington*, vol. x, 106.
290 Chateaubriand, 91.
291 Stewart, John Hall, *The Restoration Era in France*, 21.
292 Savary, *Memoirs of the Duke of Rovigo*, vol. iv, Part I, 232.
293 Savary, *Memoirs of the Duke of Rovigo*, vol. iv, Part I, 232; see also Méneval, *Memoirs*, vol. iii, 325, and Cubberly, Ray Ellsworth, *The Role of Fouché During the Hundred Days*, 6.
294 Houssaye, *1815: La première restauration*, 114.
295 Fouché to Napoleon, April 23, 1814, reproduced in *Wellington's Supplementary Dispatches*, vol. ix, 145.
296 *Wellington's Supplementary Despatches*, vol. xi, 144; Cubberly, 66-69. Étienne-Denis Pasquier, Napoleon's prefect of police for Paris prior to the First Restoration,but sympathetic to the Bourbons, also attempted to warn the regime about lax counter-measures against an escape from Elba. He notes with regard to Royalist Minister of Police Beugnot that "I was astounded at the little importance he attached to this dangerous quarter, as well as the paucity of means he made to exercise surveillance over it." He also states that Beugnot's successor, d'André, "was perfectly at ease" with the situation on Elba, and that he had had surveillance of the Emperor discontinued altogether. Pasquier, vol. iii, 58, 68.
297 Méneval, vol. iii, 444-45.
298 The pool of candidates to assassinate the Emperor included fellow Corsicans, Italians, *Chouans,* other foreign agents placed on Elba, the Spanish government (not a signatory to the peace convention of 1814), and fierce Algierian corsairs available for hire by interested parties. Houssaye, *1815: La première_restauration*, 169-173.
299 Houssaye, *1815: La première restauration*, 118-21; Chateaubriand, 111; Dallas, Gregor, *The Final Act*, 287*;* Price, Munro, *The Perilous Crown, 73-4;* Thiers, Adolphe, *History of the Consulate and the Empire*, vol. xix, 80-81; Cubberly, 10; Savary, *Memoirs of the Duke of Rovigo*, vol. iv, Part I, 255-56; Pasquier, vol. iii, 163-64.
300 Pasquier, vol..iii, 163-64.
301 Houssaye, *1815: La première restauration*, 119.
302 Chateaubriand disparagingly comments upon the prevalent fickleness: "So many chrysalides who, between two spring-times, had put off and put on, shed and resumed the skin of the Legitimist and the Revolutionary, of the Napoleonist and the Bourbonist." 156.
303 Savary, *Memoirs of the Duke of Rovigo*, vol. iv, Part I, 257.
304 Robiquet, Paul, "Fouché Pendant Les Cent Jours," *La Révolution Francaise*, vol. 71, 1918, 129; Dallas, 292-93; Cubberly, 68.
305 Bardoux, A., *Madame de Custine D'Après des Documents Inédits*, 225
306 Cubberly, 20.
307 Bardoux, A., 227; Robiquet, Paul, 129.
308 Mansell, 224.
309 Chateaubriand, 123.
310 Le Clère, 288.

311 Pasquier cynically notes: "So here was M. Fouché once more Minister of Police! The persecution he had suffered during the past few days had doubtless helped him to obtain this mark of favor." Vol. iii, 174.

312 Savary, vol. iv, Part I, 266; Cubberly, 15.

313 Savary, vol. iv, Part I, 261. One wonders why Savary, if he was indeed knowledgeable at the time about the real objectives of the "Conspiracy of the North," did not bring them to Napoleon's attention.

314 Savary, vol. iv, Part I, 265.

315 Pasquier, vol. iii, 182.

316 *Le Moniteur Universel*, April 4, 1815, 582.

317 Chateaubriand, 151.

318 For the former proposition, see the *Mémoires* of one of Napoleon's secretaries, Fleury de Chaboulon, vol. ii, 32-33, who believed that Napoleon's first act after a favorable military outcome in Flanders "would probably have been the dismissal of the Duke of Otranto." For the latter, see Pasquier, who states that "He [Fouché] has always claimed that the advance and overtures he ventured upon were naught but a manner of sounding people's intentions, and a means of rendering better service to his master. What is certain is that Napoleon was his dupe . . . ." Vol. iii, 209.

319 Pasquier, vol..iii, 208.

320 Tondeur, Jean-Philippe, *Charleroi: la journée du 15 Juin 1815*, 53-54.

321 Roberts, Andrew, *Napoleon and Wellington*, 188, 220.

322 Tondeur, Jean-Philippe, *Charleroi: la journee du 15 Juin 1815*, 55.

323 Falloux du Coudray, comte de, Memoirs of the Count de Falloux, vol. i, 103.

324 See Caulincourt [sic], Duke of Vicenza, *Napoleon and His Times*, vol. ii, 156, in which Napoleon's Foreign Minister states to a fellow minister, Carnot, about Fouché: "He has spies and agents everywhere. He has received the news, no matter by what means; and his object is to devise some diabolical plan for repressing the national feeling which would be excited by the loss of the battle."

325 Barante, Amable-Guillaume Prosper, *Souvenirs de Baron de Barante*, vol. ii, 156.

326 De Chaboulon, vol. ii, 168; Cubberly, 79.

327 Baron Despatys, *Un Ami de Fouché, d'Après les Mémoires de Gaillard*, 401-02.

328 Thibaudeau, Antoine-Claire, *Mémoires de A.-C. Thibaudeau*, 506.

329 *Mémoires, Correspondance et Manuscrits du General Lafayette*, H. Fournier (ed.), vol. v, 122-23.

330 Méneval, *Memoirs Illustrating the History of Napoleon I*, vol. iii, 455.

331 Caulincourt [sic], Armand Augustin Louis, marquis de, *Napoleon and His Times*, vol. ii, 173.

332 Pasquier, vol. iii, 281-82.

333 Bourrienne, *Memoirs of Napoleon Bonaparte*, vol. iv, 219-220; Pasquier states that Becker and Napoleon had a "private feud," vol. iii, 287. Bourrienne goes on to mention that Becker in fact treated Napoleon with due respect, while Maceroni, an aide-de camp of Murat and the perhaps unwitting agent of Fouché, asserts that Napoleon blocked Becker from joining him in the rowboat that was about to ferry him towards the British warship that would take him to St. Helena, ambiguously saying "do not come any further, lest it be said that France delivers me up to her

enemies." *Memoirs of the Life and Adventures of Colonel Maceroni, aide de camp of Murat*, vol. ii, 240.

334 The Duke of Otranto to Marshal Davout, Paris, June 27, 1815, reproduced in *Supplementary Despatches of the Duke of Wellington, etc.*, vol. x, 601.

335 Thornton, Michael, *Napoleon After Waterloo*, 8.

336 Napoleon to the Prince Regent of England (the future George IV), from the Ile d'Aix, July 14, 1815, reproduced in *Napoleon Self-Revealed*, J.M. Thompson (ed.).

337 Communication of F. Marshall, Esq. to Field Marshal the Duke of Wellington, reproduced in *Supplementary Despatches of the Duke of Wellington, etc.*, vol. x, 601.

338 Pasquier, vol. iii, 279-80.

339 The source for troop strengths given in this chapter is Esposito and Elting's *A Military History of the Napoleonic Wars.*

340 Ney, Michel, Lettre de M. le maréchal prince de la Moskowa, à S. Exc. M. le duc d'Otrante, June 26, 1815, Houghton Harvard Depository.

341 In one of the last significant combats in the Paris sector, the French cavalry commander Exelmanns caught by surprise and annihilated two regiments of Prussian cavalry at Versailles on July 1, just two days after Ney's defeatist speech to Chambers.

342 Wellington to Marshal Blücher from Gonesse, July 2,1815, *Dispatches of the Duke of Wellington*, vol. xii, 526.

343 Epstein, Robert M., *The Journal of Military History*, vol. 71, no. 2 (April 2007), 526.

344 John Gallaher, *The Iron Marshal*, 327.

345 Gallaher, 326-28; *Memoirs of the Life and Adventures of Colonel Maceroni*, vol. ii, 246.

346 Marshal Davout to the Duke of Otranto, June 28, 1815, *Correspondance du Maréchal Davout*, vol. iv, 578.

347 Reply of Fouché to Marshal Davout, reproduced in *Supplementary Despatches of the Duke of Wellington*, vol. x, 612.

348 Charrier, Pierre, *Le Maréchal Davout*, 735.

349 It was this same note that also contained the earlier-referenced promise from Fouché to "deliver up Buonaparte." See note 335.

350 F. Marshall, Esq. to Field Marshal the Duke of Wellington, June 28, 1815, published in *Supplementary Despatches of the Duke of Wellington*, vol. x, 620.

351 *Memoirs of the Life and Adventures of Colonel Maceroni*, vol. ii, 118.

352 Rain, Pierre, *L'Europe et la Restauration des Bourbons 1814-1818*, 170.

353 Rain, 171-72; Mansel, 253; Lawday, 296-97 (source of quotation).

354 *Correspondance du Maréchal Davout*, vol. iv, 286.

355 Wellington to Earl Bathurst, July 13, 1815, *Dispatches of the Duke of Wellington*, vol. xii, 557.

356 Duke of Otranto to Field Marshal the Duke of Wellington, June 27, 1815, *Supplementary Despatches of the Duke of Wellington*, vol. x, 610; Longford, 5.

357 *Memoirs of the Life and Adventures of Colonel Maceroni*, vol. ii, 249.

358 Chateaubriand, 182.

359 *Mémoires du Comte Beugnot*, 330. See also regarding Wellington's and royalists' pressures on behalf of a Fouché ministry, *Souvenirs du Baron de Barante*, vol. ii, 168.

360 *Mémoires de Vitrolles*, vol. ii, 229.

361 Rain, 175-76; Cubberly, 115.
362 *Le Moniteur Universel*, July 6, 1815, no.187.
363 Duke of Otranto to Field Marshal the Duke of Wellington, July 8, 1815, *Supplementary Despatches of the Duke of Wellington*, vol. xi, 16.
364 *Mémoires du Comte Beugnot*, 332-33.
365 *Mémoires du Comte Beugnot*, 334. Given his boyhood admiration for the Roman historian, Fouché might well have been pleased by the Count's reference.
366 Chateaubriand, 182.
367 *Le Moniteur Universel*, No. 190, 9 Juillet 1815.
368 *Recollections of Marshal MacDonald*, 442.
369 Bourrienne, *Memoirs of Napoleon Bonaparte*, vol. iv, 275.
370 Earl of Liverpool to Viscount Castlereagh, July 10, 1815, in *Supplementary Despatches of the Duke of Wellington*, vol. xi, 24.
371 Earl of Liverpool to Viscount Castlereagh, July 15, 1815, in *Supplementary Despatches of the Duke of Wellington*, vol. xi, 32.
372 Wellington to Viscount Castlereagh, September 23, 1815, in *Dispatches of the Duke of Wellington*, vol. xii, 645.
373 See Bertier de Sauvigny, Guillaume, *The Bourbon Restoration*, 120; and Pasquier, vol. iii, 366. Pasquier, despite being Minister of Justice and of the Interior under the Second Restoration, had to endure the embarrassment of his brother being arrested by the Prussians at Le Mans for refusing to turn over public funds; a cousin of Talleyrand's was likewise made a Prussian prisoner under similar circumstances occurring at Orléans. See also Houssaye's disturbing litany of episodes of what he styles as "the Prussian Terror" in *1815: La seconde abdication; la terreure blanche*, 490 et seq.
374 Wellington to the Rt. Hon. Sir Henry Wellesley, July 19, 1815, in *Dispatches of the Duke of Wellington*, vol. xii, 566.
375 *Mémoires de Vitrolles*, vol. ii, 247.
376 Pierre, Michel, *Ney: Du procès politique à la réhabilitation du "Brave des braves,"* 60.
377 See, for example, *Souvenirs du Baron de Barante*, vol. ii, 190; for a review of various estimates, see Houssaye, *1815: La seconde abdication*, 428.
378 Bertier de Sauvigny, 117.
379 Pasquier, vol. iii, 391-92.
380 Pasquier, vol. iii, 392.
381 In Joseph Conrad's novel *The Duel: A Military Tale*, the hero, a General D'Hubert, who had sat out the Hundred Days, in an act of naïve virtuousness obtains an audience with Fouché to request that the name of his bitter rival and adversary, one General Féraud, a fanatic Bonapartist, be struck from the list of the proscribed senior officers. After making D'Hubert quite uncomfortable, Conrad's Fouché advises him that he will reduce the list from twenty to nineteen individuals: "General D'Hubert stood up feeling as though he had gone through an infectious illness. 'I must beg your Excellency to keep my interference a profound secret. I attach the greatest importance to his never learning . . .' 'Who is going to inform him, I should like to know?' said Fouché, raising his eyes curiously to General D'Hubert's tense, set face. 'Take one of these pens, and run it through the name yourself. This is the

only list in existence. If you are careful to take up enough ink no one will be able to tell what was the name struck out.'" D'Hubert later comments to his sister. "'I have had to see Fouché. I have had an audience. I have been in his cabinet. There remains with one, who had the misfortune to breathe the air of the same room with that man, a sense of diminished dignity, an uneasy feeling of being not so clean, after all, as one hoped one was.'" 75-76.

382 Lamartine, Alphonse de, *The History of the Restoration of Monarchy in France*, vol. iii, 146.

383 Lamartine, vol. iii, 146-48. (Appendix I provides the entire text of the Act.) Savary boarded H.M.S. *Bellerophon* with Napoleon at Rochefort, but he was not permitted to accompany his idol to St. Helena; he was held as a prisoner of war by the British in Malta, and he therefore escaped the purges of die-hard Bonapartists in his homeland.

384 Lamartine, vol. iii, 147.

385 See, for example, the account of General Baron Thiébault in his *Mémoires*, vol. v, 377; of Victorine de Chastenay, who refers to the "alleged exchange" between Carnot and Fouché in her *Mémoires, "Deux révolutions pour une seule vie,"* 790; and a private intelligence report dated August 7, 1815, from an British agent, E.B., who states that "it is true" the exchange took place; he describes it as having been in writing, *Supplementary Despatches of the Duke of Wellington*, vol. xi, 108.

386 Bourrienne, *Memoirs of Napoleon Bonaparte*, vol. iv, 335; Pierre, 109; see also, Quynn, Dorothy Mackay, "Destination: America, Marshal Ney's attempt to escape," *French Historical Studies*, vol. 2, no. 2 (Autumn 1961), 232 et seq.

387 Pierre, 109-113. The King's remark makes for an interesting parallel to General Charles de Gaulle's comment that Marshal Henri Philippe Pétain, the head of Vichy France, should have remained in Switzerland rather than presenting himself at the French border in 1945 to stand trial for treason. The quotation, incidentally, has also been attributed to Fouché himself; see Hulot, Frédéric, *Le Maréchal Ney*, 230.

388 *Correspondance du Maréchal Davout*, #1824, vol. iv, 631-32. Marshal St.-Cyr himself struck the names of two generals from Fouché's initial list. Le Blond, Yves, *Gouvion Saint-Cyr, Maréchal de l'Empire*, 468.

389 Gallaher, 336.

390 Gallaher, 336-37. Two years later, after the political pendulum had swung back again, Davout's rank and title were returned to him and he was made a member of the Chamber of Peers.

391 See, Bertier de Sauvigny, 188-199; Pierre, 68-71, Lamartine, 324; Houssaye, *1815: La seconde abdication*, 461.

392 Pasquier, vol. iii, 429.

393 Pasquier, vol. iii, 431.

394 Pierre, 64.

395 The *Dictionnaire des Familles Francaises* states of the House of Castellane: "[T]heir vast possessions, the great number of eminent men who have made the name illustrious . . . makes it in every respect one of the first families of the French nobility." Chaix d'Est-Ange, Gustave, vol. ix, 3.

396 Molé, Louis-Mathieu, comte, *Le Comte Molé, Sa Vie Ses Mémoires*, vol. i, 276.

397 In *Les Ministres de Napoléon*, published in 1959, Jean Savant notes: "At the end of the Empire, his capital would be estimated at 14 to 20 millions (from 4 to 6 of our billions). He received around 400 of our millions a year, of which 300 was thanks to gambling. He had lands, *châteaux*, farms, and mansion houses."

398 Mansel, 265; Sapori, Julien, *L'exil et la mort de Joseph Fouché*, 19; Etèvenaux, 186. The Fondation Napoleon in Paris includes in its collection a "*nécessaire*," an ornate traveling kit rendered in mahogany, gilt silver, ebony, and gold, which Fouché commissioned and gave to his bride-to-be shortly before the wedding. Here is a partial description: ". . . [I]t contains seventy-five pieces in a hollowed-out mahogany box, decorated on the top with a palmette frieze and lyre motif, an escutcheon engraved with the monogram CF beneath a ducal crown surrounded by laurels and, on the side of the box, branch motifs and gryphons. . . . The way in which all the pieces are set into the box is remarkable and reveals Biennais's [the artistan's] virtuousity — indeed, if a single piece is wrongly inserted the box will not shut." Appropriately, it included a cleverly designed secret compartment which, when accessed via a disguised button in a mirror, reveals "an ensemble of portfolios in green and red gold-leafed morocco." www.napoleon.org/en/collectors_corner/object/files/duchesseotrante.

399 Pasquier, vol. iii, 412.

400 Horricks, Raymond, *Military Politics from Bonaparte to the Bourbons: Life and Death of Michel Ney*, 253-54.

401 *Mémoires de Vitrolles*, vol. ii, 278; Houssaye, *1815: La seconde abdication*, 530.

402 Lamartine, 186; Mansel, 265. The supposed poison seems to have been a bottle of furniture polish carelessly left in the Czar's rooms by a servant, or perhaps planted there.

403 Pasquier, vol. iii, 436; Houssaye, *1815: La seconde abdication*, 533.

404 *Mémoires de Vitrolles*, vol. ii, 272; Houssaye, *1815: La seconde abdication*, 535.

405 Kieswetter, James, "Étienne-Denis Pasquier: The Last Chancellor of France," *Transactions of the American Philosophical Society*, vol. 67, no. 1 (1977), 64; Beach, Vincent, *Charles X of France*, 152; Mansel, 323; Lamartine, 114-115.

406 Quoted in Lamartine, vol. iii, 142.

407 Pasquier (who was in attendance), vol. iii, 411.

408 Fouché, Joseph, duc d'Otrante, *Second report made to Louis XVIII*, http://opac.newsbank.com/select/shaw/35890 ; 12.

409 Houssaye, *1815: La seconde abdication*, 532.

410 The Rt. Hon. C. Arbuthnot to the Earl of Liverpool, October 30, 1815, *Wellington's Supplementary Despatches*, vol. xi, 221.

411 The Duke of Otranto to Field Marshal the Duke of Wellington, September 15, 1815, *Wellington's Supplementary Despatches*, vol. xi, 160; Wellington to General Dumouriez, September 26, 1815, *Dispatches of the Duke of Wellington*, vol. xii, 649-50.

412 Pasquier, vol. iii, 417.

413 Pasquier, vol. iii, 418; Pasquier states that it was the opinion of Talleyrand that Vitrolles was the informant, toward which suspicion he too was inclined.

414 Pasquier, vol. iii, 417.

415 Pasquier, vol. iii, 418.

416 Molé, 334.

417 *Mémoires de Vitrolles*, vol. ii, 277. Pasquier was also a witness to this charade, and he notes the irony of Fouché's having earlier recommended the United States to Napoleon as a haven (see Chapter XIV); vol. iii, 445.

418 Talleyrand, displaying the ultimate in sanctimonious hypocrisy, wrote in his *Memoirs* of the Minister of Police's misconduct: ". . . he made them [the secret reports] public, while asserting that they had been stolen from him, and that it was not he who had published them. It was impossible to maintain any relations with a man who had recourse to such measures." The Duc de Broglie, ed., vol. iii, 174

419 *Mémoires de Vitrolles*, vol. ii, 290-91.

420 *Mémoires de Vitrolles*, vol. ii, 275.

421 *Mémoires du Prince de Talleyrand*, vol. iii, 298. See also, Mansel, 266; Rain, 185-87 and 195; Dwyer, 171-73; Orieux, 498-501; and Lawday, David, *Napoleon's Master*, 305-07; the date of Talleyrand's fateful meeting with the King is given variously as September 20, 24, and 25, but three of these sources state it happened on the 24th, and that is the date which appears in the text hereof.

422 On September 21, 1815, Castlereagh wrote from Paris to Liverpool: "Fouché, probably in fear of being pursued hostilely, it is understood, takes the mission to Dresden; and Talleyrand, yesterday evening was regretting that the embassy to Vienna was filled up, as he should have wished to make it his retirement." *Wellington's Supplementary Despatches*, vol. xi, 167. See also, Lamartine, vol. iii, 220, regarding Fouché's hasty departure, and 224-25 regarding Talleyrand's last ministerial meeting with the King.

423 Brougham and Vaux, Henry Brougham, Baron, *Historical Sketches of Statesmen Who Flourished in the Time of George III*, 95. The Earl also observed in his sketch of Fouché during his brief time in Dresden: "He preserved his former habits of 'espionnage,' and remarked to me that a person who lived on the opposite side of the street sat close to the window, was much occupied in writing, was very regular in his habits, &c. He seemed to be amused in watching this unknown individual, who was afterwards discovered to be a spy sent by the French Government to observe Fouché." 110.

424 *Le Moniteur Universel*, January 14, 1816.

425 Fouché's firstborn, Nièvre, she of the republican baptism, died as a young child.

426 See, Fouché, Joseph, *Letter [of January 1, 1816] of M. Fouché, duke of Otranto, to the Duke of Wellington*, 57, in which Fouché stated that the King had assured him in writing that his absence from France would not cost him his fortune, although the date indicates that this was likely a reference to the original appointment to Dresden.

427 Despatys, 437-38; Sapori, 35-41; Rouchette, Thérèse, *Le dernier des Regicides Antoine-Claire Thibaudeau*, 368-369; Etèvenaux, 188.

428 Sapori, 47.

429 Sapori 48-50. In his work, Sapori makes excellent use of archival Austrian police records and reports.

430 Wellington to the Duc de Richelieu, April 30, 1816, *Wellington's Supplementary Despatches*, xi, 384.

431 Picaut, 239.

432 Picaut, 239-240.

433 Bertier de Sauvigny, *Metternich*, 86-87; Vidal, Florence, *Caroline Bonaparte*, 11, 75-78. Both works mention Napoleon's instructions to his sister regarding the Austrian diplomat: "Amuse this fool, we need him for the time being." As for Metternich, he commented that Caroline had "studied the character of her brother and was not under any illusions regarding his flaws" and that she "recognized perfectly well the weaknesses of her husband and she controlled him, to the extent he could be controlled." Vidal, 77.

434 Sapori, 70.

435 For a description of the effects of the *bora* and, more generally for insights about the melancholy and brooding nature of Trieste as a haven for political and self-imposed literary exiles, see Jan Morris' magisterial *Trieste and the Meaning of Nowhere*; Morris mentions among a long list of residents the Bonapartes, Casanova, James Joyce, and Stendhal, as well as Albert Einstein as a fugitive from the Reich and Adolph Eichmann as a fugitive from the avengers, but strangely she makes no mention whatsoever of Fouché. Regarding the Timavo, see also http://www.geocaching.com/seek/cache_details.aspx?guid=cc1ca888-d05b-41f3-a988-da2ea062e9bf

436 Boudon, Jacques-Olivier, *Le Roi Jérôme*, 447.

437 Boudon, 459, where he provides the following observation by Jérôme Bonaparte on Fouché in exile: "[A]t this time, he [Fouché] professed greatly his attachment and devotion to the Emperor and to his family, and vindicated himself by citing all the evils he had prevented."

438 *The St. Helena Journal of General Baron Gourgaud, 1815-1818*, ed. Norman Edwards, 14.

439 Picaut, 253.

440 *Le Moniteur Universel*, No. 241, August 28, 1820, p.1189, and No. 245, September 1, 1820, p. 1205.

441 Excerpt from letter from Planat de la Faye from Trieste to his wife, Josephine, December 19, 1820, in *Vie de Planat de la Faye*, 385.

442 Etèvenaux, 189; Sapori, 99-100.

443 Sapori, 99.

444 See, for example, Andre Castelot, *Fouché*, 382, and Madelin, *Fouché*, vol. ii, 535. In his work (119-120), Sapori attempts to disprove the legend of the avenging wind but, to this author's mind, he does not do so conclusively – an admittedly very difficult undertaking. It should also be mentioned that Sapori seems to exhibit a great deal of sympathy for Fouché's outcast plight throughout his account, which by its own objectives limits itself to the years of exile, and therefore makes very sparse mention of the preceeding years of betrayal. It is also interesting to note – although the dates do not quite mesh, as the interment took place on December 28, 1820 – that *Le Moniteur Universel* chronicles extremely severe weather conditions in Trieste during the early part of January 1821. No. 35, February 4, 1821, 145.

445 The princesses were aided in their escape from Paris in 1791 by Louis-Alexandre Berthier, then in command of the National Guard at Versailles and who later became Napoleon's miracle-working chief of staff. Tulard, *Dictionnaire Napoléon*,

203. The sisters' remains were brought back to Paris to be reinterred at Saint-Denis in 1817.

446 *Le Moniteur Universel*, No. 16, January 16, 1821, 67.

447 Sapori, 105-06.

448 *Memoirs of Joseph Fouché*, "Biographical Sketch" introducing vol. i, xxxviii, derived from the *Biographie Universelle*, Paris: Michaud 1856.

449 Vovelle, Michel, in "Presentation" introducing *Mémoires de Joseph Fouché*, 11.

450 *Memoirs of Joseph Fouché*, "Author's Preface," xi.

451 Introduction by Clement Rochel to P.J. Proudhon's *Commentaires Sur Les Mémoires de Fouché*, xxi.

452 Rochel, xx.

453 Rochel, xix.

454 Rochel, v-vii. The police report on Beauchamp, which Rochel reproduces, states that Beauchamp defended his having written with a pro-Chouan slant because he was short of funds and a prominent Chouan leader had paid him to do it, and that he also claimed that "while he would have preferred to receive funding from another source to remain more independent, he had not had that choice."

455 Rochel, x.

456 Rochel, xii-xiv.

457 Madelin, Louis, "Introduction" to *Les Mémoires de Fouché*, 22, 24.

458 *Le Moniteur Universel*, No. 6, January 6, 1825, 28; Madelin, "Introduction" to *Les Mémoires de Fouché*, 28.

459 *Memoirs of Joseph Fouché*, vol. i, 232.

460 *Memoirs of Joseph Fouché*, vol. i, 272.

461 *Memoirs of Joseph Fouché*, vol. i, 260.

462 *Memoirs of Joseph Fouché*, vol. ii, 19, 23.

463 *Memoirs of Joseph Fouché*, vol. i, 255.

464 *Memoirs of Joseph Fouché*, vol. i, 298-302.

465 *Memoirs of Joseph Fouché*, vol. ii, 231.

466 *Memoirs of Joseph Fouché*, vol. i, 138, 199-200, 226-227, 236.

467 Madelin, "Introduction" to *Les Mémoires de Fouché*, x.

468 Madelin, "Introduction" to *Les Mémoires de Fouché*, xii.

469 Arendt, Hannah, *Eichmann in Jerusalem: A Report on the Banality of Evil.*

470 Ophuls, Marcel, *The Sorrow and Pity; a film*, filmscript trans. by Mireille Johnston, 17.

471 Napoléon, *Ses Opinions et Jugements*, Damas Ginard (ed.), vol. i, 487.

472 Lavisse, Ernest, *Histoire de France Contemporaine*, vol. iii, 241.

473 Sebag Montefiore, Simon, *Stalin: The Court of the Red Tsar*, 75-6. During the March 1938 Moscow show trial of one of Beria's predecessors as NKVD chief, Stalin's state prosecutor unleashed the following invective at the doomed defendant: "Yagoda, whose duty it was to safeguard the security of the state, committed the gravest of crimes. Disguising himself, resorting to double-dealing, this traitor emulated Joseph Fouché." Vyshinsky, Andrey, "The Treason Case Summed Up," *Soviet Russia Today*, April 1938, vol. 7, no. 2, transcribed by *Red Flag Magazine*, 25.

65036586R00181

Made in the USA
Lexington, KY
28 June 2017